W9-CUO-669

'The goal of any believer is to know God and to know Him intimately. This goal is Dr. Mayhue's life passion – in *Seeking God* he leads us on that wonderful path through scripture to help us understand the heart of God in a powerful, more personal way.'

Joni Eareckson Tada
Author and artist

'The most important category of truth is that which relates to the nature of God. One's view of God is the single greatest central element in spiritual experience. Nothing is more important than seeking to know Him. Dick Mayhue surely understands this and charts a course that will lead the reader to a true understanding of God which will dramatically change his life.'

John MacArthur, Jnr.
Grace Community Church,
Sun Valley,
California

To
Mike and Lee Carson
Wade and Tracy Mayhue
with your father's prayer
that you passionately pursue
a growing intimacy with God.
2 Peter 3:18

To
Iain Michael Carson
with your grandfather's prayer
that you grow up to
honour Christ
with holiness of life, a pure love,
and unceasing spiritual service
which marked your biblical namesakes.
2 Corinthians 7:1

Seeking God

The Pathway of True Spirituality

Richard Mayhue

Christian Focus

Christian Focus Publications publishes biblically-accurate books for adults and children. The books in the adult range are published in three imprints.

Christian Heritage contains classic writings from the past.

Christian Focus contains popular works including biographies, commentaries, doctrine, and Christian living.

Mentor focuses on books written at a level suitable for Bible College and seminary students, pastors, and others; the imprint includes commentaries, doctrinal studies, examination of current issues, and church history.

For a free catalogue of all our titles, please write to
Christian Focus Publications,
Geanies House, Fearn,
Ross-shire, IV20 1TW, Great Britain

For details of our titles visit us on our web site
http://www.christianfocus.com

ISBN 185792 540 8

First published in 2000
by Christian Focus Publications
Geanies House, Fearn, Ross-shire,
IV20 1TW, Great Britain

Cover design by Owen Daily

CONTENTS

Part Four

SPIRITUAL PASSIONS

Part Five

SPIRITUAL PURSUITS

PREFACE

This book on 'spirituality' has blossomed over the last twenty-five years in the context of preaching, teaching, and discipling. It is designed to address the major elements in a close walk with God and to take into account the wide scope of Scriptural content for every topic. Each chapter provides an overview which lays the groundwork for the reader to pursue deeper and wider studies later.

This volume is primarily intended to be used as a tool to disciple a new believer in the Lord Jesus Christ. However, it could also easily be employed to point an unbeliever to Christ as the only Saviour. Other endeavours might include the restoration process of a repentant Christian, the refreshment and strengthening of a weary saint, or just the daily encouragement of any Christian who needs to be reminded of these grand truths.

This book could also serve as a text in a local church or Bible Institute setting. Christians of all ages should find it a helpful tool to learn what the Bible teaches about 'spirituality'. Seeking God can be studied individually or in a group. While basically designed to be followed in the order of the chapters, this volume can afford fruitful reading in any one of the parts or individual chapters.

Special thanks are in order to my secretary, Joan Osborne, and my personal assistant, Bob White, for their various helps in preparing this material. I am greatly indebted to Malcolm Maclean who encouraged me to put these studies in their present form.

May the Lord be pleased to glorify Himself through the study of this material and subsequent personal practice of godliness as the result.

Richard Mayhue
The Master's Seminary
Sun Valley, CA
rmayhue@tms.edu

Whom have I in heaven but You?
And besides You, I desire nothing on earth.
My flesh and my heart may fail,
but God is the strength of my heart and my portion forever.
Psalm 73:25-26

INTRODUCTION

'As the deer pants for the water brooks, so my soul pants for You, O
God' (Ps. 42:1). The psalmist yearned for God with the same intensity
as the publican who cried out 'God, be merciful to me, the sinner!'
(Luke 18:13)—though each had a different reason.

One sought for a deeper relationship; the other, a new relationship.
But both cried out for spiritual intimacy with God. Perhaps you can
identify with one of them.

Augustine wrote in *The City of God*, 'There is a God-shaped
vacuum in every man that only Christ can fill.'[1] That's where spiritual
intimacy begins, but it is by no means where it ends. It extends on in
time and maturity until: we become God's friend like Abraham (James
2:23); we walk with God like Enoch (Gen. 5:22, 24); we enjoy intimate
fellowship with God as did Job (Job 29:4, NIV); we, like David,
grow into a man or woman after God's own heart (Acts 13:22, KJV);
we know the high esteem of God similar to Daniel (Dan. 10:11, 19);
or become a favoured one of God like Mary (Luke 1:28). Just like
them, we have the treasured opportunity to become 'intimates of God'.

Spiritual Intimacy

An intimate relationship is marked by very close association, contact,
or familiarity. Expanding on that, an intimate friendship includes
warmth, tenderness, love, closeness, transparency, security,
vulnerability, strength, commitment, knowledge, and understanding.

Our chaotic world breeds a brutal, self-seeking attitude devoid of
intimacy. That is why marriages crumble, families disintegrate, and
friendships fail. To a world that callously disregards even the dignity
of human life, God calls out with a word of love (John 3:16; Rom.
5:8) and beckons us to become intimate with Him.

In our 'liberated' day, the intimate act of marriage has degenerated
into cheap sex, both in and out of marriage. Mothers regularly kill
their babies through abortion and children increasingly rebel against
their parents in homes where family intimacy has long ago been
abandoned. By ignoring God, society emotionally starves itself to
death while all along God promises to love us forever and give us
our fill of spiritual affection.

We live under continual threat of nuclear holocaust and experience
daily, life-threatening violence. Newspaper headlines fill our minds
with thoughts of euthanasia, infanticide, and genocide. These barbaric
vulgarities can only be neutralized by spiritual intimacy with a

compassionate God who alone can do all things and never fails. Our generation's greatest need is to reclaim a dominant sense of intimacy with God which will reshape our souls and redirect our lives.

Portraits of Love

For most of us, the thought of being intimate with God defies our understanding since He is God and we, mere humans. So God in His Word uses three illustrations to help us understand the intimacy He desires with us.

A shepherd with his sheep. So close and so loving is the good shepherd to His flock that He is willing to die for their well-being (John 10:11). When the sheep hear the shepherd's voice, they know it well and follow Him (vv. 4, 16, 27).

A man and his wife. Nearer to most people's experience is the picture of marriage. God the Father stands as Israel's husband (Isa. 54:5; Jer. 31:32) and Christ serves as the bridegroom for His beloved church (Eph. 5:25-32). With everlasting love and covenant faithfulness, the Lord intimately bestows His grace upon those who are His through faith in Christ.

A parent-child relationship. God is our Heavenly Father. As His redeemed children, it is our unique privilege to experience the depths of His love and call Him by the most intimate of endearments— Abba, the Aramaic equivalent for 'Daddy' (Rom. 8:15; Gal. 4:6). In Christ, we become little children (Matt. 18:3; 1 John 2:1). God knows us to the uttermost detail (Ps. 139:13-16) and reveals Himself in a knowing relationship that goes far beyond information – so far beyond that it results in eternal transformation (2 Cor. 3:18; Phil. 3:21; 1 John 3:2).

To balance out our thinking, we must not forget that a tension should always exist between responding in awe to the King of kings and coming in love to our Heavenly Father. Too much emphasis on kingship robs us of intimacy, while excess attention to our family privilege leads us to presumption. Our relationship with God must always be kept in focus as one between the human and the divine.

Our Pilgrimage

Does this confession sound familiar?

> As a young man I must have tried a dozen techniques that people said were sure to guarantee a measure of passion that would transport me

above the ordinary and ineffective. In each case I eagerly embraced whatever it was that I was supposed to do or say. But the results, if any, were short-lived, and what I discovered was that there are no shortcuts, no gimmicks, no easy ways to cultivate an intimacy with God and attain the resulting passion that should carry one through life's journey.[2]

Seeking God does not propose a 'formula' approach to closeness with God. Rather, by coming to God through His Word, we seek to dynamically be and do those things which promote a holy environment for fellowship with Him. It's both a lifetime commitment and a spiritual style of living.

In some sense, we follow by analogy the advice of John Wooden, the successful former basketball coach at UCLA. When asked by a reporter to explain his success, Wooden replied, 'I merely taught my players to master the fundamentals.'

Our study in this book is all about the fundamentals of spiritual intimacy and maturity with God. By God's grace, in Christ as a new creation, and through the Holy Spirit's power, we can 'master the fundamentals'. It must be our consuming passion to so highly prize God that we diligently cultivate His friendship and love.

Spiritual Maturity

Four men preparing for ministry at The Master's Seminary and I invested several hours a week together throughout an entire semester focusing on spirituality. Our discipleship lab worked through a highly recommended book written by a well-known Christian. But much to our surprise, the author never defined what he meant by spirituality, even though the word appeared prominently in the title.

Because this omission struck us as serious but probably all too common, we spent the remaining time searching the Scriptures to determine the biblical meaning of spirituality. We settled on this working definition after weeks of lively inquiry and discussion:

> *Christian spirituality involves growing to be like God in character and conduct, by personal submission to the transforming work of God's Word and God's Spirit.*

The author of Hebrews rejoiced that Jewish Christians had taken well to the intimacy of a child (5:12-13) but deplored their lack of advancement to maturity. So he exhorted, 'Therefore leaving the elementary teaching about the Christ, let us press on to maturity' (6:1). Paul wrote with similar disappointment to the Corinthians (1 Cor. 3:1-3).

Intimacy deals fundamentally with our initial personal relationship with the Father, Son, and Holy Spirit in godwardness. Maturity, on the other hand, reflects God's abiding, growing presence in us in godliness (John 15:1-11).

Just as a baby or young child, although not yet mature, can enjoy intimacy with a parent, so should a new Christian with the freshly found Saviour. But early on in the relationship, intimacy normally serves as the catalyst to initiate the maturing process, whereby a child begins to grow into parental likeness.

Intimacy without maturity results in infantile spiritual behaviour instead of spiritually adult responses. In contrast, maturity without intimacy results in a stale, joyless Christianity that can easily deteriorate into legalism and sometimes even a major fall into sin.

However, Scripture teaches that when intimacy and maturity combine, a strong, vibrant Christian life pattern results. Genuine spirituality, then, cannot just be one or the other; it requires both.

The foundation for understanding spiritual maturity really begins with Scripture. Jesus, Paul, and James each directly communicated God's clear and frequent pressing demand for spiritual development in the true believer. The following passages include one or more of the key New Testament words for spiritual maturity.

Therefore you are to be perfect, as your heavenly Father is perfect (Matt. 5:48).

And He gave some as apostles, and some as prophets, and some as evangelists, and some as pastors and teachers, for the equipping of the saints for the work of service, to the building up of the body of Christ; until we all attain to the unity of the faith, and of the knowledge of the Son of God, to a mature man, to the measure of the stature which belongs to the fullness of Christ (Eph. 4:11-13).

And we proclaim Him, admonishing every man and teaching every man with all wisdom, so that we may present every man complete in Christ (Col. 1:28).

All Scripture is inspired by God and profitable for teaching, for reproof, for correction, for training in righteousness; so that the man of God may be adequate, equipped for every good work (2 Tim. 3:16-17).

Consider it all joy, my brethren, when you encounter various trials, knowing that the testing of your faith produces endurance. And let endurance have its perfect result, that you may be perfect and complete, lacking in nothing (James 1:2-4).

Acceptable Christianity

As you can see, prolonged infant behaviour is not accepted as normal in Scripture; maturity is everywhere expected, never optional. And where maturity's expectation is matched by maturity's experience, God's commendation follows.

The quickest way to grasp the essence of maturity is to read about the obedience of people such as Abel, Noah, Abraham, Sarah, Isaac, Jacob, and Joseph in Genesis. But don't quit there. Sixty-five more books of the Bible contain additional stirring accounts of spiritual maturity.

This Hall of Faith serves as the ultimate in God's affirmation of intimate faith and mature faithfulness. Hebrews 11 chronicles spiritual maturity at its best. But notice that an exhortation immediately follows Hebrews 11 for the same kind of maturity in those who received the letter (12:1-3). It is accompanied by a warning about the Father's discipline of those who live out their Christianity immaturely (12:4-11). What's imperfectly true of earthly parenthood is but a reflection of God's flawlessly consistent response to those of us who by faith in the Lord Jesus Christ have been born again into God's family (John 1:12-13).

These crucial truths took on a new dimension of understanding for me when God blessed the Mayhue family with our first grandchild—Iain Michael Carson. I shared intimate moments with him, although at infancy he was incapable of maturity.

As time has gone on, our intimacy has deepened; but, more importantly, his maturity has begun to develop. If it did not, his juvenile delinquency (spiritually speaking) would eventually erode our intimacy. It is also this way in our relationship with the Heavenly Father.

A saint of old, Epaphras, prayed that the Christians at Colossae would stand perfect and fully assured in all the will of God (Col. 4:12). May God, in similar fashion, commend these compelling biblical truths about spiritual maturity to our stewardship of worship and obedience for His own great glory.

God's Grace

Whether you rebel against God like the prodigal son (Luke 15:11-32), sincerely seek to know God like Cornelius and his family (Acts 10:1-2), commit sin and interrupt your intimacy like David (Ps. 51), or desire to reach a new level of communion with God like Paul (Phil. 3:12-14), these basics in building a growing, personal relationship with God will guide and equip you to satisfy your longings.

I pray that your spiritual journey and mine will be marked by the psalmist's childlike confidence in his side-by-side walk through life with God.

> The LORD is my shepherd, I shall not be in want.
>> He makes me lie down in green pastures,
> he leads me beside quiet waters,
>> he restores my soul.
> He guides me in paths of righteousness
>> for his name's sake.
> Even though I walk
>> through the valley of the shadow of death,
> I will fear no evil,
>> for you are with me;
> your rod and your staff,
>> they comfort me.
> You prepare a table before me
>> in the presence of my enemies.
> You anoint my head with oil;
>> my cup overflows.
> Surely goodness and love will follow me
>> all the days of my life,
> and I will dwell in the house of the LORD forever
>> (Psalm 23:1-6, NIV).

Additional Resources

If you are interested in other books on the general topic of spirituality, I recommend the following:

Jerry Bridges. *The Practice of Godliness*. NavPress.
Jerry Bridges. *The Pursuit of Holiness*. NavPress.

W. Bingham Hunter. *The God Who Hears*. InterVarsity Press.
John MacArthur, Jr. *The Ultimate Priority*. Moody Press.
Richard Mayhue. *Fight the Good Fight*. Christian Focus.
Kenneth Prior. *The Way of Holiness*. Christian Focus.
J.C. Ryle. *Holiness*. Revell.
A.W. Tozer. *The Knowledge of the Holy*. Harper and Row.
A.W. Tozer. *The Pursuit of God*. Horizon Books.

Part One

SPIRITUAL PROGRESS

Therefore if anyone is in Christ, he is a new creature; the old
things passed away; behold, new things have come.
2 Corinthians 5:17

Wherever there is joy in the world, wherever there is hope, wherever
there is a spirit of moral victory, I find behind it evangelical believers
for whom God has become personally real in their lives.[1]
Carl F.H. Henry

Search me, O God, and know my heart;
Try me and know my anxious thoughts;
And see if there be any hurtful way in me,
And lead me in the everlasting way.
Psalm 139:23-24

1

KNOWING GOD

Record-setting former Los Angeles Dodgers pitcher Orel Hershiser recalled the occasion when entertainer Frank Sinatra gave him and his wife, Jamie, an autographed photo.

'He signed it, "To my great friends," and he spelled our names, "Oral and Jane". Goes to show you how good friends we really were.'[1]

On a human level, Orel's story portrays the extent to which many think they can know God. Casually at best, and details just don't matter. However, that does not represent what the Bible teaches about knowing God.

God desires that we know Him intimately and that He knows us in the closest possible spiritual relationship. God issues this invitation to all: 'Cease striving and know that I am God' (Ps. 46:10).

A. W. Tozer explains that either we can know the facts about God or we can enter into a personal relationship with God and even develop a deep intimacy with Him.

> You and I are in little (our sins excepted) what God is in large. Being made in His image we have within us the capacity to know Him. In our sins we lack only the power. The moment the Spirit has quickened us to life in regeneration our whole being senses its kinship to God and leaps up in joyous recognition. That is the heavenly birth without which we cannot see the kingdom of God. It is, however, not an end, but an inception, for now begins the glorious pursuit, the heart's happy exploration of the infinite riches of the Godhead . . .
>
> To have found God and still to pursue Him is the soul's paradox of love, scorned indeed by the too-easily satisfied religionist, but justified in happy experience by the children of the burning heart.[2]

For a few, this discussion raises a fundamentally important question . . .

Is There a God to Know?

Col. James Irwin, *Apollo 15* astronaut, tells this true story concerning Yuri Gagarin, the first Russian cosmonaut. Gagarin sarcastically commented upon his return to earth that he did not see God in space. The implication—God does not exist.

A young Russian girl heard about the remark and wrote Yuri a letter. She asked, 'Are you pure in heart? For if you are, you would have seen God.' She drew her conclusions from Matthew 5:8, 'Blessed are the pure in heart, for they shall see God.'

Significantly, the Bible never proves the existence of God.

Scripture simply begins, 'In the beginning God created the heavens and the earth' (Gen. 1:1).

In contrast, God's Word pulls no punches when it comments on those who deny the existence and reality of God: 'The fool has said in his heart, "There is no God." They are corrupt, they have committed abominable deeds; there is no one who does good' (Ps. 14:1; see 10:4; 53:1).

Whether you examine the macro-world of space or the human body with its intricate details, logic demands that we conclude the existence of God. When there is design, there must be a designer. For every effect, surely there is a cause. Life demands a life-giver. Centuries ago Sir Isaac Newton wrote, 'In the absence of other proofs, the thumb alone would convince me of God's existence.'

God's existence becomes the only reasonable conclusion for a thinking person with an open mind. To say there is no God admits that the world came into existence by random chance, better described as an accident.

With accident logic, you could believe that a Pulitzer Prize-winning novel originated by throwing a type tray into the air and having it land in the exact words of the book, or that a 747 jet came into being when a tornado went through a junkyard. These illustrations seem absurd, but they are less so than questioning the existence of God. Blind absurdity leads to atheism. Reasonable faith concludes that God exists.

The position of an atheist results in dramatic, even traumatic, conclusions about life. If you know someone who entertains atheistic thought, here are several questions with which you can test that person's certainty:

1. Have you travelled everywhere in the universe and beyond to verify there is no God?
2. If God were invisible and you could not see Him, does that deny His reality?
3. Do you know enough about God to recognize Him if you did see Him?
4. Have you read all that there is to read about God, including the Bible, to make sure your conclusions come from a complete set of facts?

Is God Knowable?

Religious people usually waffle on this one. Take the Athenians in Paul's day, for example. They admitted to many gods, including the unknown god.

> So Paul stood in the midst of the Areopagus and said, 'Men of Athens, I observe that you are very religious in all respects. For while I was passing through and examining the objects of your worship, I also found an altar with this inscription, "TO AN UNKNOWN GOD." Therefore what you worship in ignorance, this I proclaim to you. The God who made the world and all things in it, since He is Lord of heaven and earth, does not dwell in temples made with hands; nor is He served by human hands, as though He needed anything, since He Himself gives to all people life and breath and all things; and He made from one man every nation of mankind to live on all the face of the earth, having determined their appointed times, and the boundaries of their habitation, that they would seek God, if perhaps they might grope for Him and find Him, though He is not far from each one of us; for in Him we live and move and exist, as even some of your own poets have said, 'For we also are His children.'
>
> 'Being then the children of God, we ought not to think that the Divine Nature is like gold or silver or stone, an image formed by the art and thought of man. Therefore having overlooked the times of ignorance, God is now declaring to men that all people everywhere should repent, because He has fixed a day in which He will judge the world in righteousness through a Man whom He has appointed, having furnished proof to all men by raising Him from the dead' (Acts 17:22-31).

God surrounds us on all sides with knowledge about Himself. When we look up at the heavens, they declare God's glory (Ps. 19:1). A knowledge of God resides intuitively evident within mankind (Rom. 1:19). Scripture everywhere tells of God from Genesis 1:1 to Revelation 22:21. The person of Jesus Christ explained God the Father (John 1:18). God certainly does not engage in a game of hide-and-seek, but rather has gone out of His way to be obvious.

What's more, God made known His salvation (Pss. 16:11; 98:2) through Jesus Christ.

> All things have been handed over to Me by My Father; and no one knows the Son except the Father; nor does anyone know the Father except the Son, and anyone to whom the Son wills to reveal Him (Matt. 11:27).

However, if we search for God through human resources alone, the data will be misinterpreted and mankind will bypass the obvious.

> For since in the wisdom of God the world through its wisdom did not come to know God, God was well-pleased through the foolishness of the message preached to save those who believe (1 Cor. 1:21).

Knowing about God

For those who admit the existence of God and that God can be known, they experience a seeking process during which they crave to know about God, to know who He is, how He operates, and where He can be found.

Some, like Pharaoh, admit they do not know God (Ex. 5:2), while others, like Nebuchadnezzar, know God in interesting ways (Dan. 4:34-37). But knowing God factually is not enough. Listen to Paul's commentary on a whole category of God knowers:

> For even though they knew God, they did not honor Him as God, or give thanks; but they became futile in their speculations, and their foolish heart was darkened (Rom. 1:21).

They knew facts about God but their knowledge never progressed to knowing God personally.

On the other hand, many seek God the best way and in the most sincere manner possible. Take Cornelius, for example. Even though he came from a Gentile background, he was nevertheless a devout man, one who feared God, gave many alms, and prayed continually (Acts 10:2). Cornelius wanted more than facts or philosophical speculations; he desired to go beyond the mere intellectual side of knowing God to the spiritual. The same proved true of Lydia who as a worshipper of God had not yet moved from the knowledge of God to a relationship with Him (16:12-15).

Let me illustrate from the lives of two men who greatly differ in religious backgrounds. Listen to Gandhi who admitted to being a devout admirer of Jesus Christ but rejected a personal relationship with Him:

> The convention lasted for three days. I could understand and appreciate the devoutness of those who attended it. But I saw no reason for changing my belief—my religion. It was impossible for me to believe that I could go to heaven or attain salvation only by becoming a Christian. When I

frankly said so to some of the good Christian friends, they were shocked. But there was no help for it.

My difficulties lay deeper. It was more than I could believe that Jesus was the only incarnate son of God, and that only he who believed in Him would have everlasting life. If God could have sons, all of us were His sons. If Jesus was like God, or God Himself, then all men were like God and could be God Himself. My reason was not ready to believe literally that Jesus by His death and by His blood redeemed the sins of the world. Again, according to Christianity only human beings had souls, and not other living beings, for whom death meant complete extinction; while I held a contrary belief. I could accept Jesus as a martyr, an embodiment of sacrifice, and a divine teacher, but not as the most perfect man ever born. His death on the Cross was a great example to the world, but that there was anything like a mysterious or miraculous virtue in it my heart could not accept. The pious lives of Christians did not give me anything that the lives of men of other faiths had failed to give. I had seen in other lives just the same reformation that I had heard among Christians. Philosophically there was nothing extraordinary in Christian principles. From the point of view of sacrifice, it seemed to me that the Hindus greatly surpass the Christians. It was impossible for me to regard Christianity as a perfect religion or the greatest of all religions.

I shared this mental churning with my Christian friends whenever there was an opportunity, but their answers could not satisfy me.[3]

Compare that with Rabbi Max Wertheimer who knew about God factually but one day discovered that this knowledge alone could not provide eternal life:

Born in Germany of devout Jewish parents, my first fifteen years were saturated with training in Orthodox Judaism. Then I began my studies toward a career and was apprenticed to a manufacturer doing office work. Although I continued to read the prayers and attend the synagogue, my worldly associates led me into sinful pleasures, and I drifted from the faith of my fathers.

My parents sent me to America to pursue a classical education . . . Four years after completing my undergraduate work I received my Master's Degree.

Having become proficient in the translation of Hebrew into the vernacular and with a complete knowledge of Jewish history, I was ordained and inducted into rabbinical office. I served ten years in my first charge, receiving many tokens of affection from my flock. I contributed much to their knowledge of the social, industrial, and economic problems of the day. I spoke of monotheism, ethical culture, and the moral systems of the Jews. On Sabbath mornings I gave addresses on the Pentateuch, and on Sundays I taught from eight in the morning to five in the evening with only an hour's break for dinner.

Suddenly, there came a change. My wife became seriously ill and soon died, leaving me a distraught widower with two small children. I could not sleep. I walked the streets striving to find something that would make me forget the void in my life. My dreams were shattered. Where was comfort to be found? I called on the God of my fathers, but the heavens seemed as brass. How could I speak words of comfort to others when my own sorrow had brought me to despair? I delved into Spiritism, Theosophy, and Christian Science, only to find them futile and hopeless.

Again I studied Judaism, but it answered no questions; it satisfied no craving in my heart. Then I began to read the New Testament, comparing it with the Old. As I pondered over and meditated on many passages, one in particular made a definite impression, ' . . . my righteous servant,' found in the eleventh verse [Isa. 53:11]. This was the only mention of that phrase I could find in either Testament. We have, 'David, my servant,' 'Isaiah, my servant,' 'Daniel, my servant,' but here it is, 'My righteous servant.'

I could hold out in unbelief no longer. I was convinced of the truth of God as it is in Christ Jesus. I cried, 'Lord, I believe that Thou as Jehovah Yesous hast made the atonement for me. I believe that Jehovah Yesous died for me! From henceforth I will publicly confess Yeshua as my Savior and Lord!' Thus, after months of searching, I was convinced that Jesus was the righteous servant of Jehovah, Jehovah-tsidkenu, 'The Lord our righteousness.'[4]

Knowing God Personally

To the Jews, like Rabbi Wertheimer, who knew all about God historically, Jesus came so that they could know God personally. John writes in his Gospel, 'He was in the world, and the world was made through Him, and the world did not know Him . . . And this is eternal life, that they may know You, the only true God, and Jesus Christ whom You have sent' (John 1:10; 17:3).

Paul frequently spoke about people who knew facts about God but had not entered into a relational knowledge of God: 'However at that time, when you did not know God, you were slaves to those which by nature are no gods' (Gal. 4:8; see also 1 Thess. 4:5; 2 Thess. 1:8).

Now look at Galatians 4:9: 'But now that you have come to know God, or rather to be known by God . . .' Paul does not question the Galatians' factual knowledge nor God's omniscience, but rather contrasts the time when a personal relationship did not exist with the time when they put their faith in Christ (2:15-16) and entered into a personal relationship. They knew and were known.

John presents this truth very directly: 'And we know that the Son of God has come, and has given us understanding, so that we may know Him who is true, and we are in Him who is true, in His Son Jesus Christ. This is the true God and eternal life' (1 John 5:20).

That's exactly what the Prophet Hosea meant when he wrote, 'For I delight in loyalty rather than sacrifice, and in the knowledge of God rather than burnt offerings' (Hosea 6:6).

At this point, let me issue a warning: Always proceed from the step of factual knowledge to the step of relationship on God's terms alone. There have been those who foolishly tried their own way (with great sincerity), but in the end God did not acknowledge their acquaintance. The issue is not only 'Do I know God?' but also 'Does God know me?'

> Not everyone who says to Me, 'Lord, Lord,' will enter the kingdom of heaven; but he who does the will of My Father who is in heaven will enter. Many will say to Me on that day, 'Lord, Lord, did we not prophesy in Your name, and in Your name cast out demons, and in Your name perform many miracles?' And then I will declare to them, 'I never knew you; depart from Me, you who practice lawlessness' (Matt. 7:21-23).

Paul tells the Cretians, 'They profess to know God, but by their deeds they deny Him, being detestable and disobedient, and worthless for any good deed' (Titus 1:16).

Be confident, God knows. He knows the ones who are righteously related to Him in Jesus Christ. 'For the LORD knows the way of the righteous, but the way of the wicked will perish' (Ps. 1:6).

God makes the difference. Myra Brooks Welch expresses this grand truth beautifully in 'The Touch of the Master's Hand.'

Twas battered and scarred, and the auctioneer
Thought it scarcely worth his while
To waste much time on the old violin,
But held it up with a smile.
'What am I bidden, good folks,' he cried,
'Who will start bidding for me?
A dollar, a dollar' – then, 'Two!' 'Only two?

Two dollars, once; three dollars, twice;
Going for three –' But no,
From the room, far back, a gray-haired man
Came forward and picked up the bow;
Then, wiping the dust from the old violin,
And tightening the loose strings,
He played a melody pure and sweet
As sweet as a caroling angel sings.

The music ceased, and the auctioneer,
With a voice that was quiet and low,
Said, 'What am I bidden for the old violin?'
And he held it up with the bow.
'A thousand dollars, and who'll make it two?
Two thousand! And who'll make it three?
Three thousand, once; three thousand, twice;
And going, and gone!' said he.
The people cheered, but some of them cried,
'We do not quite understand
What changed its worth?' Swift came the reply:
'The touch of the master's hand.'

And many a man with life out of tune,
And battered and scarred with sin,
Is auctioned cheap to the thoughtless crowd,
Much like the old violin.
A 'mess of pottage,' a glass of wine;
A game—and he travels on.
He's 'going' once, and 'going' twice,
He's 'going' and 'almost gone.'
But the Master comes, and the foolish crowd
Never can quite understand
The worth of a soul, and the change that's wrought
By the touch of the Master's hand.[5]

Knowing God Intimately

In the *New King James Version*, Genesis 4:1 reads: 'Now Adam knew Eve his wife, and she conceived.' Adam did not only know his wife factually or just personally but also in the most intimate sense. As they knew intimacy at its deepest level maritally, we can know God in the richest way spiritually. That should be our desire, like the psalmist who pleaded, 'Search me, O God, and know my heart; try me and know my anxious thoughts' (Ps. 139:23).

For humans to know and understand God unquestionably causes God's delight (see also 1 Cor. 1:31; 2 Cor. 10:17):

> Thus says the LORD, 'Let not a wise man boast of his wisdom, and let not the mighty man boast of his might, let not the rich man boast of his riches; but let him who boasts boast of this, that he understands and knows Me, that I am the LORD who exercises lovingkindness, justice, and righteousness on earth; for I delight in these things,' declares the LORD (Jer. 9:23-24).

The New Testament uses Abba only three times in reference to God (Mark 14:36; Rom. 8:15; Gal. 4:6). That's the most tender word of endearment possible which expresses an element of our childlike delight in the Father. These three uses correspond in emphasis to the three Hebrew words translated 'delight' in the Old Testament which speak of our relationship with God.

First, there is the personal delight in God spoken of in Psalm 37:4: 'Delight yourself in the LORD; and He will give you the desires of your heart.' It expresses a delicate or close relational delight or intimacy (see also Isa. 58:2). It corresponds to the Abba of Galatians 4:6: '*And because you are sons, God has sent forth the Spirit of His Son into our hearts, crying, "Abba! Father!"* '

Next our delight should be in God's Word, illustrated in Psalm 1:2: 'But his delight is in the law of the LORD, and in His law he meditates day and night.' This delight of our will focuses on what God has said to us. Note its counterpart in Romans 8:15: 'For you have not received a spirit of slavery leading to fear again, but you have received a spirit of adoption as sons by which we cry out, "Abba! Father!" '

The third delight of intimacy comes in doing God's will, spoken of in Psalm 40:8: 'I delight to do Your will, O my God; Your Law is within my heart.' This emotional expression has its parallel in Christ's Gethsemane prayer recorded in Mark 14:36: 'And he was saying, "Abba! Father! All things are possible for You; remove this cup from Me; yet not what I will, but what You will." '

Ibrahim's true story relates the depth of intimacy and commitment which a Christian can have, by God's grace, with our Heavenly Father.

This 22-year-old former Muslim from the Central African Republic had to choose his own punishment for accepting Christ. Lose his mind. Be inflicted with an incurable sickness. Or death.

After hearing about Ibrahim putting his faith in the Lord Jesus Christ, the Islamic council of his town called a meeting. There they sought Allah's forgiveness for Ibrahim's departure, while accusing him of leading three other Muslims to hell. Finally they gave him his choice from any of the three punishments because of his 'apostasy.' By God's protective hand, he was able to escape from his religious torture; but either way Ibrahim knew an Abba intimacy with God, for he delighted in God personally, in God's Word, and in God's will. Even if it would have cost him his life.

Significant Questions

An old preacher and a professional actor both attended a social gathering to honour the actor. The actor received many requests to recite portions of well-known works. The preacher requested Psalm 23. The actor agreed only if the preacher would recite the piece too. After the actor concluded, the crowd clapped for his professional delivery and flawless expression. Then came the preacher's turn. He read haltingly with a raspy voice, but when he finished the audience wept. Someone leaned over and asked the actor, 'What caused the difference?' He candidly admitted, 'I know the psalm but he knows the Shepherd.'

Do you know only *about* the Shepherd? Or do you know Him personally? Perhaps intimately? Do you live life *coram deo*, consciously in the presence of God?

It all begins with a right relationship. Jesus extends this invitation to all: 'Come to Me, all who are weary and heavy-laden, and I will give you rest. Take My yoke upon you, and learn from Me, for I am gentle and humble in heart; and you will find rest for your souls. For My yoke is easy, and my burden is light' (Matt. 11:28-30).

Think about your personal relationship with God in terms of a prisoner being set free (Col. 1:13-14). John Mohr paints the picture with these striking words.

All are born prisoners of war.
Victims, yet fully responsible.
Then, the news of liberation.
Stories of prisoners escaping to freedom.

Some believe.
Some refuse.
And then, the rumor:
'The prison doors have been unlocked.'
Some believe—and escape.
Some believe, but for fear remain.
I remained.
One day a cellmate took courage,
Tried the door, and found it open.
He called back, 'It's true . . . there is freedom . . . come
and see!'
Now, I knew.
Still I refused.
The price paid for truth refused
Is always too great to bear.
Until one day, in misery and desperation,
I threw myself against the cell door . . .
Eyes blind with tears
Could scarcely believe.
I lay in brokenness
Outside the prison walls.
The sun shone warm on my shivering soul.
The air, buoyant with peace.
I stood.
I inhaled freedom,
And for the very first time,
Filled my lungs without a ragged breath.[6]

Now, as a liberated child of the Heavenly Father, you can desire with Paul, 'That I may know Him, and the power of His resurrection and the fellowship of His sufferings, being conformed to His death; in order that I may attain to the resurrection from the dead' (Phil. 3:10-11).

Also, as one who has been forgiven your sins and spared from their penalty by God's grace in Jesus Christ, you can exclaim:

Oh, the depth of the riches both of the wisdom and knowledge of God! How unsearchable are His judgments and unfathomable His ways! For who has known the mind of the Lord, or who became His counselor? Or who has first given to Him that it might be paid back to Him again? For from Him and through Him and to Him are all things. To Him be the glory forever. Amen (Rom. 11:33-36).

And can it be that I should gain
An interest in the Saviour's blood?
Died He for me, who caused His pain?
For me, who Him to death pursued?
Amazing love! How can it be
That Thou, my God, shouldst die for me?[1]

Charles Wesley

2

TAKING THE FIRST STEP

Sportscaster Jim Nance asked America's legendary golf great, Jack Nicklaus, at a recent Masters tournament, 'What has made the difference in your improved golf game?' The Golden Bear responded, 'I went back to the fundamentals.'

Like Nicklaus, we return to the fundamentals here before proceeding to the more advanced. Although our aim is spiritual maturity, we are first looking at spiritual infancy to outline all of the wonderful things God has done on our behalf in order for us to first understand what our salvation really involved.

Perhaps you can remember when you were saved. For me, it was on a Monday night, April 6, 1970, at Scott Memorial Baptist Church in San Diego. 'B' and I struggled in our three-year-old marriage because I loved my career as a naval officer and she loved our eighteen-month-old daughter. But we had little love for each other.

Fortunately, our Christian neighbours had built a friendship with us to the point that they started inviting us to their local church. Every time we politely refused. Finally, just to appease them, I said yes to a Monday night family seminar. We figured nothing spectacular could happen on a weekday night at a Baptist church.

That evening we heard a simple gospel presentation. I know I had heard the gospel before, but it had never made much sense; plus, in my estimation, I really did not live badly enough to be considered a thoroughgoing sinner.

But this night proved different. Everything I heard computed. All that the preacher, Kenny Poure, said had the authority of Scripture. My sinfulness became clear in light of God's holiness – I was lost and needed to be rescued. Christ's death on my behalf and God's offer of eternal life were graciously irresistible. By the end of the service, I figured that the only logical thing to do was to accept what I so clearly needed and what God had so mercifully provided, and so I did. P.S., so did 'B'.

If you had asked me immediately after the service what happened, I would have reported that I heard the facts, I considered the alternatives, and I wisely chose eternal life in Christ over eternal damnation in hell. At that time, it seemed as if the whole event revolved around and depended on me.

Over the years, however, Scripture has taught me that God played the major role that night and, at best, I responded in a minor way.

In as clear and basic a way as possible, we want to review the fundamentals of salvation from God's perspective, so that we can understand what happened to us, who did what, and most importantly how salvation has changed us. We will never fully understand Christian maturity if we do not first comprehend Christian infancy!

The Rich Young Ruler

Let's first look in on a religiously oriented person who erroneously believed, as I did at one time, that salvation depended primarily on himself rather than on God. We both centred our hopes on human achievement rather than divine accomplishment.

The rich young ruler, highly interested in life beyond death, ran with urgency to publicly inquire of Jesus, 'What shall I do to inherit eternal life?' (Mark 10:17) . Our Lord's answer has baffled people through the centuries because He did not respond with a simple, 'Believe on Me and you will have eternal life.' Rather, He exposed the young man's counterfeit interest.

The inquirer betrayed his apparent sincerity by four common mistakes people make in regard to the true nature of salvation. First, he would not acknowledge his own spiritual bankruptcy by admitting that he could do nothing to merit eternal life (10:17). Only God could accomplish his salvation. Second, he did not acknowledge the Lord Jesus as God. He saw Him only as a good teacher who could explain the way of God (10:18). Third, he failed to recognize and repent of his own personal sinfulness (10:19-20). Rather, he extolled the self-righteous virtues of his life from his youth up. Fourth, he refused to accept the exchanged life of following the will of Christ as Saviour and Lord, rather than continuing to pursue his own agenda (10:21-22).

Don't be confused here—Jesus did not teach a salvation by works. Rather, just the opposite was true. The rich young ruler tried to gain eternal life through human effort; but the Lord, through a series of questions and commands, pointed him to the real heart of true salvation extended by the mercy and grace of God. Receiving the free gift of eternal life involves at least these four elements.

1. Admitting that only God can save us
2. Acknowledging Jesus Christ as God in human flesh
3. Agreeing to our personal sin which needs God's forgiveness
4. Accepting God's terms of salvation

This encounter stands in contrast to other occasions where salvation did occur because the above truths were involved. Look at these two prime examples.

> But the tax collector, standing some distance away, was even unwilling to lift up his eyes to heaven, but was beating his breast, saying, 'God, be merciful to me, the sinner!' I tell you, this man went to his house justified rather than the other; for everyone who exalts himself will be humbled, but he who humbles himself will be exalted (Luke 18:13-14).

> And he called for lights and rushed in, and trembling with fear, he fell down before Paul and Silas, and after he brought them out, he said, 'Sirs, what must I do to be saved?' They said, 'Believe in the Lord Jesus, and you will be saved, you and your household.'... And he brought them into his house and set food before them, and rejoiced greatly, having believed in God with his whole household (Acts 16:29-31, 34).

The life of Paul unmistakably illustrates this point. Paul and the rich young ruler both thought identically about salvation in their youth. Before Paul met Christ, he approached salvation from a self-righteous perspective. He thought that God owed him eternal life because of who he had become and what he had done (Phil. 3:4-6).

Later, Paul recognized that he could offer nothing worthy of God, and that his best fell enormously short of meriting salvation. At that point, according to Paul's personal testimony in Philippians 3, he counted his religious past to be filthy and as repulsive as excrement. Paul then considered his whole life up to that time as a total spiritual loss in order that he might gain the things of Christ (3:7-8).

Until then he had held to a form of godliness but denied its power (2 Tim. 3:5). Now, Paul turned his back on self-righteousness through human achievement, and by faith embraced Christ's righteousness through God's accomplishment. In so doing, he inherited eternal life (Phil. 3:9-11).

For confirmation of this analysis, reflect back on the historical descriptions of Paul's salvation (Acts 9:3-9; 22:6-11; 26:12-20). In the Acts 9 account, Paul acknowledged Christ's lordship and obeyed His instructions. Acts 22:10 informs us that Paul asked, 'What shall I do, Lord?' Similar in words to the rich young ruler but quite different in meaning, Paul actually submitted to the will of the One whom he called Lord. 'I did not prove disobedient to the heavenly vision,' summarizes Paul's response to God's demands (26:19).

He gave up everything of self and this life in exchange for embracing everything of God and eternal life. Although I could not have explained it at the time, that's exactly what happened to me that April evening on the corner of Oregon and Madison in San Diego. I abandoned self and fully embraced Christ.

Generation

In order to understand why human beings need to be spiritually rescued by God, let's go back to Genesis 1–2. A holy God spoke a holy world and sinless human race into existence. At the conclusion of His six days of creation, 'God saw all that He had made, and behold, it was very good. And there was evening and there was morning, the sixth day' (Gen. 1:31).

Into this perfect world He placed a male and female, both created in the image of God (1:27). Although created in the image of God, they were not deity, but they shared some of the divine ability to know and think. Over this perfect world, God gave Adam and Eve dominion with the freedom to be fruitful, multiply, and fill the earth. They received only one negative command:

> The LORD God commanded the man, saying 'From any tree of the garden you may eat freely; but from the tree of the knowledge of good and evil you shall not eat, for in the day that you eat from it you will surely die' (Gen. 2:16-17).

Imagine a flawless world which you could enjoy forever, with only one thing that you should not do. That was the world of Adam and Eve. The human race had been 'generated' by God's creative energy to enjoy God's blessing and holiness forever.

Degeneration

But the story does not end there. Satan shortly thereafter deceived Eve (2 Cor. 11:3) and both Eve and Adam violated God's prohibition (Gen. 3:1-6). As God promised, they both died, first spiritually and later physically.

For Adam and Eve, death involved separation. Later on their physical bodies would be separated from their spiritual beings when what we commonly think of as death occurred (Gen. 5:5). But a far more important death took place immediately after they ate—a spiritual death. At that point, their sin of disobedience separated them from unbroken communion with their holy God. The indications of this are given in Genesis 3:7-13.

1. Being self conscious
2. Hiding from God
3. Fearing God
4. Adam blaming Eve for his own actions
5. Eve blaming Satan for her own actions

As a result, God cursed Satan, the woman, and Adam. Then they were evicted from the garden which housed the tree of eternal life (3:14-24).

Let's stop for a moment and put the entire Bible in perspective. Scripture can be outlined in three parts around this most important historical occurrence which resulted in God's curses.

I. Pre-curse history   Genesis 1–2
II. Curse history   Genesis 3–Revelation 20
III. Post-curse history   Revelation 21–22

Out of the 1,189 chapters in the Bible, only four speak of a time when the curse of Genesis 3 did not prevail. When the new heaven and new earth arrive (Rev. 21:1), there will no longer be any curse (Rev. 22:3). The remaining 1,185 chapters contrast man's utter sinfulness and inability to save himself with God's unblemished holiness, His provision in Jesus Christ for human redemption for sin and regeneration to eternal life.

As a result of Adam's sin, the entire human race has been born in sin. Although originally generated in holiness, because of Adam and Eve's fall the whole human race is now degenerate and eternally separated from God.

Behold, I was brought forth in iniquity, and in sin my mother conceived me (Psalm 51:5).

For all have sinned and fall short of the glory of God (Romans 3:23).

Scripture variously describes this spiritual death:

1. Darkness of mind that needs to be enlightened by God's truth of redemption (Acts 26:18; Col. 1:13).

2. Depravity of will that needs to be submitted to the orders of God (Rom. 6:11-20).
3. Death of our being that needs spiritual resurrection (Eph. 2:1-7).

All of the human race needs to face the fact that we are born dead to spiritual communion with God. Thus, we have but two alternatives for the future. The first is to be born again, this time into the family of God for eternal fellowship.

> Now there was a man of the Pharisees, named Nicodemus, a ruler of the Jews; this man came to Jesus by night, and said to Him, 'Rabbi, we know that You have come from God as a teacher; for no one can do these signs that You do unless God is with him.' Jesus answered and said to him, 'Truly, truly, I say to you, unless one is born again, he cannot see the kingdom of God.' Nicodemus said to Him, 'How can a man be born when he is old? He cannot enter a second time into his mother's womb and be born, can he?' Jesus answered, 'Truly, truly, I say to you, unless one is born of water and the Spirit, he cannot enter into the kingdom of God. That which is born of the flesh is flesh, and that which is born of the Spirit is spirit. Do not be amazed that I said to you, 'You must be born again.' The wind blows where it wishes and you hear the sound of it, but do not know where it comes from and where it is going; so is everyone who is born of the Spirit' (John 3:1-8).

The second alternative is to expect the second death which involves eternal separation from God in torment.

> Then I saw a great white throne and Him who sat upon it, from whose presence earth and heaven fled away, and no place was found for them. And I saw the dead, the great and small, standing before the throne, and books were opened; and another book was opened, which is the book of life; and the dead were judged from the things which were written in the books, according to their deeds. And the sea gave up the dead which were in it, and death and Hades gave up the dead which were in them; and they were judged, every one of them according to their deeds. Then death and Hades were thrown into the lake of fire. This is the second death, the lake of fire. And if anyone's name was not found written in the book of life, he was thrown into the lake of fire (Rev. 20:11-15).

Regeneration

With the seriousness of the second death in mind, we certainly must press on to God's salvation plan for regenerating, or generating a second time, a holy people for eternal fellowship with Him.

Degeneration demands regeneration if any human being hopes to enjoy communion with God forever.

The Image of God. God created Adam and Eve in His image (Gen. 1:26-27; 5:1; 1 Cor. 11:7; James 3:9). Sin has marred this glorious image which God in salvation renews and conforms us to the image of His Son (Rom. 8:29), by transforming us into the same image from glory to glory (2 Cor. 3:18).

Salvation not only saves us from eternal separation from God (2 Thess. 1:9-10), but also initiates a renewal back to the original 'man in the image of God condition' before the fall of Adam. Just as Christ is the image of the invisible God (Col. 1:15), so we will be changed into the likeness of Christ's perfect humanity (Col. 3: 9-11).

God's Initiative. Who is responsible for individual salvation—God or the person? Put another way, Did God sovereignly elect us and save us? Or did He act in accord with what He knew we would do? In other words, Who makes the first move?

Let me summarize what Scripture teaches about God's role in salvation. I recommend that you look up each passage so you can sense the overwhelming nature of the biblical answer.

God wills	John 1:12-13; Ephesians 1:5,11
God draws	John 6:44
God grants	John 6:65
God calls	1 Peter 2:9; 2 Timothy 1:9
God appoints	Acts 13:48
God predestines	Romans 8:29; Ephesians 1:5,11
God prepares	Romans 9:23
God causes	1 Corinthians 1:30
God chooses	Ephesians 1:4; 2 Thessalonians 2:13
God purposes	Ephesians 1:11
God delivers and transfers	Colossians 1:13
God saves	2 Timothy 1:9; Titus 3:5
God makes us alive	Ephesians 2:5
God pours out His Spirit	Titus 3:6
God justifies	Romans 8:30; Titus 3:7

Man's Responsibility. Does this mean that God totally overrides the human will to impose His will? Our answer is 'No!' There are other passages that teach about man's responsibility for his own sins. Think about these.

> He who believes in Him is not judged; he who does not believe has been judged already, because he has not believed in the name of the only begotten Son of God (John 3:18).

> It remains for some to enter it, and those who formerly had good news preached to them failed to enter because of disobedience (Heb. 4:6).

> And I saw the dead, the great and the small, standing before the throne, and books were opened; and another book was opened, which is the book of life; and the dead were judged from the things which were written in the books, according to their deeds. And the sea gave up the dead which were in it, and death and Hades gave up the dead which were in them; and they were judged, every one of them according to their deeds (Rev. 20:12-13).

People who reject the gospel are held accountable for their sin, rather than being excused because they are the non-elect. While this is humanly impossible to completely reconcile, it nonetheless is what Scripture teaches, and so we must accept it by faith. Jesus was able to hold God's sovereignty and man's responsibility in tension without any mental reservation. Listen to Him preach the gospel.

> All things have been handed over to Me by My Father; and no one knows the Son, except the Father; nor does anyone know the Father, except the Son, and anyone to whom the Son wills to reveal Him. Come to Me, all who are weary and heavy-laden, and I will give you rest. Take My yoke upon you, and learn from Me, for I am gentle and humble in heart; and you will find rest for your souls. For My yoke is easy, and My burden is light (Matt. 11:27-30).

Christ's Death. We have redemption through Christ's blood (Eph. 1:7). God made peace through the blood of His cross (Col. 1:20) in order that believers might be reconciled to God through Christ. He did not count their trespasses against them but rather against Christ (2 Cor. 5:18-19).

Christ's death was limited in the sense that it does not extend to angels or animals. Nor is it redemptively applied to all humans, but only to those who believe in the Lord Jesus Christ according to the glorious gospel.

On the other hand, and in some senses, the atonement of Christ was unlimited in that

1. It is suitable for the whole human race.
2. It benefits all the elect in salvation.
3. Its message is extended to all in proclamation.
4. It makes common grace available to all men in non-eternal ways.

These brief thoughts suggest that what was pictured as the atonement in the Old Testament paralleled in basic ways Christ's atonement in the New Testament. The yearly atonement in the Old (Lev. 16) anticipated Christ's once-for-all atonement in the New (Heb. 9:1-28). It also brought common grace to the unsaved in that God's mercy allowed them to live yet another day rather than being immediately judged for their sins.

The Holy Spirit's Renewal. The work of God in salvation vitally involves the Holy Spirit. Most Christians do not know this, or if they do, they haven't fully realized all that this means. Have you ever wondered why we are baptized in the name of the Father and the Son and the Holy Spirit? (Matt. 28:19) It is symbolic identification with each member of the Godhead in relationship to His part in our actual personal salvation. The Spirit of God plays a significant role in salvation.

It is the Spirit who gives life; the flesh profits nothing; the words that I have spoken to you are spirit and are life (John 6:63).

But as at that time he who was born according to the flesh persecuted him who was born according to the Spirit, so it is now also (Gal. 4:29).

He saved us, not on the basis of deeds which we have done in right-eousness, but according to His mercy, by the washing of regeneration and renewing by the Holy Spirit, whom He poured out upon us richly through Jesus Christ our Saviour, so that being justified by His grace we would be made heirs according to the hope of eternal life (Titus 3:5-7).

The Spirit's work in salvation is sometimes called sanctification, in the sense of the setting apart from sin to God that takes place at salvation (1 Cor. 6:11; 2 Thess. 2:13; 1 Peter 1:2). Other terms, including 'washing' and 'justification,' are used to show the work of

God's Spirit in salvation (Rom. 8:6,9,23; 1 Cor. 6:11; Gal. 3:2-3,14; 4:29; 6:8; 1 Thess. 1:5).

You might be asking how someone who is spiritually dead can be made alive? Or someone blind be made to see? Or someone overcome with evil made pure? Jesus illustrated this in the Gospels when He performed miracles of raising the dead (John 11:17-46), giving sight to the blind (John 9:1-41) and freeing people from the evil of demons (Mark 5:1-20). These miracles picture in the physical realm what occurs spiritually in salvation. Salvation begins and ends with God miraculously doing for us what we cannot do for ourselves. It is His work, not ours. It is for His glory and no one else's.

> For by grace you have been saved through faith; and that not of yourselves, it is the gift of God; not as a result of works, so that no one may boast. For we are His workmanship, created in Christ Jesus for good works, which God prepared beforehand, so that we would walk in them (Eph. 2:8-10).

God has made us alive, i.e., has raised us out of being dead in sins and trespasses by the regenerating work of the Holy Spirit. As we will see shortly, what God begins with His Spirit in salvation, He continues with His Spirit in the Christian life (Phil. 1:6; Gal. 5:25). These two aspects of the new life—birth and growth—always go together in Scripture.

A New Creation
True salvation is not a decision made today which will bring change only later in eternity. Regardless of how one feels or what one understands at the moment of salvation, it promises to bring with it radical change now: 'Therefore if any man is in Christ, he is a new creature; the old things passed away; behold, new things have come' (2 Cor. 5:17). Whereas I was dead, now I'm alive. Before I was blind, but now I can see. Although I was incurably stricken with sin, God has miraculously cured my transgression problem. Before I was in darkness, but today I walk in the light. Previously Satan ruled me in his domain; now I am a resident of God's kingdom. Now I am at peace with God, where before I was estranged from Him. I am a new creation (Gal. 6:15).

A saved person has laid aside the old self and has put on the new self (Col. 3:9-10). He continues to be exhorted to lay aside the former

manner of life, or old self, and put on the new (Eph. 4:24). Because
we are 'new' in Christ:

> We sing a *new* song (Pss. 33:3; 96:1; 98:1; 144:9; 149:1; Rev. 5:9).
> We walk in *newness* of life (Rom. 6:4).
> We serve in *newness* of spirit (Rom. 7:6).
> We will receive a *new* name (Rev. 2:17).

Put Off – Put On

As new creatures in Christ, we are clothed in Christ (Gal. 3:27) and,
as a result, we are to put on Christ-like behaviour (Rom. 13:14). This
figure of speech involves taking off the filthy rags of our old behaviour
and dressing our new life with the garments of righteous behaviour.
Here is what to put off:

Deeds of Darkness	Romans 13:12
Falsehood	Ephesians 4:25
Anger	Ephesians 4:31; Colossians 3:8
Unwholesome words	Ephesians 4:29
Bitterness	Ephesians 4:31
Wrath	Ephesians 4:31; Colossians 3:8
Clamor	Ephesians 4:31
Slander	Ephesians 4:31; Colossians 3:8; 1 Peter 2:1
Malice	Colossians 3:8; 1 Peter 2:1
Abusive speech	Colossians 3:8
Lying	Colossians 3:9
Every encumbrance	Hebrews 12:1
Easily entangling sin	Hebrews 12:1
Filthiness	James 1:21
Wickedness	James 1:21
Guile	1 Peter 2:1
Hypocrisy	1 Peter 2:1
Envy	1 Peter 2:1

God doesn't want us to stand around spiritually naked, now that we
have begun to shed our old lifestyle. Instead, He invites us to dress
for spiritual success and provides a righteous wardrobe for our
wearing (Eph. 4:24; Col. 3:10). It includes:

The armour of light	Romans 13:12
The full armour of God	Ephesians 6:11
Truth	Ephesians 4:25
Honest labour	Ephesians 4:28
Timely words of grace	Ephesians 4:29
Kindness	Ephesians 4:32; Colossians 3:12
Tenderheartedness	Ephesians 4:32
Forgiveness	Ephesians 4:32; Colossians 3:13
A heart of compassion	Colossians 3:12
Humility	Colossians 3:12
Gentleness	Colossians 3:12
Patience	Colossians 3:12
Love	Colossians 3:14
Peace of Christ	Colossians 3:15
Thankfulness	Colossians 3:15
The Word of God	Colossians 3:16
A gentle and quiet spirit	1 Peter 3:4
Submissiveness to husband	1 Peter 3:5

Reasonable Conclusions

Two great truths must be drawn before we depart from the fundamentals of Christian infancy and dive headlong into 'Growing in Grace.'

First, since God initiates and sustains our salvation, true salvation can never be forfeited. We might be short on our personal assurance, but never on the God-determined reality of our salvation.

> For I am confident of this very thing, that He who began a good work in you will perfect it until the day of Christ Jesus (Phil. 1:6).

> My sheep hear My voice, and I know them, and they follow Me; and I give eternal life to them, and they will never perish; and no one will snatch them out of My hand. My Father, who has given them to Me, is greater than all; and no one is able to snatch them out of the Father's hand (John 10:27-29).

> But in all these things we overwhelmingly conquer through Him who loved us. For I am convinced that neither death, nor life, nor angels, nor principalities, nor things present, nor things to come, *nor powers, nor height, nor depth, nor any other created thing, will be able to* separate us from the love of God, which is in Christ Jesus our Lord (Rom. 8:37-39).

Faithful is He who calls you, and He also will bring it to pass (1 Thess. 5:24).

The second great truth is that since true salvation involves being raised from spiritual death and being made alive in Jesus Christ, then a true believer will show unmistakable signs of spiritual vitality and growth (James 2:14-26).

Finish then Thy new creation,
Pure and spotless let us be;
Let us see Thy great salvation
Perfectly restored in Thee.
Changed from glory into glory,
'Till in heav'n we take our place,
'Till we cast our crowns before Thee,
Lost in wonder, love and praise![1]

Charles Wesley

3

GROWING IN GRACE

After 'B' and I were saved, we discovered some wonderful new changes in our lives and marriage. Immediately, we knew that divorce would not solve our marriage problems. Rather, we needed to start all over again in order to build our home according to God's blueprint outlined in Scripture.

We also understood that our lives could no longer be lived just for ourselves; we were now servants of the God who had saved us. To the best of our remembrance, no one taught us this. It just was what we read in those fresh days of studying Scripture for the first time. We wanted to let God be God in all of our life.

Unfortunately, there are many today who believe or teach very differently about the Christian life. Listen to noted church historian, Richard Lovelace, summarize the present problem.

> Like American liberalism, the modern evangelical movement has a weakened sense of the holiness of God and the depth of personal sin. The Reformation stress on justification has been retained, and also the Puritan motif of the need for regeneration. But the process of being born again is much easier than the Puritans made it; a simple immediate response of faith and commitment, often after a very short presentation of the gospel. The possibility of losing the assurance of one's salvation is not even intimated. In fact, converts are urged to believe they are saved, as though this were one of the main doctrines of the faith. The themes of holiness and continued sanctification are very much muted compared to the Puritan and awakening eras. Evangelicals are once again suffering from a sanctification gap.[2]

What Lovelace rightly diagnoses is the notion that there is no necessary or vital Christian experience after salvation and before glorification. As a result, many a Christian's life between his second birth and physical death has been seriously ignored or misunderstood by otherwise sincere Christians.

Let me illustrate what I mean with a story from the life of famous artist Michelangelo. After carefully reviewing a painting by one of his better students, the master artist wrote across the work '**AMPLIUS**' which in Latin means 'larger.'

The painting needed to be expanded—the size of the canvas enlarged. The picture, as originally done by the student, did not do justice to its grand themes and magnificent detail. A painting of worth should not be confined to such a small space that its exquisite detail could not be admired by all.

In the same manner, God would need to write '**AMPLIUS**' across the miniature canvas of many a Christian life. We live in a time when growth, commitment, loyalty, fervency, sacrifice, and boldness are often taught as optional Christian qualities for the elite few, when in fact God has designed every Christian to be a portrait of Christ.

I believe the biblical correction to this 'sanctification gap' begins with understanding God's holy character and His holy purposes for our lives. Paul stated it this way:

> So then, my beloved, just as you have always obeyed, not as in my presence only, but now much more in my absence, work out your salvation with fear and trembling; for it is God who is at work in you, both to will and to work for His good pleasure (Phil. 2:12-13).

God's Holiness
We have been saved to be holy and to live a holy life.

> As obedient children, do not be conformed to the former lusts which were yours in your ignorance, but like the Holy One who called you, be holy yourselves also in all your behaviour; because it is written, 'You shall be holy, for I am holy' (1 Peter 1:14-16).

What does it mean to be holy? Both the Hebrew and Greek words (with about 2,000 appearances in Scripture) basically mean 'to be set aside for something special'. In the case of God, He sets Himself apart from creation, humanity, and all pagan gods by the fact of His deity and His sinlessness. That's why the angels sing of God, 'Holy, Holy, Holy' (Isa. 6:3; Rev. 4:8).

> Exalt the LORD our God,
> And worship at His holy hill;
> For holy is the LORD our God (Psalm 99:9).

> I am the LORD, your Holy One,
> The Creator of Israel, your King (Isa. 43:15).

Thus the idea of holiness takes on a spiritual meaning among the people of God, based on the holy character of God. For instance, the high priest of God had inscribed across his headpiece, 'Holy to the LORD' (Ex. 39:30). The High Priest had been especially set apart by God to intercede on behalf of a sinful nation to a holy God for the forgiveness of their transgressions.

Holiness embodies the very essence of Christianity. Our holy Saviour has saved us to be a holy people (1 Peter 2:4-10). That's why one of the most common biblical names for a believer is 'saint' which simply and wonderfully means, 'saved and set apart.'

> To all who are beloved of God in Rome, called as saints: Grace to you and peace from God our Father and the Lord Jesus Christ (Rom. 1:7).

> To the church of God which is at Corinth, to those who have been sanctified in Christ Jesus, saints by calling, with all who in every place call on the name of our Lord Jesus Christ, their Lord and ours (1 Cor. 1:2).

When we consider that a Holy God saved us, it is no surprise to learn that He gives His Holy Spirit to every believer at salvation as a gift. A primary purpose of this gift is to equip believers with the power to live a holy life.

> For God has not called us for the purpose of impurity, but in sanctification. So, he who rejects this is not rejecting man but the God who gives His Holy Spirit to you (1 Thess. 4:7-8).

> The one who keeps His commandments abides in Him, and He in him. We know by this that He abides in us, by the Spirit whom He has given us (1 John 3:24; 4:13).

So God wants us to share His holiness (Heb. 12:10) and to present ourselves as slaves of righteousness. This will result in holiness (Rom. 6:19). Listen to this challenge which contains both a negative and a positive aspect. Both are required to know holiness.

> Therefore, having these promises, beloved, let us cleanse ourselves from all defilement of flesh and spirit, perfecting holiness in the fear of God (2 Cor. 7:1).

And so it is that the author of Hebrews writes, 'Make every effort to live in peace with all men and to be holy; without holiness no one will see the Lord' (12:14, NIV). Holiness is the core of a Christian's experience.

Scottish theologian John Brown boils holiness down to a definition that we can all understand and then pursue. Out of holiness springs spiritual maturity.

Holiness does not consist of mystic speculations, enthusiastic fervours, or uncommanded austerities; it consists in thinking as God thinks, and willing as God wills. God's mind and will are to be known from His word; and, so far as I really understand and believe God's word, God's mind becomes my mind, God's will becomes my will, and according to the measure of my faith, I become holy.[3]

Christian Purity

Closely connected with holiness is sanctification. In many New Testament uses, the word means salvation (Acts 20:32; 1 Cor. 1:2). Sanctification, or being set apart in salvation, should result in our being set apart for Christian living:

> Sanctification is an immediate work of the Spirit of God on the souls of believers, purifying their natures from the pollution and uncleanness of sin, renewing in them the image of God, and thereby enabling them, from a spiritual and habitual principle of grace, to yield obedience to God, according to the tenor of the new covenant, by virtue of the life and death of Jesus Christ. Or more briefly, it is the universal renovation of our natures by the Holy Spirit, into the image of God, through Jesus Christ.[4]

Sanctification includes not only the immediate act and fact of salvation, but additionally involves a progressive or growing experience of greater holiness and less sinfulness. It expresses God's will and fulfills the purpose of God's salvation call:

> For this is the will of God, your sanctification; that is, that you abstain from sexual immorality; that each of you know how to possess his own vessel in sanctification and honor . . . for God has not called us for the purpose of impurity, but in sanctification (1 Thess. 4:3-4, 7).

Sanctification includes our responsibility to participate in continuing what God's Spirit began in salvation.

> Therefore, if anyone cleanses himself from these things, he will be a vessel for honor, sanctified, useful to the Master, prepared for every good work (2 Tim. 2:21).

> Let the one who does wrong, still do wrong; and the one who is filthy, still be filthy; and let the one who is righteous, still practice *righteousness; and the one who is holy, still keep himself holy* (Rev. 22:11).

Christians are constantly exhorted to pursue in their Christian experience what God has declared to be true of them in salvation. We are also promised that what is not now complete, God will ultimately finish in glory.

> So then, my beloved, just as you have always obeyed, not as in my presence only, but now much more in my absence, work out your salvation with fear and trembling; for it is God who is at work in you, both to will and to work for His good pleasure (Phil. 2:12-13).

> Now may the God of peace Himself sanctify you entirely; and may your spirit and soul and body be preserved complete, without blame at the coming of our Lord Jesus Christ (1 Thess. 5:23).

This expresses one of the great paradoxes of Scripture— 'We are to become what we already are and one day will be.'

> Whoever will call on the name of the Lord will be saved (Rom. 10:13).

> For the word of the cross is foolishness to those who are perishing, but to us who are being saved it is the power of God (1 Cor. 1:18).

> Do this, knowing the time, that it is already the hour for you to awaken from sleep; for now salvation is nearer to us than when we believed (Rom. 13:11).

Sanctification involves the spiritual process which is pictured by a body growing into adulthood (Heb. 5:11-14) or a seed developing into a tree or flower (Ps. 1:1-6). Growth is not always easy or uniform; however, it should be the direction of a true Christian's life.

Several obstacles face the believer in this lifelong pursuit. We need to know them and be on guard to avoid or correct them as they become a part of our thinking.

1. We may think more highly of ourselves than we ought and not pursue holiness as we should (Rom. 12:3).
2. We may presume on salvation and assume that since we are saved, holy living is optional (Rom. 6:1-2).
3. We may have been erroneously taught about the nature of Christian living and so neglect the lordship of Christ (1 Peter 3:15).

4. We may be wearied by life and lack the zeal or energy to make holiness a priority (2 Cor. 7:1).

5. We may think we are saved but in reality are not, then we try to live holy lives in the power of the flesh (Matt. 13:5-7, 20-22).

A Believer's Growth

Nature teaches us that growth is normal and to be expected; conversely, a lack of growth should sound an alarm that something is seriously wrong. Scripture also teaches this, in a spiritual sense. Frequently we read in Acts that the early church grew and expanded (cf. 2:41; 4:4; 5:14; 6:7; 9:31,35,42; 11:21; 14:1,21; 16:5; 17:12).

We also read about God's expectations for individual growth in the Christian's life. We need to take these exhortations of Scripture seriously.

> But grow in the grace and knowledge of our Lord and Savior Jesus Christ. To Him be the glory, both now and to the day of eternity. Amen (2 Peter 3:18).

> Like newborn babies, long for the pure milk of the word, so that by it you may grow in respect to salvation (1 Peter 2:2).

The chief agents for this growth are God's Word (John 17:17; 1 Peter 2:2) and God's Spirit (Eph. 5:15-21). When the growth occurs, we can quickly acknowledge God as the cause.

> I planted, Apollos watered, but God was causing the growth. So then neither the one who plants nor the one who waters is anything, but God who causes the growth (1 Cor. 3:6-7).

> And not holding fast to the head, from whom the entire body, being supplied and held together by the joints and ligaments, grows with a growth which is from God (Col. 2:19).

Salvation's Assurance

The Holy Spirit plays a prominent role in providing a true believer with the assurance of salvation and His assurance connects directly with growth.

> The Spirit Himself testifies with our spirit that we are children of God, and if children, heirs also, heirs of God and fellow heirs with Christ, if

indeed we suffer with Him so that we may also be glorified with Him (Rom. 8:16-17).

The one who keeps His commandments abides in Him, and He in him. We know by this that He abides in us, by the Spirit whom He has given us (1 John 3:24).

Having formerly been spiritually dead but now made alive unto God, the believer can check his own vital signs to substantiate the fact that he is indeed alive, because he walks in the works which God has prepared (Eph. 2:1-10).

Some would teach that we only need to look at our 'birth certificate' to validate new life in Christ. That is to say we need only remember the moment we put our trust in Christ and then claim the biblical promise for eternal life. They would say that how one lives after this salvation experience has little or nothing to do with validating the genuineness of one's supposed salvation.

While that is partially true, it is not biblically complete. What happens if we lose the certificate or can't remember the details of personal salvation? What if the certificate turns out to be counterfeit? The only conclusive proof is current vital signs of a spiritual nature that point to a real, continuing life.

If you want to check your spiritual health, here are some of the most important vital life signs of a true Christian.

Christian fruit (John 15:8)
Love for God's people (John 13:35)
Concern over personal holiness (1 Peter 1: 13-21)
Love for God's Word (1 Peter 2: 1-3)
Desire to obey (John 14: 15,21,23)
Sense of intimacy with God (Rom. 8: 14-17)
Perseverance (Phil. 1: 27-28)
Fellowship with God's people (Heb. 10: 19-25)
Desire to glorify God (Matt. 5: 13-16)
Witness to Christ's reality in you (1 Peter 3:15)

Normal Christianity

And He gave some as apostles, and some as prophets, and some as evangelists, and some as pastors and teachers, for the equipping of the saints for the work of service, to the building up of the body of Christ;

until we all attain to the unity of the faith, and of the knowledge of the Son of God, to a mature man, to the measure of the stature which belongs to the fullness of Christ. As a result, we are no longer to be children, tossed here and there by waves, and carried about by every wind of doctrine, by the trickery of men, by craftiness in deceitful scheming; but speaking the truth in love, we are to grow up in all aspects into Him, who is the head, even Christ, from whom the whole body, being fitted and held together by what every joint supplies, according to the proper working of each individual part, causes the growth of the body for the building up of itself in love (Eph. 4:11-16).

No passage in the Bible equals this paragraph in expressing God's intention for the true believer to mature in the faith.

Three significant words are used in 4:12-13 which speak emphatically of the normal process when God's servants herald the Word of God to Christians. It is for the *equipping* of the saints who then will do the work of ministry resulting in the building up of the body of Christ. The goal is that each individual becomes a *mature* person.

As a result, Christians are not to linger or remain at the childhood level, but are to *grow up* in all things. As this individual maturity or *growth* occurs, it extends to the building up and growth of the corporate body of Christ (vv. 14-16).

Make no mistake about this process. It involves *God's Spirit* taking *God's Word* and maturing *God's people* through the ministry of *God's servants* for the *spiritual growth* of individual believers which results in the *growth of Christ's body*.

God has no alternative plan for His spiritual children.

For consider Him who has endured such hostility by sinners against Himself, so that you will not grow weary and lose heart. You have not yet resisted to the point of shedding blood in your striving against sin; and you have forgotten the exhortation which is addressed to you as sons. 'My son, do not regard lightly the discipline of the Lord, nor faint when you are reproved by Him; for those whom the Lord loves He disciplines, and He scourges every son whom He receives.'

It is for discipline that you endure; God deals with you as with sons; for what son is there whom his father does not discipline? But if you are without discipline, of which all have become partakers, then you are illegitimate children and not sons. Furthermore, we had earthly fathers to discipline us, and we respected them; shall we not much rather be subject to the Father of spirits, and live? For they disciplined us for a short time as seemed best to them, but He disciplines us for our good, that we may share His holiness. All discipline for the moment seems not to be joyful, but sorrowful; yet to those who have been trained by it, afterwards it yields the peaceful fruit of righteousness (Heb. 12:3-11).

IF

No better human expression of growing in grace has been written than by Amy Carmichael in her classic devotional *IF*.[5]

It fleshes out the ultimate in Christian maturity. Enjoy this sampling and then set your heart to grow in Christ.

IF I hold on to choices of any kind, just because they are my choice; if I give any room to my private likes and dislikes, then I know nothing of Calvary love.

IF I feel injured when another lays to my charge things that I know not, forgetting that my sinless Saviour trod this path to the end, then I know nothing of Calvary love.

IF there be any reserve in my giving to Him who so loved that He gave His Dearest for me; if there be a secret 'but' in my prayer – 'anything but that, Lord' then I know nothing of Calvary love.

Immortal, invisible,
God only wise,
In light inaccessible
Hid from our eyes,
Most blessed, most glorious,
The Ancient of Days,
Almighty, victorious -
Thy great name we praise.[1]

Walter Chalmers Smith

4

WHAT IS GOD LIKE?

No more appropriate lyrics have been sung to honour the person of God than these by the four living creatures and the twenty-four elders in heaven.

> Holy, Holy, Holy, is the Lord God, the Almighty, who was and who is and who is to come (Rev. 4:8).

> Worthy art You, our Lord and our God, to receive glory and honor and power; for You created all things, and because of Your will they existed, and were created (Rev. 4:11).

These verses describe the unblemished character of our omnipotent, sovereign God who created the universe out of nothing by a spoken word. He eternally exists before time, through time, and beyond time. Comprehending these lofty thoughts is more challenging than attempting to physically ascend Mt. Everest. God's fullness can never be fully scaled by our human minds. Writers of Scripture use the following superlatives in trying to describe God who cannot be limited or equalled.

Unsearchable	Romans 11:33
Immortal	1 Timothy 1:17
Inscrutable	Isaiah 40:28
Incorruptible	Romans 1:23
Invisible	1 Timothy 1:17
Unapproachable light	1 Timothy 6:16
Unfathomable	Romans 11:33

The Psalms abound in descriptions of God's character and works. Stop and survey this sampler in order to mentally and emotionally bask in the glorious majesty of God.

Psalm 2	Psalm 73	Psalm 139
Psalm 8	Psalm 90	Psalm 144
Psalm 18	Psalm 99	Psalm 145
Psalm 24	Psalm 104	Psalm 146
Psalm 29	Psalm 105	Psalm 147
Psalm 33	Psalm 106	Psalm 148
Psalm 50	Psalm 121	Psalm 149
Psalm 63	Psalm 135	Psalm 150

The Names of God

The names of people do not always correspond to their characters or their accomplishments. But the names of God always reveal something true about Him.

1. For instance, *Elohim* or 'God' tells us that He is supreme above all things and all people (Gen. 1:1). He is eternal while all else is temporal. He is the Creator; all has been made by Him.

2. *Jehovah* or 'LORD' occurs over 6,800 times in the Old Testament and speaks of God's eternal and unchanging nature. It literally means, 'I AM.' God used it to instruct Moses (Ex. 3:13-14); and Christ confounded the Pharisees with this name (John 8:58).

3. *El-Shaddai* or 'God Almighty' points to God's invincibility and His omnipotence or all-powerfulness (Gen. 17:1-2). Nothing is too hard for God and no enemy will ever defeat Him. He can do all things.

4. A fourth name is *Adonai* which means 'Master' or 'Lord' (Deut. 10:17). It indicates authority and ownership. Therefore, God deserves our worship, allegiance, and obedience, because from Him we have received our very existence, as well as our eternal redemption in Christ.

5. Abraham unforgettably learned about *Jehovah-Jireh*, 'the LORD will provide', when God substituted the sacrifice to replace Isaac (Gen. 22:14). The name pictures God as seeing, and thus anticipating His divine provision of the right supply at just the right time. His omniscience or all-knowingness and wisdom are in view here.

6. *Jehovah-Rophe* points to God as healer (Ex. 15:26). The Shepherd's mercy, compassion, and loving-kindness shows through this name. God's healing is to be understood both in a physical and spiritual sense.

7. God's holiness can be seen in *Jehovah-M'kaddesh* which means 'the LORD who sanctifies' (Lev. 20:7-8). He stands as our redeemer and our sanctifier. The name reminds us that He hates sin.

8. Gideon built an altar and called it *Jehovah-Shalom* (Judg. 6:24). For him it signified the quality of peace which is central to God's nature. Closely associated in a redemptive sense is *Jehovah-Tsidkenu* or 'Jehovah our righteousness' (Jer. 23:5-6).

9. *Jehovah-Rohi*, 'the LORD is my Shepherd' (Ps. 23:1), and *Jehovah-Shammah*, 'the LORD is there' (Ezek. 48:35), describe God's presence to guide, protect, and make provision for our needs.

The Attributes of God

An *attribute* or 'characteristic quality' helps to describe the nature of something or someone. In the case of God, His attributes tell us who He is, in terms that we can understand.

Theologians categorize God's attributes in various ways; but for our purposes, we will use the descriptive phrases *noncommunicable* and *communicable*. God's noncommunicable qualities are those characteristics which are unique to deity. In contrast, communicable attributes can be reproduced, at least in part, in human beings.

1. Noncommunicable Attributes. These major characteristics of God exclusively pertain to His deity. They will never be experienced by anyone else.

Omnipotence	Jeremiah 32:17
Omniscience	Psalm 139:1-6
Omnipresence	Psalm 139:7-10
Immutability	Psalm 102:27
Sovereignty	1 Chronicles 29:11-12
Eternality	Psalm 90:2
Immortality	1 Timothy 1:17
Greatness	Psalm 135:5
Self-existence	Isaiah 41:4

While we can never aspire to these qualities, they do tell us something significant about God in His relationship with us. For example, since God is all-powerful or omnipotent, nothing in life will defeat Him, and we will encounter no one or anything over which God is unable to be victorious. No problem of mine is too hard for God to solve.

Since God is omniscient, and is everywhere or omnipresent, then nothing surprises Him and He misses nothing in our lives. He will be with us both in good and bad times.

His unchangeableness or immutability, sovereignty, eternality, immortality, greatness, and self-existence all point to the exclusiveness of His deity which will be shared by no one else. Thus, we worship the one true God who is ever consistent with Himself from eternity to eternity, is dependent on nothing, will be victorious over all, and whose eternal purposes will be completely accomplished.

2. Communicable Attributes. These qualities find their ultimate expression in God. However, humans can experience them to a limited degree but never in their fullest form. They include:

Wisdom	Romans 16:27
Faithfulness	1 Corinthians 10:13
Truthfulness	Exodus 34:6
Love	1 John 4:8
Goodness	Psalm 100:5
Righteousness	Psalm 92:15
Mercy	Psalm 86:15
Compassion	Lamentations 3:22-23
Holiness	Psalm 99:9
Graciousness	Psalm 116:5
Patience	2 Peter 3:15
Peace	Hebrews 13:20
Kindness	Psalm 100:5
Gentleness	2 Corinthians 10:1
Joy	John 17:13
Forgiveness	Exodus 34:7
Justice	Deuteronomy 10:18

At this point, you might be wondering how the attributes of God are important in our lives. Let me illustrate with a recent event at The Master's Seminary. During the recession of the early 1990s, our school needed to cut back on salaries in order to exercise good stewardship of our professors and staff, plus raising tuition for students.

As Vice President and Dean, I had to explain this to our Seminary family. I did so in the context of God's faithfulness. I reminded them from Scripture that God is faithful (Deut. 7:9; 32:4; Pss. 36:5; 100:5). He is faithful in:

His word/promises	Hebrews 10:23
His salvation	1 Thessalonians 5:24
His protection	2 Thessalonians 3:3
His Son	Revelation 19:11
His provision	Lamentations 3:22-23

I told them that because of God's faithfulness, we had two obligations. First, we could completely trust God, even though we might not see how our family budget could be balanced with a reduced salary, or how we could afford higher tuition. But as God had been faithful to accomplish His purpose in us before, so he would in the future. Therefore, we must trust Him in the same way.

Second, we could use this life opportunity to cultivate faithfulness in our own lives, families, ministries, and Seminary involvement (Prov. 12:22; 20:6). Thus we could prepare for the day when we will stand before Christ to give an account of our stewardship, when we hope we will hear the words, 'Well done, good and faithful slave' (Matt. 25:21, 23). By understanding God's absolute dependability, trustworthiness, and reliability, we not only wait for His provision by faith, but also develop these same qualities in our lives.

Close Encounters of a Spiritual Kind
Experiencing God up close often turns into a terrifying event. Whether we look at the disciples in the boat during a stormy night on the sea of Galilee (Mark 4:41), at Adam in the garden (Gen. 3:8-10), or Israel at Sinai (Ex. 20:18-21), we see a holy trauma.

1. Job's Encounter. Job was blameless, upright, fearing God, and turning away from evil (Job 1:1). But when God chose to reveal Himself in a fresh way to Job, the result was fear and repentance.

You can read through the two-part oral examination that God administered to Job (38:1-40:5; 40:6-42:6). Confronted by the overwhelming noncommunicable attributes of God, Job cried out:

> I know that You can do all things, and that no purpose of Yours can be thwarted. Who is this that hides counsel without knowledge? Therefore I have declared that which I did not understand, things too wonderful for me, which I did not know. Hear, now, and I will speak; I will ask You, and You instruct me. I have heard of You by the hearing of the ear; but now my eye sees You; therefore I retract, and I repent in dust and ashes (Job 42:2-6).

2. Isaiah's Encounter. When this faithful prophet of God heard the seraphim sing, 'Holy, Holy, Holy, is the LORD of hosts, the earth is full of His glory' (Isa. 6:3), and when he glimpsed the King's majesty, his world crumpled. Isaiah lamented:

> Woe is me, for I am ruined! Because I am a man of unclean lips, and I live among a people of unclean lips; for my eyes have seen the King, the LORD of Hosts (Isa. 6:5).

Because Isaiah responded rightly over his own sin in the presence of his holy God, the Lord dispatched him on a continuing ministry of proclamation to Israel (Isa. 6:8-13). Later on God entrusted Isaiah to record some of the most moving declarations of God's attributes (Isa. 40-46). You would be greatly blessed to stop studying at this point and read these great chapters by Isaiah.

3. Habakkuk's Encounter. Habakkuk could not figure out why God acted as He did, in light of who he knew God to be (Hab. 1:2-4, 12-17). So on two occasions the Lord gave His prophet some postgraduate instructions on how and why God's action is always consistent with His attributes (1:5-11; 2:2-20).

The prophet's response was remarkable. First, he prayed that God would accomplish His purpose (3:1-7). Then, he recited a psalm of God's heroic deeds (3:8-15). He concluded the whole episode with these words,

> I heard and my inward parts trembled; at the sound my lips quivered. Decay enters my bones, and in my place I tremble. Because I must wait quietly for the day of distress, for the people to arise who will invade us (Hab. 3:16).

Finally, Habakkuk promised God that regardless of what came, he would trust the Lord as his strength (3:17-19).

4. Paul's Encounter. One of the really magnificent statements in Scripture about God's character was written by the Apostle Paul.

> Oh, the depth of the riches both of the wisdom and knowledge of God! How unsearchable are His judgments and unfathomable His ways! For who has known the mind of the Lord, or who became His counselor? Or who has first given to Him that it might be paid back to him again? For from Him and through Him and to Him are all things. To Him be the glory forever. Amen (Rom. 11:33-36).

Where did Paul learn this? I submit that this was indelibly etched in Paul's mind during his visit to the third heaven (2 Cor. 12:2).

While in Paradise, he undoubtedly saw and heard things he was unable to directly communicate (2 Cor. 12:4). But Paul knew enough to believe that when God said, 'My grace is sufficient for you, for power is perfected in weakness' (2 Cor. 12:9), he needed to believe and obey. So we are not surprised to read this and other wonderful expressions about God's greatness from Paul's pen.

> Now to the King eternal, immortal, invisible, the only God, be honor and glory forever and ever. Amen (1 Tim. 1:17).

> The Lord will rescue me from every evil deed, and will bring me safely to His heavenly kingdom; to Him be the glory forever and ever. Amen (2 Tim. 4:18).

The Ultimate Perspective

Reading about God in a book is secondhand at best. If that's all we have, so be it. But for most, if not all of us, we want to know more about God in an immediate way. Thus the Lord Jesus Christ gives us the answer:

> No one has seen God at any time; the only begotten God, who is in the bosom of the Father, He has explained Him (John 1:18).

Jesus came to explain or demonstrate God by His life. If you really want to understand the attributes of God, then carefully observe Christ in the Gospels. The attributes are all there—both noncommunicable and communicable.

Paul wrote that Christians have been predestined to become conformed to the image of the Lord Jesus Christ (Rom. 8:29). As we become like Christ, then we become like God in His communicable attributes. In so doing, the effect of the curse will be continually reversed and the image of God in man will be progressively restored.

Be Thou my vision, O Lord of my heart;
Naught be all else to me, save that Thou art -
Thou my best thought, by day or by night,
Waking or sleeping, Thy presence my light.[1]

Unknown

5

TO BE LIKE GOD!

Several Christmases ago my wife introduced me to a hobby that we now dearly enjoy together—model railroading. Our 'N' gauge layout represents the actual Pennsylvania Railroad on which my Grandfather Mayhue served forty years as a brakeman.

'N' gauge trains (about half the size of HO) are $1/160$ th the size of the real thing or prototype. As you might guess, replica models do not contain every detail of a full-size diesel engine or freight car, but no one would mistake the fact that they have been scale-modelled after the originals.

These electric trains help us to illustrate godliness. God is the prototype after whom Christians are fashioned to be scale models. We will never be identical in size to God—only miniatures; we will never possess all the characteristics of God, only those which are communicable. Put another way, we will never become or ever approach deity, but we are exhorted by Scripture to be godlike. God intends Christians to be representative copies of Himself.

Spiritual Renovation
The Bible variously describes salvation and the Christian life as going from darkness to light (Col. 1:12-13), from Satan to God, (Acts 26:18), from death to life (Col. 2:13), from lust to purity (1 Peter 1:14-16), from old to new (2 Cor. 5:17), and from brokenness to being whole (Col. 2:10). Every true Christian currently experiences God's renovation or reformation. God announced the end at the beginning—we are saved. Yet He does not finish the project until the end when we are glorified. Paul described this process to the Colossians who had 'put on the new self who is being renewed to a true knowledge according to the image of the One who created him' (Col. 3:10).

He told the Galatians that he laboured again on their behalf until Christ be formed in them (Gal. 4:19). Paul prayed that the Ephesians would be filled up with all the fullness of God (Eph. 3:19). God's image in man, severely marred by sin, is made renewable by salvation so that the Christian life involves progressive restoration toward the original (Adam and Eve before the Fall) which was characterized by perfect godliness. However, the total perfection of godliness in a Christian will not be experienced until we are in God's presence (Phil. 1:21; 2 Cor. 5:8). Listen to Peter's explanation of salvation's effect.

Grace and peace be multiplied to you in the knowledge of God and of Jesus our Lord; seeing that His divine power has granted to us everything pertaining to life and godliness, through the true knowledge of Him who called us by His own glory and excellence. For by these He has granted to us His precious and magnificent promises, so that by them you may become partakers of the divine nature, having escaped the corruption that is in the world by lust (2 Peter 1:2-4).

Jerry Bridges captures the essence of being godly with this insightful explanation.

Godliness consists of two distinct but complementary traits, and the person who wants to train himself to be godly must pursue both with equal vigour. The first trait is God-centredness, which we call devotion to God; the second is God-likeness, which we call Christian character. Godly character flows out of devotion to God and practically confirms the reality of that devotion.[2]

Bridges suggests that godliness involves first a commitment or devotion to God (God-centredness) which then yields godlikeness in character. Both stand inseparably linked.

I would like to take his definition one more step. Mature godliness involves three, not two, elements which bloom sequentially much like a beautiful rose.

1. Godward consecration.
2. Godlike character.
3. Godly conduct.

Now, let's see if the biblical evidence bears this out.

Biblical Godliness

The basic idea of both the Hebrew and Greek words translated 'godly' centres around the general thought of devotion. The Old Testament's play on words (God's covenant loving-kindness and man's godliness) involves the concept that as God is devoted to those with whom He made a covenant, so they in turn will be devoted to Him, the Covenant-Maker.

1. Old Testament. Three elements of God's relationship to a godly person emerge in the Old Testament. First, God has set the godly one apart for Himself (Ps. 4:3). Second, God preserves the way of the godly (Prov. 2:8). And third, God vindicates the godly by judging the ungodly (Ps. 149:9). Interestingly, this corresponds first to the nature of salvation, then steadfastly living out the Christian life, and finally receiving eternal results.

Although the biblical information is scant, the following activities mark a godly person. Note their God-centredness followed by both character and conduct implications.

Rejoicing in good	2 Chronicles 6:41
Singing and praising God	Psalms 30:4; 132:9,16; 148:14
Blessing God	Psalm 145:10
Praying to God	Psalm 32:6
Loving God	Psalm 31:23

2. New Testament. Ungodliness finds a ringing condemnation from the pen of New Testament writers.

For the wrath of God is revealed from heaven against all ungodliness and unrighteousness . . . (Rom. 1:18).

But realize this, that in the last days difficult times will come. For men will be lovers of self, lovers of money, boastful, arrogant, revilers, disobedient to parents, ungrateful, unholy, unloving, irreconcilable, malicious gossips, without self-control, brutal, haters of good, treacherous, reckless, conceited, lovers of pleasure rather than lovers of God; holding to a form of godliness, although they have denied its power. Avoid such men as these (2 Tim. 3:1-5).

It was also about these men that Enoch, in the seventh generation from Adam, prophesied, saying, 'Behold, the Lord came with many thousands of His holy ones, to execute judgment upon all, and to convict all the ungodly of all their ungodly deeds which they have done in an ungodly way, and of all the harsh things which ungodly sinners have spoken against Him' (Jude 14-15).

In contrast, devotion or consecration which marks godliness is strongly promoted by the New Testament writers.

But flee from these things, you man of God; and pursue righteousness, godliness, faith, love, perseverance and gentleness (1 Tim. 6:11).

Now for this very reason also, applying all diligence, in your faith supply moral excellence, and in your moral excellence, knowledge; and in your knowledge, self-control; and in your self-control, perseverance; and in your perseverance, godliness; and in your godliness, brotherly kindness; and in your brotherly kindness, love. For if these qualities are yours and are increasing, they render you neither useless nor unfruitful in the true knowledge of our Lord Jesus Christ. For he who lacks these qualities is blind or short-sighted, having forgotten his purification from his former sins. Therefore, brethren, be all the more diligent to make certain about His calling and choosing you; for as long as you practice these things, you will never stumble; for in this way the entrance into the eternal kingdom of our Lord and Savior Jesus Christ will be abundantly supplied to you (2 Peter 1:5-11).

We're not surprised to also see the final element—conduct—as a prominent feature in the New Testament discussion of godliness.

Likewise, I want women to adorn themselves with proper clothing, modestly and discreetly, not with braided hair and gold or pearls or costly garments, but rather by means of good works, as is proper for women making a claim to godliness (1 Tim. 2:9-10).

Indeed, all who desire to live godly in Christ Jesus will be persecuted (2 Tim. 3:12).

Since all these things are to be destroyed in this way, what sort of people ought you to be in holy conduct and godliness (2 Peter 3:11).

Paul's instruction to Titus summarizes all three aspects of godliness—consecration, character, and conduct.

For the grace of God appeared, bringing salvation to all men, instructing us to deny ungodliness and worldly desires and to live sensibly, righteously and godly in the present age, looking for the blessed hope and the appearing of the glory of our great God and Savior, Christ Jesus; who gave Himself for us to redeem us from every lawless deed, and to purify for Himself a people for His own possession, zealous for good deeds (Titus 2:11-14).

God's Character

In a real way, character sums up the Christian life. If our character conforms to the character of God through our continual consecration to or centredness in Him, then the result will be conduct worthy of God.

You'll remember that God's character or attributes divide into two categories. His noncommunicable attributes are unique to His deity and found exclusively in Him. His communicable attributes can be formed in us by God's Spirit. God's most significant attributes which He would develop in us include:

Wisdom	Mercy	Kindness
Faithfulness	Compassion	Gentleness
Truthfulness	Holiness	Joy
Love	Graciousness	Forgiveness
Goodness	Patience	Justice
Righteousness	Peace	

Biblical godliness involves centring our focus on God, whose character can be formed in us. This produces godly behaviour in the true Christian. It all begins with God's grace and ultimately results in God's glory.

Godliness Illustrated

Let's take the communicable attribute of truthfulness. Everywhere Scripture declares that God is truthful. Isaiah calls Him 'the God of truth' (65:16). Titus declares that God cannot lie (1:2). The psalmist asserts that 'the sum of Your Word is truth' (119:160). God is not a man that He should lie (Num. 23:19; 1 Sam. 15:29).

Apart from God's intervention to bring salvation, man is inherently untruthful (Rom. 3:10-18). But in salvation, we turn our attentions from Satan the father of lies, and from a world full of deceit, to concentrate on God. In so doing, we begin to value truth as God values it.

Put away from you a deceitful mouth,
And put devious speech far from you (Prov. 4:24).

Two things I asked of You,
Do not refuse me before I die:
Keep deception and lies far from me,

Give me neither poverty nor riches;
Feed me with the food that is my portion,
That I not be full and deny You and say, 'Who is the Lord?' (Prov. 30:7-9a).

As our character conforms to God's character of truthfulness, then our lives are lived with greater truthfulness.

Therefore, laying aside falsehood, speak truth, each one of you, with his neighbour, for we are members of one another (Eph. 4:25).

To the degree that our lives reflect truthfulness, we reflect godliness. Keep in mind that godliness is not being God, but rather it is bearing a likeness to God.

A Testimony of Godliness

Look for all three elements of godliness in David's wonderful expression of allegiance to God—consecration, character, and conduct. You will understand then why God called David 'a man after My heart' (Acts 13:22).

1   And David spoke the words of this song to the Lord in the day that the Lord delivered him from the hand of all his enemies and from the hand of Saul.
  2   He said,
      "The Lord is my rock and my fortress and my deliverer;
  3   My God, my rock, in whom I take refuge,
      My shield and the horn of my salvation, my stronghold and my refuge;
      My savior, You save me from violence.
  4   "I call upon the Lord, who is worthy to be praised,
      And I am saved from my enemies.
  5   "For the waves of death encompassed me;
      The torrents of destruction overwhelmed me;
  6   The cords of Sheol surrounded me;
      The snares of death confronted me.
  7   "In my distress I called upon the Lord,
      Yes, I cried to my God;
      And from His temple He heard my voice,
      And my cry for help *came* into His ears.
  8   "Then the earth shook and quaked,
      The foundations of heaven were trembling
      And were shaken, because He was angry.

9   "Smoke went up out of His nostrils,
    Fire from His mouth devoured;
    Coals were kindled by it.

10 "He bowed the heavens also, and came down
    With thick darkness under His feet.

11 "And He rode on a cherub and flew;
    And He appeared on the wings of the wind.

12 "And He made darkness canopies around Him,
    A mass of waters, thick clouds of the sky.

13 "From the brightness before Him
    Coals of fire were kindled.

14 "The LORD thundered from heaven,
    And the Most High uttered His voice.

15 "And He sent out arrows, and scattered them,
    Lightning, and routed them.

16 "Then the channels of the sea appeared,
    The foundations of the world were laid bare
    By the rebuke of the LORD,
    At the blast of the breath of His nostrils.

17 "He sent from on high, He took me;
    He drew me out of many waters.

18 "He delivered me from my strong enemy,
    From those who hated me, for they were too strong for me.

19 "They confronted me in the day of my calamity,
    But the LORD was my support.

20 "He also brought me forth into a broad place;
    He rescued me, because He delighted in me.

21 "The LORD has rewarded me according to my righteousness;
    According to the cleanness of my hands He has recompensed me.

22 "For I have kept the ways of the LORD,
    And have not acted wickedly against my God.

23 "For all His ordinances *were* before me,
    And *as for* His statutes, I did not depart from them.

24 "I was also blameless toward Him,
    And I kept myself from my iniquity.

25 "Therefore the LORD has recompensed me according to my
    righteousness,
    According to my cleanness before His eyes.

26 "With the kind You show Yourself kind,
    With the blameless You show Yourself blameless;

27 With the pure You show Yourself pure,
    And with the perverted You show Yourself astute.

28 "And You save an afflicted people;

But Your eyes are on the haughty *whom* You abase.

29 "For You are my lamp, O Lord;
And the Lord illumines my darkness.

30 "For by You I can run upon a troop;
By my God I can leap over a wall.

31 "As for God, His way is blameless;
The word of the Lord is tested;
He is a shield to all who take refuge in Him.

32 "For who is God, besides the Lord?
And who is a rock, besides our God?

33 "God is my strong fortress;
And He sets the blameless in His way.

34 "He makes my feet like hinds' *feet,*
And sets me on my high places.

35 "He trains my hands for battle,
So that my arms can bend a bow of bronze.

36 "You have also given me the shield of Your salvation,
And Your help makes me great.

37 "You enlarge my steps under me,
And my feet have not slipped.

38 "I pursued my enemies and destroyed them,
And I did not turn back until they were consumed.

39 "And I have devoured them and shattered them, so that they did not rise;
And they fell under my feet.

40 "For You have girded me with strength for battle;
You have subdued under me those who rose up against me.

41 "You have also made my enemies turn *their* backs to me,
And I destroyed those who hated me.

42 "They looked, but there was none to save;
Even to the Lord, but He did not answer them.

43 "Then I pulverized them as the dust of the earth;
I crushed *and* stamped them as the mire of the streets.

44 "You have also delivered me from the contentions of my people;
You have kept me as head of the nations;
A people whom I have not known serve me.

45 "Foreigners pretend obedience to me;
As soon as they hear, they obey me.

46 "Foreigners lose heart,
And come trembling out of their fortresses.

47 "The Lord lives, and blessed be my rock;
And exalted be God, the rock of my salvation,

48 The God who executes vengeance for me,

And brings down peoples under me,
49 Who also brings me out from my enemies;
    You even lift me above those who rise up against me;
    You rescue me from the violent man.
50 "Therefore I will give thanks to You, O LORD, among the nations,
    And I will sing praises to Your name.
51 "*He* is a tower of deliverance to His king,
    And shows lovingkindness to His anointed,
    To David and his descendants forever."

A Closing Prayer

An ancient saint captures the heart of godliness in his prayer. I commend it to us all.

Day by day, dear Lord,
of Thee three things I pray:
To see Thee more clearly
To love Thee more dearly
To follow Thee more nearly.
(Richard of Chichester, 1197-1253)

Part Two

SPIRITUAL POWER

Therefore having such a hope, we use great boldness in our speech, and are not as Moses, who used to put a veil over his face that the sons of Israel would not look intently at the end of what was fading away. But their minds were hardened; for until this very day at the reading of the old covenant the same veil remains unlifted, because it is removed in Christ. But to this day whenever Moses is read, a veil lies over their heart; but whenever a person turns to the Lord, the veil is taken away. Now the Lord is the Spirit; and where the Spirit of the Lord is, there is liberty. But we all, with unveiled face, beholding as in a mirror the glory of the Lord, are being transformed into the same image from glory to glory, just as from the Lord, the Spirit.
2 Corinthians 3:12-18

I have had a deep conviction for many years that practical holiness and entire self-consecration to God are not sufficiently attended to by modern Christians in this country. Politics or controversy or party spirit or worldliness have eaten out the heart of lively piety in too many of us. The subject of personal godliness has fallen sadly into the background. The standard of living has become painfully low in many quarters. The immense importance of 'adorning the doctrine of God our Saviour' (Titus 2:10), and making it lovely and beautiful by our daily habits and tempers, has been far too much overlooked. Worldly people sometimes complain with reason that 'religious' persons, so-called, are not so amiable and unselfish and good-natured as others who make no profession of religion.

Yet sanctification, in its place and proportion, is quite as important as justification. Sound Protestant and Evangelical doctrine is useless if it is not accompanied by a holy life. It is worse than useless: it does positive harm. It is despised by keen-sighted and shrewd men of the world as an unreal and hollow thing, and brings religion into contempt. It is my firm impression that we want a thorough revival about Scriptural holiness, and I am deeply thankful that attention is being directed to the point.[1]

J.C. Ryle

Breathe on me, Breath of God,
Fill me with life anew,
That I may love what Thou dost love,
And do what Thou wouldst do.
Breathe on me, Breath of God,
Until my heart is pure,
Until my will is one with Thine,
To do and to endure.[1]

Edwin Hatch

6

INVADED BY GOD'S SPIRIT[2]

In February 1991, I travelled to the former Soviet Union with several of my colleagues from The Master's Seminary to inaugurate a new seminary outside of Kiev in Ukraine. While there, I taught this material on the Holy Spirit. The joy of the students in knowing the truth about His work in the believer's life still lingers prominently in my memory. I trust that your joy will be as great because you have studied Scripture about God's Holy Spirit.

Now, just as there can be no salvation without the work of the Holy Spirit (Eph. 1:13-14; Titus 3:5-6), so there can be no holy living without the ministry of the Spirit (Gal. 5:16-26; Rom. 8:1-11). The Holy Spirit is central to, and indispensable in, the Christian life and spiritual maturity.

Unfortunately, throughout all of church history, the Spirit of God has all too often been neglected by Christians. This despite the fact that the Holy Spirit first appears in Scripture at Genesis 1:2 and is last mentioned in Revelation 22:17, with hundreds of mentions in between. Christians have frequently under-rated His involvement in the kingdom plans of God.

Over the centuries some have been troubled whether or not the Holy Spirit is deity and then whether or not there are three persons who comprise the triune Godhead. With regard to His deity, the Apostle Peter explicitly declares the Holy Spirit is God:

> But Peter said, 'Ananias, why has Satan filled your heart to lie to the Holy Spirit, and to keep back some of the price of the land? While it remained unsold, did it not remain your own? And after it was sold, was it not under your control? Why is it that you have conceived this deed in your heart? You have not lied to men, but to God' (Acts 5:3-4).

One needs only to read a passage such as Matthew 3:16-17, which speaks of Christ being baptized, the Father pronouncing His approval from heaven, and the Holy Spirit descending on Jesus, to conclude that there are three Persons who are each Deity. That's why Jesus instructed the church to baptize in the name of the Father and of the Son and of the Holy Spirit (Matt. 28:19). Only this explanation allows for Paul's benediction to the Corinthians:

> The grace of the Lord Jesus Christ, and the love of God, and the fellowship of the Holy Spirit, be with you all (2 Cor. 13:14).

With these basic truths of the Holy Spirit's deity and triune relationship with the Son and Father reaffirmed, we need to examine the special truths of Scripture about the Spirit's ministry to believers in living out the Christian life. Without the Holy Spirit's continual work in a believer, there can be no true spirituality.

Spirit Indwelling – Presence
The Holy Spirit actively worked in Old Testament times. He was in Joshua (Num. 27:18) and Moses (Num. 11:17). The Spirit energized Samson (Judg. 13:25; 14:6,19; 15:14). The Spirit departed from Saul (1 Sam. 16:14), and David pleaded for God not to take the Spirit from him (Ps. 51:11).

But never do we sense from Old Testament narratives that God's Spirit dwelt in every believer. In the Gospels Jesus hinted at a change that could be understood only if a new dimension of the Spirit's ministry was to begin after Christ's departure to heaven (John 14:16-17; 16:7-11). God's standard for personal holiness did not change; however, just like the progressive revelation of Scripture, there appeared to be a new level of divinely provided resource for holy living.

In the New Testament, there is explicit teaching that with the New Covenant comes a new level of divine expectation for holy living:

> However, you are not in the flesh but in the Spirit, if indeed the Spirit of God dwells in you. But if anyone does not have the Spirit of Christ, he does not belong to Him. If Christ is in you, though the body is dead because of sin, yet the spirit is alive because of righteousness. But if the Spirit of Him who raised Jesus from the dead dwells in you, He who raised Christ Jesus from the dead will also give life to your mortal bodies through His Spirit who indwells you (Rom. 8:9-11).

Paul's direct statement to the fact that the Holy Spirit indwells all believers finds corroboration in other passages such as 2 Timothy 1:14 and 1 Peter 4:14:

> Or do you not know that your body is a temple of the Holy Spirit who is in you, whom you have from God, and that you are not your own? For you have been bought with a price: therefore glorify God in your body (1 Cor. 6:19-20).

Guard, through the Holy Spirit who dwells in us, the treasure which has been entrusted to you (2 Tim. 1:14).

If you are reviled for the name of Christ, you are blessed, because the Spirit of glory and of God rests on you (1 Peter 4:14).

As a result, the presence of God's Spirit allows Him to be:

Our source of unity	Ephesians 4:3-4
Our source of life and peace	Romans 8:6
Our source of assurance	Romans 9:1
Our source of intercession	Romans 8:26-27
Our source of instruction	1 John 2:20, 27
Our source of giftedness	1 Corinthians 12:4-11
Our source of liberty	2 Corinthians 3:18
Our source of strength	Ephesians 3:16
Our source of fruit	Galatians 5:22-23
Our source of true worship	Philippians 3:3
Our source of fellowship	Philippians 2:1
Our source of direction	Romans 8:14
Our source of ministry power	1 Corinthians 2:4

Spirit Baptism – Participation

Attendant with the Spirit's presence in our lives comes our entrance into and participation in the church universal, the body of Christ, with Spirit baptism.

For even with one Spirit we all were baptized into one body, whether Jews or Greeks, whether slaves or free people; all were made to drink of one Spirit (1 Cor. 12:13, author's translation).

This simply means that, by Christ's doing, Christians are immersed into the assembly of those who are saved. God has sovereignly willed this, regardless of our thoughts on the subject.

John the Baptist alerted the disciples to the forthcoming ministry of Jesus who would baptize with the Holy Spirit:

John was clothed with camel's hair and wore a leather belt around his waist. . . . And he was preaching, and saying, 'After me One is coming who is mightier than I, and I am not fit to stoop down and untie the thong of His sandals. I baptized you with water; but He will baptize you with the Holy Spirit' (Mark 1:6-8).

John testified saying, 'I have seen the Spirit descending as a dove out of heaven, and He remained upon Him. I did not recognize Him, but He who sent me to baptize in water said to me, "He upon whom you see the Spirit descending and remaining upon Him, this is the One who baptizes in the Holy Spirit." I myself have seen, and have testified that this is the Son of God' (John 1:32-34).

Jesus testified to the same truth just before He ascended into heaven:

Gathering them together, He commanded them not to leave Jerusalem, but to wait for what the Father had promised, 'Which,' He said, 'you heard of from Me; for John baptized with water, but you will be baptized with the Holy Spirit not many days from now' (Acts 1:4-5).

When Cornelius, the Gentile centurion, was saved along with his household, Peter remembered this promise and used it to explain how he knew salvation had come to those people.

'And as I began to speak, the Holy Spirit fell upon them, just as He did upon us at the beginning. And I remembered the word of the Lord, how He used to say, "John baptized with water, but you will be baptized with the Holy Spirit." Therefore if God gave to them the same gift as He gave to us also after believing in the Lord Jesus Christ, who was I that I could stand in God's way?' When they heard this, they quieted down, and glorified God, saying, 'Well then, God has granted to the Gentiles also the repentance that leads to life' (Acts 11:15-18).

We need to understand several features about Jesus baptizing us with the Holy Spirit.

1. Spirit baptism is inseparably linked with salvation.
2. Spirit baptism, like salvation, occurs only once.
3. In Spirit baptism, Christ does the baptizing and the Holy Spirit is the medium into which we are immersed.
4. The isolated historical instances where tongues speaking was accompanied with Spirit baptism were associated with the apostolic era and are not normal for today (Acts 2:4; 10:46; 19:6).
5. God initiates Spirit baptism; we do not have to seek it.
6. Spirit baptism is the means by which God places us in His church (1 Cor. 12:13).

Spirit Sealing – Promise
Just as a young man gives a young lady an engagement ring to validate his promise to marry her, so God gives every believer the Holy Spirit as a salvation down payment. This assures us of His promise to complete what He began with regard to our marriage to Christ resulting in eternal life.

> Now He who establishes us with you in Christ and anointed us is God, who also sealed us and gave us the Spirit in our hearts as a pledge (2 Cor. 1:21-22).

> Now He who prepared us for this very purpose is God, who gave to us the Spirit as a pledge (2 Cor. 5:5).

> In Him, you also, after listening to the message of truth, the gospel of your salvation—having also believed, you were sealed in Him with the Holy Spirit of promise, who is given as a pledge of our inheritance, with a view to the redemption of God's own possession, to the praise of His glory (Eph. 1:13-14).

> Do not grieve the Holy Spirit of God, by whom you were sealed for the day of redemption (Eph. 4:30).

These passages on the sealing of our souls by God with the Holy Spirit leads us to several conclusions.

1. We are never commanded or told to seek sealing.
2. God sovereignly seals us with the Holy Spirit as a part of our salvation.
3. Sealing identifies us as an everlasting possession of God.
4. Sealing promises God's protection against spiritual enemies.
5. Sealing guarantees our ultimate redemption by God who saved and sealed us for the purpose of eternal life.
6. Sealing is to the praise of God's glory.

Spirit Fruit – Production
The clearest passage on this wonderful ministry of the Holy Spirit occurs in Galatians 5:13-26:

> For you were called to freedom, brethren; only do not turn your freedom into an opportunity for the flesh, but through love serve one another. For the whole Law is fulfilled in one word, in the statement, 'You shall

love your neighbor as yourself.' But if you bite and devour one another, take care that you are not consumed by one another.

But I say, walk by the Spirit, and you will not carry out the desire of the flesh.

For the flesh sets its desire against the Spirit, and the Spirit against the flesh; for these are in opposition to one another, so that you may not do the things that you please. But if you are led by the Spirit, you are not under the Law.

Now the deeds of the flesh are evident, which are: immorality, impurity, sensuality, idolatry, sorcery, enmities, strife, jealousy, outbursts of anger, disputes, dissensions, factions, envyings, drunkenness, carousings, and things like these, of which I forewarn you just as I have forewarned you, that those who practice such things will not inherit the kingdom of God.

But the fruit of the Spirit is love, joy, peace, patience, kindness, goodness, faithfulness, gentleness, self-control; against such things there is no law. Now those who belong to Christ Jesus have crucified the flesh with its passions and desires. If we live by the Spirit, let us also walk by the Spirit. Let us not become boastful, challenging one another, envying one another.

Paul contrasted the deeds of the flesh, i.e. carnality, with the fruit of the Spirit, i.e. spirituality. He insisted that the believer must walk by the Spirit (vv.16, 25), and be led by the Spirit (v.18). Several chapters earlier, he had challenged the Galatians.

This is the only thing I want to find out from you: did you receive the Spirit by the works of the Law, or by hearing with faith? Are you so foolish? Having begun by the Spirit, are you now being perfected by the flesh? (Gal. 3:2-3).

At times they, like we, wanted to return to the works of the law and the deeds of the flesh. To do this, however, would be to give up their freedom in salvation and be enslaved once more to sin.

Note carefully that the flesh and the Spirit stand in direct opposition to one another (5:17). Because of this contrast, to walk by the Spirit is to avoid walking in the flesh. When we start to walk in the flesh, the warning signs are evident (5:19). They do not correspond to kingdom behaviour (5:21).

Later on I define each element in the fruit of the Spirit from the Greek text. The definitions are personalized in action form. I encourage you to review that material, in Chapter 15, before going on.

Now, let me take us a step further and compare the fruit of the
Spirit with the character of God and then with His commands in
order that we live out His character in our lives.

The Character of God

Love	God is love (1 John 4:16)
Joy	The town of My joy (Jer. 49:25)
Peace	The God of peace (Heb. 13:20)
Patience	God is patient with us (2 Peter 3:9)
Kindness	God's kindness to us (Eph. 2:7)
Goodness	The goodness of the Lord (Ps. 27:13)
Faithfulness	God is faithful (1 Cor. 10:13)
Gentleness	Christ is gentle and humble in heart (Matt. 11:29)
Self-control	The divine nature includes self-control (2 Peter 1:4,6)

The Commands of Scripture

Love	You shall love (Matt. 22:37, 39)
Joy	Rejoice in the Lord (Phil. 4:4)
Peace	Seek peace and pursue it (1 Peter 3:11)
Patience	Be patient with all men (1 Thess. 5:14)
Kindness	Put on ... kindness (Col. 3:12)
Goodness	Let us do good to all men (Gal. 6:10)
Faithfulness	Be faithful until death (Rev. 2:10)
Gentleness	Make a defense ... with gentleness (1 Peter 3:15)
Self-control	Add to your knowledge self-control (2 Peter 1:6)

Spirit Giftedness—Provision
Countless volumes have been written on spiritual gifts. But in short
order, I want to outline the basics with four questions and the
appropriate biblical answers.

What Do I Need to Know about Spiritual Gifts?
1. Salvation is a 'charisma' or free gift (Romans 6:23).
2. God's Holy Spirit is a gift as a part of salvation (Rom. 5:5; 1 Thess. 4:8; 1 John 3:24; 4:13).
3. Every believer has received a spiritual gift—spiritual in source and nature (1 Peter 4:10; 1 Cor. 1:7; 7:7).

4. God's will, not man's, is the criterion for who gets what gift (1 Cor. 12:11, 18).
5. Spiritual gifts are diverse (1 Cor. 12:12-27). Of the several gift lists in the New Testament, no two are the same (Rom. 12:6-8; 1 Cor. 7:7-8; 12:8-10; 12:28-30; 13:1-3, 8).
6. In the qualities desired for church leaders and mature believers, spiritual gifts are never mentioned (1 Cor. 13:4-7; Gal. 5:22-23; 1 Tim. 3:1-7; Titus 1: 5-9).
7. The kind of spiritual gifts people are given do not necessarily indicate their level of spirituality.

How Can I Identify My Spiritual Gift?
1. Believing that God has uniquely gifted you, the focus should be more on gift than gifts (1 Peter 4:10).
2. Your spiritual gift will come as a result of salvation.
3. You will be able to maximize ministry with minimum effort.
4. Sooner or later, others will recognize and comment on your spiritual gift.
5. Your spiritual gift will be used most effectively in the context of the local church.
6. If you can't identify your spiritual gift, still get involved.
7. Your inclinations and the observations of others will lead you to fruitful ministry.

What Should I Do with My Spiritual Gift?
1. Build up the church (1 Cor. 14:12).
2. Serve one another (1 Cor. 12:7; 1 Peter 4:10).

What Errors Should I Avoid in Exercising My Spiritual Gift?
1. Self-edification rather than the edification of others (1 Peter 4:10).
2. Self-exercise rather than being Spirit-exercised (1 Peter 4:11).
3. Self-exaltation rather than for God's glory (1 Peter 4:11).

Spirit Filling – Power
The concept of filling does not *first* appear in the New Testament, but rather in Exodus 31:3 and 35:31 when it refers to a special enablement of Bezalel by God to craft the tabernacle. And in Luke 1, before the birth of Jesus, we discover the Spirit-filled family: Zacharias (1:67), Elizabeth (1:41), and John the Baptist while yet in the womb (1:15).

Most instructive is that which was said about Christ.

Jesus, full of the Holy Spirit, returned from the Jordan and was led about by the Spirit in the wilderness (Luke 4:1).

Jesus was totally controlled by God's Spirit, which is the basic idea of 'full of the Holy Spirit'. Therefore, *He was led about by the Spirit.* Simply put, Christ totally submitted to the leadership of the Spirit and was perfectly obedient to the Spirit's direction in His wilderness experience. Please do not make this wonderful truth difficult or complex. What Christ lived out in His humanity, we also are to live out in our Christian experience.

You might ask, 'Why should I be filled with the Spirit?' We are never commanded to be baptized, indwelt, sealed, or gifted by the Spirit. But we are commanded to be filled.

Therefore be careful how you walk, not as unwise men, but as wise, making the most of your time, because the days are evil. So then do not be foolish, but understand what the will of the Lord is.

And do not get drunk with wine, for that is dissipation, but be filled with the Spirit, speaking to one another in psalms and hymns and spiritual songs, singing and making melody with your heart to the Lord; always giving thanks for all things in the name of our Lord Jesus Christ to God, even the Father; and be subject to one another in the fear of Christ (Eph. 5:15-21).

God's will involves God's Spirit literally controlling our lives and giving us spiritual direction. How does He do this and how can we cooperate in this spiritual venture? Look at Colossians 3:16-17, and you'll discover that letting the Word of God dwell in you richly produces the same spiritual qualities as letting God's Spirit control you. The simple but profound conclusion is that God's Word energizes man's mind to obey God's Spirit.

If we do this, what will it produce? First, godly conversation (Eph. 5:19). We will communicate heavenward with songs of praise to God and horizontally to each other with words of spiritual joy. Second, a thankful reaction to all of life (5:20). Third, a submitted relationship to one another in the fellowship of Christ that will extend from our marriage and family life (5:22-6:4) to the work world (6:5-9) and beyond (6:10-20).

This answers the 'how' and 'what' raised by Peter's exhortation 'to live the rest of the time in the flesh no longer for the lusts of men, but for the will of God' (1 Peter 4:2). We fuel the process by taking megadoses of God's Word. We check our progress by looking at three areas of life: (1) our rhetoric, (2) our reactions, and (3) our relationships. If you need a mentor in these areas, let Barnabas be your model (Acts 11:22-24).

Teach me, O LORD, the way of Your statutes,
And I shall observe it to the end.
Give me understanding, that I may observe Your law,
And keep it with all my heart.
Make me walk in the path of Your commandments,
For I delight in it.
Psalm 119:33-35

7

LISTENING TO GOD

A well-known Christian author recently wrote , 'Anyone who comes to the Bible with a primary purpose of gaining knowledge about theology misses its message. We must come with the purpose of understanding ourselves better so we can know God better.'[1]

At first glance that sounds OK. We all agree that studying Scripture should not stop with information but continue on to personal transformation. Now think a little longer. Do we understand God better by first understanding ourselves? After all, who created whom?

God, through the Prophet Isaiah, declared, 'My thoughts are not your thoughts, nor are your ways My ways.... For as the heavens are higher than the earth, so are My ways higher than your ways, and My thoughts than your thoughts' (Isa. 55:8-9). Since His ways and thoughts differ radically from ours, we should start with Him—not ourselves—if we're to know and be what He wants us to be. To know God, we must start with Scripture for that is where He gives the most intimate glimpses of Himself and His design for spiritual well-being.

Cultivating Intimacy

One of the most effective ways to cultivate a deeper relationship with God is talking to Him (prayer). Learn to speak freely with God about your concerns for others, your circumstances, your sin (confession), and your need for Him. Let your desire to be intimate with Him show by how you communicate with Him. Numerous other activities help cultivate a deeper relationship with God: worshipping in spirit and in truth, being filled with God's Sprit, praising God with thanksgiving, giving sacrificially to build Christ's church, walking in God's will, and framing your life with a desire to glorify Him in all things.

But your pursuit of intimacy can be detoured, ineffective, or even wasteful if you have not entered at the right gateway. All those wonderful practices presuppose that you know what God desires from His children and that you are acting in accord with His specific instructions in the Bible.

The key to a great relationship with your spouse and children is good communication—particularly listening. That is also true of our relationship with God. Through Scripture, we can listen to and know the mind of God (Ps. 119; 1 Thess. 2:13).

Good communication heightens with intimacy. God's Word reveals all that we need to know about Him, His plan, and our relationship with Him. The Bible is God's way of talking to us.

Scripture is like a photo album of other family members, a diary of past events, a calendar of future plans, a letter from home, a revealing portrait of God, and descriptions of acceptable family behaviour.

Only in Scripture do we get intimate glances into the history of God's involvement with this world (Genesis to Esther). Or glimpses into the diaries of men like Job, the Psalmists, or Solomon. Proverbs and Ecclesiastes contain the treasures of God's wisdom. In the prophets, we learn of God's faithfulness to reward obedience and punish sin. The New Testament introduces us to God's Son in the Gospels, His church in Acts and the Epistles, and earth's ultimate destiny in Revelation.

Without Scripture, we would know relatively little about Him. Our level of intimacy would be extremely limited. To be specific, our praise would be incomplete (Ps. 119:164), our lives lacking the Spirit's power (Eph. 5:18-21; Col. 3:16-17), our prayers aimless (1 John 1:3), and worship of Him misdirected since it should be based on walking in the light of His Word (John 4:24).

Mankind's original intimacy with God collapsed because Adam and Eve listened to another's word and disobeyed God's Word (Gen. 3:1-19). Spiritual intimacy returns only when our attitudes and actions are based on Scripture.

The Bible clearly illustrates the connection between knowing God and knowing Scripture. God looks with favour on humble individuals who tremble at His Word (Isa. 66:2,5). Just as God spoke to Moses as a friend (Ex. 33:11), so God will speak to Christians through His Word as a special friend. Here is an illustrious listing of individuals who counted on the certainty of these truths: Daniel (Dan 9:1-23); Jeremiah (Jer. 15:16); Jesus (Matt. 4:4); Job (Job 23:12); Joshua (Josh. 1:8-9); Josiah (2 Kings 23:3); Paul (2 Tim. 3:16-17); and Solomon (Eccl. 12:13-14).

How well we would do to stand in their company by trembling at the Lord's Word.

Opening the Gate
The thought of personal Bible study intimidates many Christians. It seems so formidable when you have little or no formal training. Yet Psalm 119 beckons every true worshipper to feed on the spiritual nourishment provided by the Holy Scriptures, and thereby grow in spiritual intimacy with God.

Whether you are a pastor with several theological degrees or a new babe in Christ, this series of simple steps for fruitful Bible study will successfully lead you into the Word of God. You can come away with the deep satisfaction of knowing that the living God has spoken to you through His Word, that you understand the message, and that you have drawn closer to your Heavenly Father's side.

Step 1—Affirmation: Prayerfully acknowledge before God that you recognize His book, the Bible, to be the only written expression of His will given to mankind. Thus it is the absolute authority for both your beliefs and behaviour (Matt. 5:18; 24:35; 2 Tim. 3:16).

Step 2—Preparation: Prayerfully ask God to open your eyes (Ps. 119:18), teach you His statutes (v. 12), and establish your ways by His Word (v. 5).

Step 3—Observation: Carefully read your Bible to discover what it says. Study it systematically. Good Christian books and magazines that supplement your Bible reading are also helpful, but there is no substitute for reading Scripture itself.

Step 4—Investigation: Consult Bible commentaries, dictionaries, encyclopedias, and atlases to see what other godly people have observed.

Step 5—Interpretation: Analyze all those observations to discover what God meant by what He said. Use the normal rules for literary interpretation—as you would for any other piece of literature—and seek the Spirit's illuminating help (Ps. 119:102; 1 John 2:27).

Step 6—Correlation: Use the cross-references in your Bible or a work like *The Treasury of Scripture Knowledge*[2] to discover the totality of what God has said about a particular theme or idea that you're interested in. You will understand the whole only when you've taken time to assemble all the parts.

Step 7—Appropriation: Your Bible study is never complete until you apply what you have learned to your life. Transfer the fruit of your labours from the head and heart to the hands and feet. James 4:17 (NIV) says, 'Anyone, then, who knows the good he ought to do and doesn't do it, sins.'

Step 8—Proclamation: Ask God to bring someone into your life on a daily basis with whom you can share your exciting discoveries in God's Word. Don't be silent about the most precious book ever written-someone's life might depend on it.[3]

Take heed to our Lord's conversation with Mary and Martha (Luke

10:38-42). It's a great statement on the number-one priority of the Word. Jesus commended Mary for 'listening to the Lord's Word' (v. 39), but scolded Martha for putting her service above her God (vv. 41-42).

Fuelling God's Spirit
The Bible promises tremendous spiritual blessing to those who devote their time to it.

> This book of the law shall not depart from your mouth, but you shall meditate on it day and night, so that you may be careful to do according to all that is written in it; for then you will make your way prosperous, and then you will have success (Josh. 1:8).

> But his delight is in the law of the LORD, and in His law he meditates day and night. He will be like a tree firmly planted by streams of water (Ps. 1:2-3).

> Blessed is he who reads and those who hear the words of the prophecy, and heed the things which are written in it; for the time is near (Rev. 1:3).

But so few people seem to experience what God wants to deliver. Why?

Look carefully at these next two passages. What feature do they share in common? What features distinguish them?

> Let the word of Christ richly dwell within you, with all wisdom teaching and admonishing one another with psalms and hymns and spiritual songs, singing with thankfulness in your hearts to God. Whatever you do in word or deed, do all in the name of the Lord Jesus, giving thanks through Him to God the Father (Col. 3:16-17).

> And do not get drunk with wine, for that is dissipation, but be filled with the Spirit, speaking to one another in psalms and hymns and spiritual songs, singing and making melody with your heart to the Lord; always giving thanks for all things in the name of our Lord Jesus Christ to God, even the Father; and be subject to one another in the fear of Christ (Eph. 5:18-21).

The results are almost identical, but the means seem to be different. Let me suggest that both means—the Holy Spirit and the Bible—

blend together in the total process. Think about it! As believers, we all have the Holy Spirit, but we do not have equal experiences with the Word. I'm suggesting that it is the combination of Scripture along with the Holy Spirit that produces vitality in the believer's life.

Let me illustrate by comparing this spiritual process to starting a car. God's Spirit is the engine, your will serves as the ignition key, and God's Word acts as fuel. If you have an engine without fuel, you can turn the ignition key all you want but the car will not start. Without the Word, the power of the Holy Spirit will go unignited.

You can have the best of engines and a tank full of the best fuel, but until the ignition is turned there will be no energy. So the Holy Spirit and the Word without the cooperation of the human will are essentially dormant.

However, with a perfect engine, a tank of high-octane fuel, and timely ignition, you have all the power needed to drive. Likewise, with the Holy Spirit, rich portions of the Word, and your will desiring God's will, you have all of the spiritual energy and blessing you could ever want. All three elements need to be in sync before anything significant happens.

God's Word at Work

You might be wondering, 'If all three elements are true in my life, what actual results can I expect?' Note Paul's broad answer—the Word performs spiritual work: 'For this reason we also constantly thank God that when you received the word of God, which you heard from us, you accepted it not as the word of men, but for what it really is, the word of God, which also performs its work in you who believe' (1 Thess. 2:13).

Now carefully consider some of the specifics of how it:

1. SAVES US
   1 Peter 1:23—'For you have been born again not of seed which is perishable but imperishable, that is, through the living and enduring word of God.'
2. TEACHES US
   2 Timothy 3:16—'All Scripture is inspired by God and profitable for teaching . . .'
3. REBUKES US
   2 Timothy 3:16—'for reproof . . .'

4. CORRECTS US
   2 Timothy 3:16-17—'for correction . . .'
5. DISCIPLES US
   2 Timothy 3:16-17—'for training in righteousness . . .'
6. EQUIPS US
   2 Timothy 3:17—'that the man of God may be adequate, equipped for every good work.'
7. GUIDES US
   Psalm 119:105—'Your word is a lamp to my feet, and a light to my path.'
8. COUNSELS US
   Psalm 119:24—'Your testimonies also are my delight; they are my counselors.'
9. REVIVES US
   Psalm 119:154—'Plead my cause and redeem me; revive me according to Your word.'
10. RESTORES OUR SOUL
    Psalm 19:7—'The law of the LORD is perfect, restoring the soul; the testimony of the LORD is sure, making wise the simple.'
11. WARNS US/REWARDS US
    Psalm 19:11—'Moreover, by them Your servant is warned; in keeping them there is great reward.'
12. NOURISHES US
    1 Peter 2:2—'Like newborn babies, long for the pure milk of the word, that by it you may grow in respect to salvation.'
13. JUDGES US
    Hebrews 4:12—'For the word of God is living and active and sharper than any two-edged sword, and piercing as far as the division of soul and spirit, of both joints and marrow, and able to judge the thoughts and intentions of the heart.'
14. SANCTIFIES US
    John 17:17—'Sanctify them in the truth; Your word is truth.'
15. FREES US
    John 8:31-32—'Jesus was saying to those Jews who had believed Him, 'If you continue in My word, then you are truly disciples of Mine; and you will know the truth, and the truth will make you free.''
16. ENRICHES US
    Colossians 3:16—'Let the word of Christ richly dwell within

you, with all wisdom teaching and admonishing one another with psalms and hymns and spiritual songs, singing with thankfulness in your hearts to God.'

17. PROTECTS US

Psalm 119:11—'Your word I have treasured in my heart, that I may not sin against You.'

18. STRENGTHENS US

Psalm 119:28—'My soul weeps because of grief; strengthen me according to Your word.'

19. MAKES US WISE

Psalm 119:97-100—'O how I love Your law! It is my meditation all the day. Your commandments make me wiser than my enemies, for they are ever mine. I have more insight than all my teachers, for Your testimonies are my meditation. I understand more than the aged, because I have observed Your precepts.'

20. REJOICES OUR HEART

Psalm 19:8—'The precepts of the LORD are right, rejoicing the heart; the commandment of the LORD is pure, enlightening the eyes.'

People of God's Word

Let me introduce you to some people in Scripture who exemplified a key element in having a right relationship to God's Word. If you will incorporate each of these examples into your experience, you can lead the normal Christian life.

First, *Job* hungered for and craved God's Word. He prioritized spiritual nourishment higher than the physical. 'I have not departed from the command of His lips; I have treasured the words of His mouth more than my necessary food' (Job 23:12).

Second, *Caleb* fully obeyed God's Word. He understood the Word as orders from above with the obligation to follow in every detail. 'But My servant Caleb, because he has had a different spirit and has followed Me fully, I will bring into the land which he entered, and his descendants shall take possession of it' (Num. 14:24).

Third, the *post-captivity Jews* honoured God's Word. When the Word was opened, it was as though God entered their presence. They responded with appropriate respect. 'Ezra opened the book in the sight of all the people for he was standing above all the people; and when he opened it, all the people stood up. Then Ezra blessed the LORD the great God. And all the people answered, 'Amen, Amen!' while lifting up their hands; then they bowed low and worshipped the LORD with their faces to the ground' (Neh. 8:5-6).

Fourth, *Ezra* studied God's Word. He viewed Scripture not as a shallow stream to wade in but rather a deep river in which to swim. 'For Ezra had set his heart to study the law of the LORD, and to practice it, and to teach His statutes and ordinances in Israel' (Ezra 7:10).

Fifth, *Apollos* understood God's Word. Accuracy became his hallmark. 'Now a Jew named Apollos, an Alexandrian by birth, an eloquent man, came to Ephesus; and he was mighty in the Scriptures. This man had been instructed in the way of the Lord; and being fervent in spirit, he was speaking and teaching accurately the things concerning Jesus, being acquainted only with the baptism of John' (Acts 18:24-25).

Sixth, *Paul* discipled faithful and able men in the Scriptures. He realized the responsibility to hand the Word on to coming generations. 'The things which you have heard from me in the presence of many witnesses, entrust these to faithful men who will be able to teach others also' (2 Tim. 2:2).

A Daily Pursuit

Intimacy with God is not limited to ancient history. God's Word remains fresh and powerful (Ps. 119:89-90; Isa. 55:11). However, according to a recent Gallup poll, only a small percentage of American Christians spend time daily in God's Word. If your Bible wrote a diary about its use, how would it read? Here is an imaginary report of one such Bible:

> *Jan. 15—Been resting for a week. A few nights after the first of the year my owner opened me, but no more. Another New Year's resolution gone awry.*
>
> *Feb. 3—Owner picked me up and rushed off to Sunday School.*
>
> *Feb. 23—Cleaning day. Was dusted and put back in my place.*
>
> *April 2—Busy day. Owner had to present the lesson at a church society meeting. Quickly looked up a lot of references.*
>
> *May 5—In Grandma's lap again, a comfortable place.*
>
> *May 9—She let a tear fall on John 14:1-3.*
>
> *May 10—Grandma's gone. Back in my old place.*
>
> *May 20—Baby born. They wrote his name on one of my pages.*

July 1—Packed in a suitcase—off for a vacation.

July 20—Still in the suitcase. Almost everything else taken out.

July 25—Home again. Quite a journey, though I don't see why I went.

Aug. 16—Cleaned again and put in a prominent place. The minister is to be here for dinner.

Aug. 20—Owner wrote Grandma's death in my family record. He left his extra pair of glasses between my pages.

Dec. 31—Owner just found his glasses. Wonder if he will make any resolutions about me for the New Year.

If you wouldn't want anyone to read your Bible's diary, let me suggest two helps that will encourage you to have a daily visit with God in His Word. *The Daily Walk* (from Walk Thru the Bible Ministries) and *The One Year Bible* (Tyndale) have proved invaluable to me; I highly recommend them to you as well. Then develop the daily habit of reading and studying not just for information but for intimacy.

The framed words of this wonderful charter hang on the wall at the entrance to my study. They always remind me that in the Bible, I have all of God's provision for intimacy with Him:

This book contains: the mind of God, the state of man, the way of salvation, the doom of sinners, and the happiness of believers.

Its doctrine is holy, its precepts are binding, its histories are true, and its decisions are immutable.

Read it to be wise, believe it to be safe, and practice it to be holy.

It contains light to direct you, food to support you, and comfort to cheer you.

It is the traveler's map, the pilgrim's staff, the pilot's compass, the soldier's sword, and the Christian's charter.

Here heaven is opened, and the gates of hell disclosed.

Christ is its grand subject, our good its design, and the glory of God its end.

It should fill the memory, rule the heart, and guide the feet.

Read it slowly, frequently, and prayerfully.

It is a mine of wealth, health to the soul, and a river of pleasure.

It is given to you here in this life, and will be opened at the Judgment, and is established forever.

It involves the highest responsibility, will reward the greatest labor, and condemns all who trifle with its contents.

Intimacy with God is not reserved for a select group of initiates but is within the grasp of every believer. There's no magic formula to achieving intimacy. In fact, there are no shortcuts, only one, well-marked path—the Word of God. Study it. Make its truths yours. It is the only gateway to your growing intimacy with God.

Holy Bible, Book divine
Precious treasure, thou art mine;
Mine to tell me whence I came;
Mine to teach me what I am.
Mine to chide me when I rove;
Mine to show a Saviour's love.
Mine thou art to guide and guard;
Mine to punish or reward.[1]

John Burton

8

IMPACTED BY GOD'S WORD

Let's start this discussion with an 'agree/disagree' question. 'When it comes to spiritual matters, all we need to know is revealed in God's Word and ministered to us by His Spirit.'

Think twice about the statement before you finalize your answer. Where you stand on this ultimately decides where you land on every spiritual issue. What do you think the Apostle Paul would say? Undoubtedly, he would tell us what he said to Timothy:

> All Scripture is inspired by God and profitable for teaching, for reproof, for correction, for training in righteousness; so that the man of God may be adequate, equipped for every good work (2 Tim. 3:16-17).

And what about King David?

> The law of the LORD is perfect, restoring the soul;
> The testimony of the LORD is sure, making wise the simple.
> The precepts of the LORD are right, rejoicing the heart;
> The commandment of the LORD is pure, enlightening the eyes.
> The fear of the LORD is clean, enduring forever;
> The judgments of the LORD are true; they are righteous altogether.
> They are more desirable than gold, yes, than much fine gold;
> Sweeter also than honey and the drippings of the honeycomb.
> Moreover, by them Your servant is warned;
> In keeping them there is great reward (Ps. 19:7-11).

Both David and Paul would uncompromisingly answer, 'Agree!' On the other hand, what would the implication be if someone disagreed? To answer that, let's look in on a group of people who did answer that way and hear what the Lord Jesus Christ thought of their response.

When Jesus received the Pharisees' rebuke that His disciples did not wash according to Jewish tradition, He confronted them with the consequences of rejecting the all-sufficiency of God's Word and relying on a mixture of man's religious traditions and God's truth.

Christ indicted the Pharisees on two counts. First, He rebuked them, 'Neglecting the commandment of God, you hold to the tradition of men' (Mark 7:8).

Second, He said they had *rejected* God's Word (7:9-12). 'You are experts at setting aside the commandment of God in order to keep your tradition' (v. 9). Jesus concluded that to both neglect and reject, which is to say Scripture alone is not sufficient in spiritual matters, results in negating the validity of Scripture (7:13).

If Scripture can be neglected and/or rejected in whole or in part, then there is no significance in a claim like Paul's or David's as to the completeness of the Bible. Therefore to disagree with our beginning question is to disagree not with John MacArthur, but with Scripture itself.[2] If you disagreed, you will be at odds with God who testified:

> Every word of God is flawless;
>> he is a shield to those who take refuge in him.
> Do not add to his words,
>> or he will rebuke you and prove you a liar (Prov. 30:5-6, NIV).

Loving God's Word[3]

The psalmists would wholeheartedly agree that Scripture is sufficient. We want to listen in on the heart and mind of a spiritually mature approach to the Bible found in the longest Psalm (176 verses) and the most complete text speaking about the whole of Scripture.

The author of Psalm 119 does not identify himself, although through the years David, Ezra, or Daniel have been suggested by godly scholars. In this study, we want to note the features of a person who has been impacted by God's Word. These qualities characterize mature Christianity as evidenced by one's response to Scripture.

The psalmist craved God's Word with an insatiable appetite. He understood that his spiritual vitality depended on an abundant intake of Scripture. These phrases from Psalm 119 stress the ultimate importance of God's Word to this believer.

Loves the Word	119:47-48, 97, 113, 127, 140, 159, 163, 165, 167
Delights in the Word	119:16, 24, 35, 47, 70, 77, 92, 143, 174
Longs for the Word	119:19-20, 40, 131
Waits for the Word	119:38, 43
Finds joy in the Word	119:111, 162
Esteems the Word	119:128
Stands in awe of the Word	119:161

The psalmist responded to the Word like the Thessalonians to whom Paul wrote:

For this reason we also constantly thank God that when you received the word of God, which you heard from us, you accepted it not as the word of men, but for what it really is, the word of God, which also performs its work in you who believe (1 Thess. 2:13).

Hating Sin

His love for God's Word resulted in a predictable corollary—he hated sin because God hates sin. A constant reading about God who is holy will give us the same attitude toward sin as we see in God.

The psalmist spoke against:

The arrogant	119:21-22
The wicked	119:53
The false way	119:104
The double-minded	119:113
The evildoers	119:115
The deceitful	119:118
The lawbreakers	119:126

Of all the characteristics of God that he mentions, one stands out far more frequently than others—the covenant lovingkindness of God to forgive those who repent of their sins and turn to God in faith for salvation (vv. 41, 64, 76, 88, 124, 149, 159). When referring to the nature of God's Word, the psalmist most often focuses on a corollary to God's covenant kindness—the righteousness of God's Word which reflects God's just character (vv. 62, 106, 123, 144, 160, 164, 172).

The psalmist so detests sin that he confesses, 'My eyes shed streams of water, because they do not keep Your law'(v. 136). In a positive response to the presence of sin, he asks a key question and then answers like this:

How can a young man keep his way pure? By keeping it according to Your word. With all my heart I have sought You; do not let me wander from Your commandments. Your word I have treasured in my heart, that I may not sin against You (Ps. 119:9-11).

Questing to Know God's Mind

The writer so deeply desired to understand God's Word that on at least six occasions he cried for God to give him understanding (vv. 27, 34, 73, 125, 144, 169), and prayerfully invited God to be his teacher (vv. 12, 26, 33, 64, 66, 68, 108, 124, 135). Listen to the resulting testimony.

> I have not turned aside from Your ordinances, for You Yourself have taught me (Ps. 119:102).

The psalmist knew that he was dependent upon God for light (v.105), sight (v.18), insight (v.99), and wisdom (v.98). This became so important to him that he promised God that he would not forget God's Word (vv.16, 93, 176). He put a premium on possessing Scripture for immediate recall; he unquestionably memorized Scripture for this to become reality.

God's ministry of illumination by which He gives us light on the meaning of Scripture (v.130) is in view here. Paul and John affirm this also in the New Testament.

> I pray that the eyes of your heart may be enlightened, so that you will know what is the hope of His calling, what are the riches of the glory of His inheritance in the saints, and what is the surpassing greatness of His power toward us who believe. These are in accordance with the working of the strength of His might (Eph. 1:18-19).

> As for you, the anointing which you received from Him abides in you, and you have no need for anyone to teach you; but as His anointing teaches you about all things, and is true and is not a lie, and just as it has taught you, you abide in Him (1 John 2:27).

The truth about God illuminating Scripture should greatly encourage us. While it does not eliminate the need for gifted men to teach us (Eph. 4:11-12; 2 Tim. 4:2), or the hard labour of serious Bible study (2 Tim. 2:15), it does promise that we do not need to be enslaved to church dogma or be led astray by false teachers. Our primary dependence for learning Scripture needs to be upon the Author of Scripture—God Himself. Thus, we can be like the Bereans who compared every teaching of man with God's Word to determine if man's words were true or not (Acts 17:11).

Meditating on God's Word

This spiritual man made Scripture his constant mental companion. He thrived on contemplating or thinking about God's Word (119:15, 23, 27, 48, 78, 97, 99, 148). His mind-set became more like God's through constant exposure and repetition. He purified his thinking by continually washing it in the pure water of God's Word. Because he thought like God, then he could progressively live according to God's will as outlined in His Word. Here is a good way to determine your success with meditation.

> We can test ourselves by asking whether our spiritual thoughts are like guests visiting a hotel, or like children living at home. There is a temporary stir and bustle when guests arrive, yet within a little while they leave and are forgotten. The hotel is then prepared for other guests. So it is with religious thoughts that are only occasional. But children belong to their house. They are missed if they don't come home. Preparation is continually being made for their food and comfort. Spiritual thoughts that arise from true spiritual mindedness are like the children of the house—always expected, and certainly enquired for if missing.[4]

Finding Comfort/Counsel in God's Truth

The psalmist did not live or minister in the best of circumstances (119:81-88, 145-152). Yet, he looked to God for comfort in the midst of affliction (vv. 49-50, 52, 76-77, 82, 84-86). He also sought counsel (v.24) which gave him more insight than all his teachers, more wisdom than his enemies, and greater understanding than the aged (vv.98-100).

It's no wonder that the Word encouraged him in tough times or gave him greater understanding than others. Listen to how the psalmist describes some of the qualities of Scripture which parallel the attributes of God.

Good	119:39
True	119:43, 142, 151, 160
Trustworthy	119:42
Faithful	119:86
Light	119:105
Pure	119:140
Eternal	119:89, 152
Unchangeable	119:89

Combining Prayer with God's Word

It is difficult in Psalm 119 to distinguish at times where testimony ends and prayer begins. The psalm resembles a two-way conversation, although we hear only the psalmist. However, we know that he has heard God in His Word and now responds in a most personal and verbal way. Listen to a few examples of his requests.

Oh that my ways may be established to keep Your statutes! (v.5).

Remove the false way from me, and graciously grant me Your law (v.29).

Incline my heart to Your testimonies, and not to dishonest gain (v.36).

I sought Your favor with all my heart; be gracious to me according to Your Word (v.58).

Establish my footsteps in Your Word, and do not let any iniquity have dominion over me (v.133).

Walking Obediently

Christians must be strongly confronted with the need for obedience. Paul found it necessary to so rebuke the Corinthians.

And I, brethren, could not speak to you as to spiritual men, but as to men of flesh, as to infants in Christ. I gave you milk to drink, not solid food; for you were not yet able to receive it. Indeed, even now you are not yet able, for you are still fleshly. For since there is jealousy and strife among you, are you not fleshly, and are you not walking like mere men? (1 Cor. 3:1-3)

They did not have the same constant companionship of the Scripture as did the psalmist. He passionately desired to walk obediently to God's commandments (Ps. 119:4, 8, 30-32, 44-45, 51, 55, 59-61, 67-68, 74, 83, 87, 101-102, 110, 112, 141, 157). Take note of his constant promises to God.

The LORD is my portion; I have promised to keep Your words (Ps. 119:57).

I am a companion of all those who fear You, and of those who keep Your precepts (v.63).

I have sworn, and I will confirm it, that I will keep Your righteous ordinances (v.106)

Your testimonies are wonderful; therefore my soul observes them (v.129).

My soul keeps Your testimonies, and I love them exceedingly. I keep

Your precepts and Your testimonies, for all my ways are before You (vv. 167-168).

Praising God Continually

Praise permeates Psalm 119. The psalmist sings (vv. 54,172), gives thanks (vv.62,108), and rejoices (vv.13-14). His gratefulness abounds (vv.65, 151-152, 160).

He testifies that seven times daily the praise of God breaks forth from his lips over the righteous ordinances of the law (v.164). He even prays that God will sustain his praise.

Let my lips utter praise, for You dost teach me Your statutes (v.171).

Let my soul live that it may praise You, and let Your ordinances help me (v.175).

When we consider the richness of God's Word, we're not surprised at the psalmist's praise. In Psalm 119, eight different terms are used to describe God's Word—each indicating a particular characteristic or function.[5]

Law	119:1
Word	119:9
Judgments	119:7
Testimonies	119:2
Commands	119:6
Statutes/decrees	119:5
Precepts	119:4
Word/promise	119:11

Valuing Scripture Highly

According to the psalmist (119:72, 127), Scripture has greater value than money. It brings more pleasure than the sweetness of honey (119:103). Maturity (119:3) and blessing (119:1-2) are the results of obedience to it. No wonder he exalted Scripture so highly—just as did the writers of Proverbs.

The one who despises the Word will be in debt to it, but the one who fears the commandment will be rewarded (Prov. 13:13).

He who gives attention to the Word will find good, and blessed is he who trusts in the LORD (Prov. 16:20).

He who keeps the commandment keeps his soul, but he who is careless of his ways will die (Prov. 19:16).

Appealing to God for Deliverance

The promise of Scripture gave the psalmist courage to squarely face life's trials (119:46,75,89-91,116-117). He believed that a righteous testing would come from keeping God's Word (119:80) and personal peace with God would be his (119:165).

One of the most constant pleas throughout Psalm 119 is for *revival*. The psalmist needed revival in the sense that life and his enemies had worn him down; so he appealed to God for renewed physical, emotional, and spiritual vitality (119:25, 37, 40, 50, 88, 93, 107, 149, 154, 156, 159).

Even more frequent than his prayer for revival is a repeated plea for deliverance. Sometimes it is not clear whether he speaks of rescue from his human enemies or salvation from sin and its damnable consequences. The latter, in its ultimate sense, would precede the former, in its final sense (119:41-42, 81, 94, 123, 134, 146, 153-154, 166).

Where did he get his courage? Certainly, it came from being saturated with a knowledge of God's character as taught in Scripture. Notice this sample of references to God in Psalm 119.

God's goodness	119:68
God's creatorship	119:73,90
God's judgment	119:75, 84, 120, 137
God's faithfulness	119:75, 90
God's compassion	119:77
God's righteousness	119:137,142
God's mercy	119:156

To close the psalm, he prays for the blessing that he wrote about in the first two verses.

Let Your hand be ready to help me, for I have chosen Your precepts. I long for Your salvation, O LORD, and Your law is my delight. Let my soul live that it may praise You, and let Your ordinances help me. I have gone astray like a lost sheep; seek Your servant, for I do not forget Your commandments (Ps. 119:173-176).

Becoming a Psalm 119 Person

Understandably, you might be a little overwhelmed by now—but that's unnecessary. Augustine supposedly commented on Psalm 119 in this fashion, 'It seems not to need an expositor, but only a reader and a listener.' His point is that anyone who is serious about God's Word can understand this psalm and apply its principles to life. It's not just for scholars; rather God intended it for anyone who takes Scripture seriously.

One personal characteristic of the psalmist stands out noticeably. From sunrise to beyond sunset, the Word of God dominated his life.

At dawn	119:147
Daily	119:97
Seven times daily	119:164
Nightly	119:55, 148
At midnight	119:62

Three simple habits can give you what the psalmist experienced.

1. Read in God's Word every day of your life.[6]
2. Think in God's Word frequently.
3. Walk in God's Word continuously.

This free-verse poem captures the spirit of our psalmist; I hope it captures your spirit also.

New Bible

This was an exciting day for me, Lord!
This morning I opened my new Bible.
Not a single word was circled,
Not a single phrase underlined.
Now with each new day
I can circle and underline again.
I can word-clutter the margins.
And I know what will happen, Lord—
I'll be asking as I read
Why didn't I see that before?
But even with the joy of a new Bible,
I'm going to miss my old one
With its tattered pages—

Its creased and torn edges.
Oh, how many personal notes
Are jotted on the margins!
How many God-whispered secrets!
Yes, Lord, I'll miss it.
But thank you for a friend's reminder:
'If your Bible is falling apart
Chances are your life isn't.'[7]

Let the words of my mouth and the meditation
of my heart be acceptable in Your sight,
O LORD, my rock and my redeemer.
Psalm 19:14

9

THINKING LIKE GOD

Jim Downing tells this insightful story.

An Oriental fable tells of three horsemen who were traveling through the desert at night. Unexpectedly they were confronted by a mysterious person. The stranger told them that they would soon cross the dry bed of a stream.

'When you arrive there,' he declared, 'get off your horses and fill your pockets and saddle bags from the river bed. At sunrise examine the stones you have picked up. You will be both glad and sorry.'

As the man predicted, the travelers came to a dry stream bed. In the spirit of adventure they put a few of the many stones they found scattered into their pockets. At sunrise the next day they examined the pebbles they had picked up. To their great astonishment they found the stones had been transformed into diamonds, rubies, emeralds, and other precious stones.

Recalling the statement of the stranger in the desert, they understood what he meant—they were glad for the pebbles they had picked up but sorry they hadn't taken more.[1]

With all of God's infallible wisdom available in unlimited quantities we, like the horsemen, wish in hindsight that we had picked up more. This sounds very much like Solomon's woes in Ecclesiastes, where he wrote, 'And I set my mind to seek and explore by wisdom concerning all that has been done under heaven. It is a grievous task which God has given to the sons of men to be afflicted with. . . . And I set my mind to know wisdom and to know madness and folly; I realized that this also is striving after wind. Because in much wisdom there is much grief, and increasing knowledge results in increasing pain' (Eccl. 1:13, 17-18).

Even though Solomon had God's wisdom abundantly available (1 Kings 3:12), he chose to think like man, not God.

Control Centre

The brain is key to human existence. It weighs only three pounds but determines what the rest of our much heavier body does. It consumes 25 percent of our blood's oxygen supply, handles 10,000 thoughts daily, regulates over 103,000 heartbeats every 24 hours, controls over 600 muscles, and coordinates over 23,000 breaths a day.

Not only does the brain control our physical life but also our emotions, our will, our thinking, and our spiritual life. What we do with our mind determines what we do with our life.

This central truth did not escape the notice of an ancient writer of Scripture, who commented, 'For as he thinks within himself, so he is' (Prov. 23:7). Another cultural proverb says:

Sow a thought, reap an act.
Sow an act, reap a habit.
Sow a habit, reap a character.

Christianity claims to be and certainly is a religion of the mind. Listen to Paul:

> For those who are according to the flesh set their minds on the things of the flesh, but those who are according to the Spirit, the things of the Spirit....Because the mind set on the flesh is hostile toward God, for it does not subject itself to the law of God, for it is not even able to do so; and those who are in the flesh cannot please God (Rom. 8:5, 7-8).

Jesus admonished Christians to love God with all of their mind (Matt. 22:37). How we think and who we think like determines the course of our lives. The brain becomes central to thinking like God and then loving God.

The Renewed Mind
When you entered into a personal relationship with Jesus Christ, you became a new creation (2 Cor. 5:17) who now sings a new song (Ps. 98:1). But that does not mean that everything becomes new in the sense of perfection. Your mind acquired a new way to think and a new capacity to clean up your old ways of thinking. God is in the business of mind renewal.

> And do not be conformed to this world, but be transformed by the renewing of your mind, that you may prove what the will of God is, that which is good and acceptable and perfect (Rom. 12:2).

> And that you be renewed in the spirit of your mind (Eph. 4:23).

> And have put on the new self who is being renewed to a true knowledge according to the image of the One who created him (Col. 3:10).

The Bible tells us to 'set our minds on the things above, not on the things that are on earth' (Col. 3:2). Paul put this concept in military terms: 'We are destroying speculations and every lofty thing raised up against the knowledge of God, and we are taking every thought captive to the obedience of Christ' (2 Cor. 10:5).

How do we do this? Scripture is the mind of God. Not all of His mind, to be sure; but all that God cared to give us. To think like God, we must think like Scripture. That's why Paul encouraged the Colossians to let the word of Christ richly dwell within them (Col. 3:16).

Harry Blamires, an Englishman with extraordinary understanding about thinking Christianly, puts this quite well:

> *To think Christianly is to think in terms of Revelation. For the secularist, God and theology are the playthings of the mind. For the Christian, God is real, and Christian theology describes His truth revealed to us. For the secular mind, religion is essentially a matter of theory: for the Christian mind, Christianity is a matter of acts and facts. The acts and facts which are the basis of our faith are recorded in the Bible.[2]*

Meditation

To hear something once for most of us is not enough. To briefly ponder something profound for most of us does not allow enough time to grasp and fully understand its significance. This proves to be most true with God's mind in Scripture.

The idea of meditating sometimes lends itself to misunderstanding, so let me illustrate its meaning. Meditation involves prolonged thought or pondering. Our American figure of speech is 'to chew' on a thought. Some have likened it to the rumination process of the cow's double stomach digestive system.

For me, the most vivid picture comes from a coffee percolator. The water goes up a small tube and drains down through the coffee grounds. After enough cycles, the flavour of the coffee beans has been transferred to the water which we then call coffee. So it is that we need to cycle our thoughts through the 'grounds' of God's Word until we start to think like God and then act godly or godlike.

Scripture commands that we meditate in three areas:

1. *God*   Psalms 27:4; 63:6
2. *God's Word*   Joshua 1:8; Psalm 1:2
3. *God's works*   Psalms 143:5; 145:5

The greatest portion of Scripture that talks about Scripture is Psalm 119. (Read Chapter Eight for an exposition of Psalm 119.) All 176 verses extol the virtue of knowing and living out the mind of God. Meditation is mentioned at least seven times as the habit of one who loves God and desires a closer intimacy with Him: 'O how I love Your law! It is my meditation all the day.... My eyes anticipate the night watches, that I may meditate on Your word' (Ps. 119:97, 148; see also vv. 15, 23, 48, 78, 99).

You can 'chew' on God's Word as you read it daily and you also can think about it during other times when your mind is free. This requires that you internalize the Word or be able to recall what you have read.

However you do it, meditating on God's Word will cleanse away the old thoughts that are not of God. Meditation places and reinforces new thoughts from Scripture. Also, it puts a protective shield around your mind to reject incoming thoughts that contradict God. That's the scriptural process of renewing your mind.

Turning On the Light
Scripture tells us that we need God's help to understand God's Word.

> Now we have received, not the spirit of the world, but the Spirit who is from God, that we may know the things freely given to us by God, which things we also speak, not in words taught by human wisdom, but in those taught by the Spirit, combining spiritual thoughts with spiritual words (1 Cor. 2:12-13).

Theologians call this 'illumination.' We use the expressions, 'It just dawned on me' or 'The light just came on' to describe darkened thoughts which later take on new understanding. God's Spirit does that for us with Scripture.

One of my favourite and most often uttered prayers as I study Scripture is, 'Open my eyes, that I may behold wonderful things from Your law' (Ps. 119:18). It acknowledges that I need God's light in Scripture. So do verses like, 'Teach me, O LORD, the way of Your statutes, and I shall observe it to the end. Give me understanding, that I may observe Your law, and keep it with all my heart' (vv. 33-34; see also v. 102).

God wants us to know and understand and obey. So He gives us all the help we need through His Holy Spirit. We, like the men to whom Jesus spoke on the road to Emmaus, need God's help: 'Then He opened their minds to understand the Scriptures' (Luke 24:45).

Christ's Mind

Ultimately and immediately, we must think like Christ. According to Paul, God gave us a good start: 'For who has known the mind of the Lord, that he will instruct Him? But we have the mind of Christ' (1 Cor. 2:16).

Possessing Christ's mind obligates us to use Christ's mind. So Paul writes to the Philippians, 'Have this attitude [mind] in yourselves which was also in Christ Jesus' (Phil. 2:5). What does that involve? Christ's mind led Him to:

1. Sacrifice (Phil. 2:7).
2. Submit (Phil. 2:8).

So we, like Christ, need to think in terms of what we can give, not what we can receive; of how we can obey, not how we can rebel. One who gives and obeys will be a servant, just like Christ. Such is the lifestyle of the person who thinks 'sacrifice' and 'submission'.

Satan's Attack

To be forewarned is to be forearmed. While a commitment to think Christianly sounds great, it is not without opposition. For Satan would have you think contrary to God's Word and then act disobediently to God's will.[3]

Understand first that before you became a Christian your mind was blinded by the devil: 'The god of this world has blinded the minds of the unbelieving so that they might not see the light of the gospel of the glory of Christ, who is the image of God' (2 Cor. 4:4).

Even after salvation, Satan continues his intellectual rampage. Paul had a great concern for the Corinthian church, for he writes, 'But I am afraid that, as the serpent deceived Eve by his craftiness, your minds will be led astray from the simplicity and purity of devotion to Christ' (2 Cor. 11:3).

Eve had allowed Satan to do some thinking for her. Then she did some of her own thinking independent of God. When her conclusions differed from God's she chose to act on her's not God's, which is sin (Gen. 3:1-7).

In warning believers about the battle with Satan, Paul on two occasions tells about the schemes or wiles of the devil. Two different Greek words are used, but they both refer to the mind:

> Put on the full armor of God, so that you will be able to stand firm against the schemes of the devil (Eph. 6:11).

> So that no advantage would be taken of us by Satan, for we are not ignorant of his schemes (2 Cor. 2:11).

No one is immune from this kind of attack. Even the Apostle Peter succumbed. Remember the Lord's words of rebuke: 'Get behind Me, Satan! You are a stumbling block to Me; for you are not setting your mind on God's interests, but man's' (Matt. 16:23).

So you really do need to heed Peter's strong encouragement to 'prepare your minds for action, keep sober in Spirit, fix your hope completely on the grace to be brought to you at the revelation of Jesus Christ' (1 Peter 1:13). You'll do that by thinking like God.

Think on These Things

Someone has said that the mind is the taproot of the soul. That being so, we need to carefully and nutritiously feed our souls by sinking our taproots deep into God's mind in Scripture. So we ask, 'What's the recommended soul food?'

Paul's gourmet menu for the mind includes those things which are:

1. True
2. Honorable
3. Right
4. Pure
5. Lovely
6. Of good repute
7. Excellent
8. Praiseworthy

We must dwell on these sorts of things with our minds (Phil. 4:8). Where do we find these kinds of thoughts? In the Bible! A book of God's word, containing God's will for God's people.

All Scripture is inspired by God and profitable for teaching, for reproof, for correction, for training in righteousness; so that the man of God may be adequate, equipped for every good work (2 Tim. 3:16-17).

The Bottom Line

You might be asking, 'What will I gain?' God anticipated your question. Carefully consider His answer.

This book of the law shall not depart from your mouth, but you shall meditate on it day and night, so that you may be careful to do according to all that is written in it; for then you will make your way prosperous, and then you will have success (Josh. 1:8).

How blessed is the man who does not walk in the counsel of the wicked, nor stand in the path of sinners, nor sit in the seat of scoffers! But his delight is in the law of the LORD, and in His law he meditates day and night. He will be like a tree firmly planted by streams of water, which yields its fruit in its season, and its leaf does not wither; and in whatever he does, he prospers (Ps. 1:1-3).

When you think like God wants you to think and act like God wants you to act, then you will receive God's blessing for obedience. Spiritually, you will be that obedient child, that pure bride, that healthy sheep in Christ's flock who experiences the greatest intimacy with God.

It's amazing how scholars and philosophers over the centuries have recognized the importance of the mind but have rejected the Creator of the mind and the Saviour of the soul. Charles Colson lets us look in on one such classic case:

It was cold and raw that day in 1610 when a French mathematician named Rene Descartes pulled his cloak around him and climbed into the side compartment of a large stove. Descartes had been wrestling for weeks with questions of doubt and reason in his search for some certainty of a philosophical system. As he warmed himself in his stove, his imagination began glowing with the light of reason, and he resolved to doubt everything that could possibly be doubted.

Hours later Descartes emerged, having determined that there was only one thing he could not doubt, and that was the fact that he doubted. A good day's work. Descartes drew the conclusion, Cogito, ergo sum: *'I think, therefore I am.' Then he went out for a cognac.*

Descartes' now-famous postulate led to a whole new promise for philosophic thought: man, rather than God, became the fixed point around which everything else revolved; human reason became the foundation upon which a structure of knowledge could be built; and doubt became the highest intellectual value. [4]

The ultimate form of idolatry would be, like Descartes, to reject the mind of God and worship at the altar of our own independent thinking. Our greatest intimacy with the Lord will be those times when His thoughts supersede ours and our behaviour then models the behaviour of Christ.

We are what we think. That exact idea come from the proverbist's pen close to 3,000 years ago (Prov. 23:7). This truth can be lived out for good or for evil. If we choose to think like God, then we will act like Him. I commend this mental and spiritual route to you with the same enthusiasm as the psalmist:

> O how I love Your law!
> It is my meditation all the day.
> Your commandments make me wiser than my enemies,
> For they are ever mine.
> I have more insight than all my teachers,
> For Your testimonies are my meditation.
> I understand more than the aged,
> Because I have observed Your precepts.
> I have restrained my feet from every evil way,
> That I may keep Your word.
> I have not turned aside from Your ordinances,
> For You Yourself have taught me.
> How sweet are Your words to my taste!
> Yes, sweeter than honey to my mouth!
> From Your precepts I get understanding;
> Therefore I hate every false way (Psalm 119:97-104).

Oh to be like Thee! blessed Redeemer,
This is my constant longing and prayer;
Gladly I'll forfeit all of earth's treasures,
Jesus, Thy perfect likeness to wear.[1]

Thomas O. Chisholm

10

TRANSFORMED BY GOD'S WISDOM

Being a former naval officer, I was delighted one day to find *A Sailor's Dictionary* while browsing through my favourite bookstore. The dust jacket read, 'A dictionary for landlubbers, old salts and armchair drifters'. It sounded inviting.

Intrigued, I picked up the book to sample the humour. Here's how it described *sailing*— 'The fine art of getting wet and becoming ill while slowly going nowhere at great expense.'[2] That's true not only of sailing but also of the spiritual life, unless we are directed by the gentle breeze of God's transforming wisdom.

Wisdom's Source

Wisdom shouts in the street, she lifts her voice in the square; at the head of the noisy streets she cries out; at the entrance of the gates in the city she utters her sayings: 'How long, O naive ones, will you love being simple-minded? And scoffers delight themselves in scoffing, and fools hate knowledge? Turn to my reproof, behold, I will pour out my spirit on you; I will make my words known to you. Because I called, and you refused, I stretched out my hand, and no one paid attention; and you neglected all my counsel, and did not want my reproof; I will also laugh at your calamity; I will mock when your dread comes, when your dread comes like a storm, and your calamity comes like a whirlwind, when distress and anguish come upon you.

'Then they will call on me, but I will not answer; they will seek me diligently, but they will not find me, because they hated knowledge, and did not choose the fear of the LORD. They would not accept my counsel, they spurned all my reproof. So shall they eat of the fruit of their own way, and be satiated with their own devices. For the waywardness of the naive will kill them, and the complacency of fools will destroy them. But he who listens to me shall live securely, and will be at ease from the dread of evil' (Prov. 1:20-33).

The writer of Proverbs puts wisdom in street language. Portrayed as a woman crying out in the city, wisdom beckons the people to turn from their sinful scoffing to the reproof of God and its attendant reward (vv. 23, 33).

Jesus parallels this same idea with His Parable of the Two Builders.

Therefore everyone who hears these words of Mine, and acts upon them, may be compared to a wise man, who built his house on the rock. And the rain fell, and the floods came, and the winds blew, and slammed against that house; and yet it did not fall, for it had been founded on the rock.

Everyone who hears these words of Mine, and does not act on them, will be like a foolish man, who built his house on the sand. The rain fell, and the floods came, and the winds blew, and slammed against that house; and it fell, and great was its fall (Matt. 7:24-27).

Our spiritual transformation begins when we receive Jesus Christ as Saviour and Lord. Paul describes Him as the one 'in whom are hidden all the treasures of wisdom and knowledge' (Col. 2:3; see 1 Cor. 1:24, 30). The Spirit of God comes to indwell us with what Isaiah calls 'The spirit of wisdom and understanding, the spirit of counsel and strength, the spirit of knowledge and the fear of the LORD' (Isa. 11:2). Paul reminds us that the one to whom glory will be given forever is 'the only wise God' (Rom. 16:27) referring to God the Father. Our relationship to Father, Son, and Holy Spirit refers to a union with pure wisdom. Thus we are transformed by the personal presence and power of wisdom in our lives.

Wisdom's Manner

God's will, His Word, and His way are all wise. Everything about God is wise; all else is foolishness. This little catechism answers several key questions about wisdom from Scripture.

Place—Where Can Wisdom Be Found?

The law of the LORD is perfect, restoring the soul; the testimony of the LORD is sure, making wise the simple (Ps. 19:7).

You, however, continue in the things you have learned and become convinced of knowing from whom you have learned them; and that from childhood you have known the sacred writings which are able to give you the wisdom that leads to salvation through faith which is in Christ Jesus (2 Tim. 3:14-15).

Pattern—What Identifies True Wisdom?

The fear of the LORD is the beginning of wisdom, and the knowledge of the Holy One is understanding (Prov. 9:10).

Profit—How Valuable Is Wisdom?

How blessed is the man who finds wisdom, and the man who gains understanding. For its profit is better than the profit of silver, and its gain than fine gold. She is more precious than jewels; and nothing you desire compares with her. Long life is in her right hand; in her left hand are riches and honor. Her ways are pleasant ways, and all her paths are peace. She is a tree of life to those who take hold of her, and happy are all who hold her fast (Prov. 3:13-18).

Promise—How Is Wisdom Obtained?

But if any of you lacks wisdom, let him ask of God, who gives to all generously and without reproach, and it will be given to him. But he must ask in faith without any doubting, for the one who doubts is like the surf of the sea, driven and tossed by the wind. For that man ought not to expect that he will receive anything from the Lord, being a double-minded man, unstable in all his ways (Jas. 1:5-8).

Precaution—Are There Warnings about Wisdom?

Thus says the LORD, 'Let not a wise man boast of his wisdom, and let not the mighty man boast of his might, let not a rich man boast of his riches; but let him who boasts boast of this, that he understands and knows Me, that I am the LORD who exercises lovingkindness, justice, and righteousness on earth; for I delight in these things,' declares the LORD (Jer. 9:23-24).

Paradox—Are There Surprises with Wisdom?

Let no man deceive himself. If any man among you thinks that he is wise in this age, he must become foolish so that he may become wise (1 Cor. 3:18).

Practice—What Should We Do with Wisdom?

Therefore be careful how you walk, not as unwise men, but as wise, making the most of your time, because the days are evil. So then do not be foolish, but understand what the will of the Lord is (Eph. 5:15-17).

Wisdom's Fruit

> Who among you is wise and understanding? Let him show by his good behavior his deeds in the gentleness of wisdom. But if you have bitter jealousy and selfish ambition in your heart, do not be arrogant and so lie against the truth. This wisdom is not that which comes down from above, but is earthly, natural, demonic. For where jealousy and selfish ambition exist, there is disorder and every evil thing. But the wisdom from above is first pure, then peaceable, gentle, reasonable, full of mercy and good fruits, unwavering, without hypocrisy. And the seed whose fruit is righteousness is sown in peace by those who make peace (Jas. 3:13-18).

James distinguished between an earthly wisdom and true godly wisdom from above. Wisdom from God will reflect good conduct with a gentle character, while the counterfeit wisdom of demons produces evil and disorder. Righteousness and peace accompany authentic wisdom. In verse 17, we see a kaleidoscope of wisdom patterns describing the transformed life of one who is spiritually mature in wisdom. James asked, 'Who among you is wise and understanding?' in verse 13, and then provided the basis for determining the answer in verse 17.

PURE. The premier feature of godly wisdom is cleanness or, put another way, the absence of sin's pollution. Wisdom and desire for sinlessness are synonymous. The church is to be pure like a chaste virgin (2 Cor. 11:2); Christians are to think on pure things (Phil. 4:8); young women are to be pure (Titus 2:5); and leaders in the church need to keep pure (1 Tim. 5:22).

The ancient church father Tertullian put purity in perspective with his statement:

> *Be clothed with the silk of honesty, the fine linen of holiness and the purple of chastity; thus adorned, God will be your friend.*

As Christ wisely withstood the impure lure of sin, so should we (Matt. 4:1-11).

PEACEABLE. Wisdom makes peace, not war. Peacemakers are called sons of God (Matt. 5:9). Peace is included in the fruit produced by God's Spirit (Gal. 5:22). We are to let the peace of Christ rule our hearts (Col. 3:15). Since Christ is called the 'Prince of Peace' (Isa. 9:6), Christians need to be ambassadors of peace (2 Cor. 5:20).

GENTLE. The Greek word we translate 'gentle' contains much more than our English word conveys. Let me try to fill it out with some descriptive phrases:

    sweet reasonableness
    going the second mile
    not demanding one's rights
    full of mercy
    discerning between the letter and spirit of the law

Gentleness should characterize the elders' behaviour in the church (1 Tim. 3:3). Believers need to be gentle with one another (Phil. 4:5). Ultimately, Christians are to be gentle with all men (Titus 3:2). As Christ wisely spoke gentle words to the thief, so should we to those who seek Christ (Luke 23:39-43).

REASONABLE. This makes us conciliatory and willing to yield when spiritual progress can be gained. If we are reasonable, no one will ever characterize us as a 'course grade' of sandpaper. Christ always yielded to His Heavenly Father; that's our example to follow.

> I can do nothing on my own initiative. As I hear, I judge; and My judgment is just, because I do not seek My own will, but the will of Him who sent Me (John 5:30).

FULL OF MERCY. Since God is rich in mercy, so should we be (Eph. 2:4). By God's great mercy we were born again and made heirs of eternal life (1 Peter 1:3; Titus 3:5). Mercy withholds judgment and extends grace without violating justice. We can follow in the footsteps of Christ's full mercy, as extended to the harlot (John 8:1-11), and to Peter (John 21:17).

FULL OF GOOD FRUITS. The idea here is not so much fruit in character as fruit in action that qualifies to be called good. Like mercy, these fruits should flow in abundance.

The pattern that James calls for follows the teaching of Jesus who demanded fruit (John 15:2), *more* fruit (John 15:2), and *much* fruit (John 15:5,8).

UNWAVERING. With regard to the things of God, we are to be single-minded, without compromise, and consistent. If we don't waver, we won't be blown around by every wind of doctrine or trickery of men (Eph. 4:14). Like Christ, we should always pray,

> Father, if You are willing, remove this cup from Me; yet not My will, but Yours be done (Luke 22:42).

WITHOUT HYPOCRISY. Sincere, genuine, unpretentious, and without a mask all describe this quality. Our love (Rom. 12:9) and our faith (1 Tim. 1:5) are to be without hypocrisy. What we claim to be we are to be. Just as Jesus claimed to be a servant (Matt. 20:28) and actually served (John 13:12-17), so we need to live with transparent honesty.

Wise Transformation

Job twice asked the significant question: 'Where can wisdom be found; where does wisdom come from?' (Job 28:12, 20). He answered his own questions,

> God understands its way; and He knows its place. For He looks to the ends of the earth, and sees everything under the heavens. When He imparted weight to the wind, and meted out the waters by measure, when He set a limit for the rain and a course for the thunderbolt, then He saw it and declared it; He established it and also searched it out. And to man he said, 'Behold, the fear of the Lord, that is wisdom; and to depart from evil is understanding' (Job 28:23-28).

So wisdom begins with the transformation wrought by salvation, but it does not end there.

Wisdom resides in God's Word (Ps. 19:7). By it believers are transformed by the renewing of their minds (Rom. 12:2). Going a step further, wisdom not only knows God's Word but obeys it.

> The conclusion, when all has been heard, is: fear God and keep His commandments, because this applies to every person (Eccl. 12:13).

True wisdom avoids being conformed to this world and its lusts (Rom. 12:2; 1 Peter 1:14), and rather pursues transformation into the image of our wise Saviour.

But we all, with unveiled face, beholding as in a mirror the glory of the Lord, are being transformed into the same image from glory to glory, just as from the Lord, the Spirit (2 Cor. 3:18).

Acquiring Wisdom

For a true Christian, true spiritual wisdom comes by at least four means. First, we can ask God for wisdom. When Solomon could have anything he wanted from God, he asked for wisdom and discernment (1 Kings 3:3-9). God commended him because he did not ask for long life or riches but wisdom. Thus Solomon became the wisest man of history (1 Kings 4:29-34). This same invitation to pray for wisdom awaits us today.

> But if any of you lacks wisdom, let him ask of God, who gives to all generously and without reproach, and it will be given to him. But he must ask in faith without any doubting, for the one who doubts is like the surf of the sea driven and tossed by the wind. For that man ought not to expect that he will receive anything from the Lord, being a double-minded man, unstable in all his ways (James 1:5-8).

Second, wisdom can also be obtained from God's Word (Ps. 119:98-100). God's invitation to this source is also available to all.

> Let the Word of Christ richly dwell within you (Col. 3:16).

Third, wisdom closely associates itself with the Holy Spirit. Bezalel was filled with the Spirit of God in wisdom (Ex. 31:3) as were the seven servants of the early church (Acts 6:3). Thus, to be filled with the Holy Spirit corresponds to being filled with wisdom.

Fourth, the crowds marvelled at Christ's wisdom (Matt. 13:54; Mark 6:2). Luke reports He increased in wisdom (2:40, 52). Thus as we abide in Christ (John 15:4-7), we abide in wisdom.

Christian spirituality involves growing to be like God in character and conduct through *the transforming work* of God's Word and God's Spirit.

Part Three

SPIRITUAL PRIORITIES

But, beloved, we are convinced of better things concerning you, and things that accompany salvation, though we are speaking in this way. For God is not unjust so as to forget your work and the love which you have shown toward His name, in having ministered and in still ministering to the saints. And we desire that each of you show the same diligence so as to realize the full assurance of hope until the end, so that you may not be sluggish, but imitators of those who through faith and patience inherit the promises.

Hebrews 6:9-12

We need to warn such persons that there is not a shortcut to holiness. It must be the business of their whole lives to grow in grace and continually to add one virtue to another. It is, as far as possible, 'to go on towards perfection' (Hebrews 6:1). 'He only that doeth righteousness is righteous' (1 John 3:7). Unless they bring forth 'the fruit of the Spirit' (Galatians 5:22), they can have not sufficient evidence that they have actually received the Spirit of Christ, 'without which they are none of His' (Romans 8:9). Unless, then, the root of the matter is found in them, they are not adorning the doctrine of God, but disparaging and discrediting it.[1]

William Wilberforce

*I said to the L*ORD*, 'You are my God;*
*Give ear, O L*ORD*,*
to the voice of my supplications.'
Psalm 140:6

11

TALKING TO GOD

An executive received notification that he would be transferred to another part of the country. His young daughter, having lived her entire life where they were, became unhappy over the pending move.

The night before the moving van arrived she said her evening prayers. She went through the usual 'God bless Mommy and Daddy,' then added, 'I guess I'd better tell You too, God, that this is good-bye. I won't be able to pray to You anymore—we're moving to New York.'

For many the mere mention of prayer produces thoughts of awkwardness, inadequacy, or embarrassment. At times, we feel as infant-like in prayer as the young girl who didn't want to move.

Or perhaps we're like the two middle-aged men who had been neighbours as farm boys and met one day on a city street. They reminisced for a few minutes, then agreed to meet again and visit their boyhood homes. The time came and they began to stroll through the fields, eventually coming to a pasture where a herd of cattle was grazing. They passed through a barbed-wire fence into a field, unafraid of the cattle.

As they walked further, a bull suddenly appeared, snorting and pawing. The men started running back toward the fence and the bull gave chase. When they realized they were not going to reach the fence in time, one man said, 'We'd better start praying,' and then, since both were unaccustomed to praying, he added, 'You had a father that prayed, or that at least said table grace, so you know more about praying that I do.' So quickly the other man said the only prayer that he could remember: 'O Lord, let us be thankful for that which we are about to receive!'

We're all at times guilty of praying only in emergencies, of turning to God only when the heat is on.

But what is the true essence of prayer? Ray Stedman explains prayer as an awareness of our helpless need and an acknowledgement of divine adequacy![1] Put more simply, prayer is the conversation between a spiritual child with his or her Heavenly Father.

It can be praise and thanksgiving, praying for someone (intercession) or praying for yourself (supplication), a confession of sin or a request for a specific need (petition). Whatever our prayer, we come to God as helpless paupers seeking His divine resources for our lives.

Biblical Keys

From the first to the last, biblical prayer marks the connecting link from man to God. Joshua prayed and the sun stood still (Josh. 10:12-13). Nehemiah prayed that the king would grant his request (Neh. 2:4). And Daniel prayed for God's deliverance of Israel (Dan. 9:4-19).

Jesus prayed constantly (Luke 3:21; 5:16; 6:12; 9:18, 28; 11:1; 22:32, 41). He never taught His disciples how to preach but He did instruct them how to pray (11:1-4). Paul constantly prayed for those whom he loved (1 Thess. 1:2-3). Prayer, perhaps more than any other activity, measures the level of intimacy we have with the Lord.

Charles Spurgeon suggested that prayer is the slender nerve that moves the muscle of God's omnipotence. We need to know how that works; how we can pray in such a way that God hears and answers.

Some have believed it is the special words or phrases we use. Others believe it is the closing of eyes or the folding of hands or kneeling on knees. The place of prayer has been suggested as the key to success. But that's not what the Bible teaches.

Prayer rises above the externals. It is based on what is inside of us, not mere words or ways. There are five biblical keys to fruitful prayer revealed in Scripture. They are:

1. Our willingness to give (James 4:1-3)
2. Our willingness to believe (James 1:5-8)
3. Our willingness to yield (1 John 5:14-15)
4. Our willingness to obey (1 John 3:22)
5. Our willingness to wait (Luke 18:1-8)

Right Reasons

Selfish prayer does not commend itself to God. Note these words in James' epistle:

> What is the source of quarrels and conflicts among you? Is not the source your pleasures that wage war in your members? You lust and do not have; so you commit murder. You are envious and cannot obtain; so you fight and quarrel. You do not have because you do not ask. You ask and do not receive, because you ask with wrong motives, so that you may spend it on your pleasures (Jas. 4:1-3).

The early church dealt with internal strife every step of the way. Jesus taught unity; they experienced division. Why? Selfishness.

These Christians lived a self-centred existence rather than focusing chiefly on God and others.

They grabbed for what they wanted and usually came up empty-handed. To their plight James responds, 'You do not have because you do not ask' (4:2). They had long ago left God out of the process.

But some did pray. However, they prayed with the same failure to receive. These asked or prayed for wrong reasons. Self-gratification and self-satisfaction drove their prayers. They possessed little concern for the kingdom of God or the household of their Heavenly Father.

If you are a parent, you can understand this better than most. If your children come with various requests, which one will you be more likely to honour? The kid who is always concerned with himself or the child who has your best interest and those of other family members in mind?

Does that mean it's wrong to pray for yourself? No! It does mean, however, that you need to ask *why* you are making a certain request of God. Here is a quick test:

1. Is this request reflecting that I am first and foremost in my life seeking God's kingdom and His righteousness? (Matt. 6:33)
2. Am I considering other people to be more important than me? (Phil. 2:3)

Take a moment to recall Jesus' account of the Pharisee and the tax collector as they prayed (Luke 18:9-14). The first prayed to justify himself; the second, to be justified by God. This most vividly illustrates the importance of praying with right motives.

Your attitude proves far more important than your ability to articulate a masterful prayer. Perhaps the simplicity of this child would be best. Her grandfather overheard her repeating the alphabet in reverent, hushed tones. 'What are you doing?' he inquired. 'I'm praying, Grandpa,' she replied. 'I can't think of the right words, so I just say all the letters. God will put them together for me because He knows what I'm thinking.'

Right Rest

A prayer without faith resembles a car without an engine—they both go nowhere. Without faith it is impossible to please God (Heb. 11:6). Also, without faith it is impossible to reach God in prayer.

> But if any of you lacks wisdom, let him ask of God, who gives to all generously and without reproach, and it will be given to him. But he

must ask in faith without any doubting, for the one who doubts is like the surf of the sea driven and tossed by the wind (Jas. 1:5-7).

To pray without faith is to question either God's existence, His ability, or His willingness. When we pray, it must be with the confidence that God is, that He is able, and that He does all things perfectly.

Faith willingly accepts God's denial of a request and believes that God has a better idea. The early church accepted James' death although they most certainly had prayed for his release as they later prayed for Peter's (Acts 12:1-2, 12). Paul accepted his thorn in the flesh in spite of praying for its removal (2 Cor. 12:7-10).

Faith can then embrace God's delivery of answered prayer. Those who had prayed so faithfully for James surely were disappointed. But think of the delight when Peter, for whom they had also prayed in exactly the same circumstances, showed up as living proof that God intervened (Acts 12:5, 16-17).

Warren Wiersbe relates four levels of prayer. In a sense, they each reflect a growing maturity of faith.

1. Grade school level–praying
2. High school level–praying for God's will
3. College level–praying as children to their Heavenly Father
4. Post-graduate level–praying for spiritual maturity

Which level best describes your prayer life?

Right Realm

Over a century ago Richard Chenevix Trench crisply wrote, 'Prayer is not overcoming God's reluctance; it is laying hold of His willingness.' Almost 2,000 years ago John recorded these words:

> This is the confidence which we have before Him, that, if we ask anything according to His will, He hears us. And if we know that He hears us in whatever we ask, we know that we have the requests which we have asked from Him (1 John 5:14-15).

God's will frames effective prayer. Central to Christ's teaching of prayer came this principle:

> Your Kingdom come. Your will be done, on earth as it is in heaven (Matt. 6:10).

Central to Christ's praying came this practice:

> And he went a little beyond them, and fell on His face and prayed saying,
> 'My Father, if it is possible, let this cup pass from Me; yet not as I will,
> but as You will' (Matt. 26:39).

The essence of prayer does not involve satisfying our personal
wishes, but rather being so changed by our communion with God
that we come to wholeheartedly crave His will for us. The psalmist
put it this way, 'Delight yourself in the LORD; and He will give you
the desires of your heart' (Ps. 37:4).

Right Response

As a parent, will you be more inclined to respond to the obedient or
disobedient child? Ponder God's response to His spiritual children:

> If I regard wickedness in my heart, the Lord will not hear (Ps. 66:18).

> And whatever we ask we receive from Him, because we keep His
> commandments and do the things that are pleasing in His sight (1 John
> 3:22).

Let me illustrate from Scripture. Daniel proved to be the epitome
of obedience. Even though he had not yet passed out of adolescence—
and despite the fact that he had been violently separated from his
parents and forced to live in a pagan culture—he still clung to an
uncompromising allegiance to God (Dan. 1:8-9). It's no wonder that
when Daniel stood on the brink of death and prayed, God delivered
him (2:18-23). This sort of experience marked the remainder of
Daniel's life. He prayed for release from the lions' den and God
delivered (6:10, 22-23). He also prayed for the release of Israel from
foreign domination and God answered (9:3-19).

Israel, on the other hand, often proved that God meant business
when He said He would not honour disobedience.

> Behold, the LORD's hand is not so short that it cannot save; nor is His ear
> so dull that it cannot hear. But your iniquities have made a separation
> between you and your God, and your sins have hidden His face from
> you, so that He does not hear. For your hands are defiled with blood,
> and your fingers with iniquity; your lips have spoken falsehood, your
> tongue mutters wickedness (Isa. 59:1-3).

The more time you spend listening to God in His Word, the more likely you will talk to God in prayer. With growing intimacy comes increased obedience.

A.T. Pierson paints this vivid picture of intimacy:

He who would keep up intimate converse with the Lord must habitually find in the Scriptures the highway of such companionship. God's aristocracy, His nobility, the princes of His realm are not the wise, mighty, and highborn of earth, but often the poor, weak, despised of men, who abide in His presence, and devoutly commune with Him through His inspired Word. Blessed are they who have thus learned to use the key which gives free access, not only to the King's treasures, but to the King Himself.[2]

Right Restraint

Impatience mocks God, who always sets the absolute, precise standard of time. The psalmist struggled with waiting (Ps. 13:1-2). Saul's unwillingness to wait led to his fall from Israel's throne (1 Sam. 13:1-14). The disciples were always in a hurry (Acts 1:6).

That tendency must be the reason behind our Lord's parable of the nasty judge and needy widow (Luke 18:1-8). It begins: 'Now He was telling them a parable to show that at all times they ought to pray and not to lose heart' (v. 1).

Delay does not mean denial. God just has a better timetable. Pray until God shows you that you are to stop.

No better example of this could be found than in the prayer life of Zacharias and Elizabeth. One day in the twilight moments of his priestly career, Zacharias ministered in the temple and heard an angel say, 'Do not be afraid, Zacharias, for your petition has been heard' (Luke 1:13). What petition? Obviously the prayer for a child (vv.13-14).

This great news shocked Zacharias, who asked, 'How shall I know of this for certain? For I am an old man, and my wife is advanced in years' (v. 18).

Imagine praying for years that God would bless your marital union with a child, knowing that society would conclude barrenness meant God's displeasure. Then, when you and your spouse were past child-bearing years, you accepted God's will of no child. So you planned to finish out your career and retire. Now in the waning days of your

service, you discover the baby is on the way. That describes Zacharias'
experience perfectly.

In your prayer, be persistent and be patient. But above all, be
prepared!

Plan of Attack
Here are some simple steps to take as you launch out on a lifetime
journey of prayer:

Admission	—	*Lord, I am unable!*
Submission	—	*Lord, You know best!*
Transmission	—	*Lord, please intervene!*
Intermission	—	*Lord, I will wait for You!*
Permission	—	*Lord, thank You for Your answer!*

The psalmist prayed at least twenty times, 'Lord, be gracious/merciful
to me/us.' That's a great place to start and to end in your prayer life.

Parting Thoughts
Ultimately, the greatest blessing of prayer is not in receiving the
answer, but rather in becoming the kind of intimate friend whom
God can trust with the answer. Listen to the psalmist's words: 'But
certainly God has heard; He has given heed to the voice of my prayer.
Blessed be God, who has not turned away my prayer, nor His
lovingkindness from me' (Ps. 66:19-20).

Prayer undoubtedly proves to be the greatest opportunity a believer
can enter into. Note these two New Testament promises:

> Therefore let us draw near with confidence to the throne of grace, so
> that we may receive mercy and may find grace to help in time of need
> (Heb. 4:16).

> Now to Him who is able to do far more abundantly beyond all that we
> ask or think, according to the power that works within us (Eph. 3:20).

One night a British soldier was caught creeping back into his
quarters from the nearby woods. He was taken before his commanding
officer and charged with holding communications with the enemy.
The man pleaded that he had gone into the woods to be alone to pray.
That was his only defense.

'Have you been in the habit of spending hours in private prayer?'

the officer growled.

'Yes, sir!'

'Then down on your knees and pray now! You never needed it so much!'

Expecting immediate death, the soldier knelt down and poured out his soul in prayer that could only be inspired by the power of the Holy Spirit.

'You may go,' said the officer simply, when the soldier had finished. 'I believe your story. If you hadn't drilled often, you could not do so well at review.'

How well would you have done?

I was glad when they said to me,
'Let us go to the house of the LORD.'
Psalm 122:1

12

WORSHIPPING GOD

A well-known worship leader, commenting on contemporary worship in America, said in my presence recently, 'People play at their worship, worship their work, and work at their play.' How tragic—how true! A.W. Tozer observed that 'worship acceptable to God is the missing crown jewel in evangelical Christianity.'[1]

If any one of these major life activities—worship, work, or play—falls prey to error, then the other two will likely be affected also. So it's imperative that we understand God's desire for our spiritual activities, sustaining energies, and social outlets.

Obviously, worship becomes the place to begin since God is our highest priority. The word *worship* originated with the Anglo-Saxon *weoscrip,* meaning 'that to which we ascribe worth or value.' In a religious sense, it can be directed to an unlimited number of created objects or persons. However, in a biblical context, worship ascribes ultimate eternal worth to God alone; and that is why God jealously demands to be the exclusive object of worship.

> You shall not make for yourself an idol, or any likeness of what is in heaven above or on the earth beneath or in the water under the earth. You shall not worship them or serve them; for I, the Lord your God, am a jealous God, visiting the iniquity of the fathers on the children, on the third and fourth generations of those who hate Me, but showing lovingkindness to thousands, to those who love Me and keep My commandments (Ex. 20:4-6).

Scripturally, the prominent Hebrew and Greek terms translated 'worship' derive from the ancient practice of bowing oneself to the ground as an outward sign of reverence. In a broad sense, then, worship expresses the recognition and celebration that God is the one, true, eternal Sovereign upon whom we are totally dependent and to whom we ascribe absolute spiritual allegiance.

True worship can be personal and corporate, but true corporate worship will always be preceded by the personal side. Worship can be either outward or inward; authentic outward expression will always be validated by a true inward attitude.

For our immediate purpose, let me broadly define worship as living in the presence of God according to His will for His pleasure and glory. Put another way, it is having spiritual fellowship with God (1 John 1:3).

God's Plan

One of the common threads running from Genesis to Revelation is God's desire to 'tabernacle' among His people and to be their God. The fellowship between God and man began in the Garden of Eden, but quickly disintegrated because Adam's sin erected a barrier between God and the human race. Both Adam and Eve were evicted from Eden where they previously had walked and talked with God.

The Lord reaffirmed His desire to fellowship with man by initiating a relationship with Israel. He visibly demonstrated this relationship by displaying His Shekinah presence in Moses' tabernacle and Solomon's temple.

> Moreover, I will make My dwelling among you, and My soul will not reject you. I will also walk among you and be your God, and you shall be My people (Lev. 26:11-12).

But God's dwelling among Israel, similar to Eden, ended due to sin on the part of Israel (Ezek. 10-11).

This tabernacling of God now takes place individually as He dwells within those who are His in Christ: 'Do you not know that you are a temple of God, and that the Spirit of God dwells in you?' (1 Cor. 3:16)

For Christians who die, the tabernacle experience continues in heaven where Christ now sits at God the Father's right hand.

> Now the main point in what has been said is this: we have such a high priest, who has taken His seat at the right hand of the throne of the Majesty in the heavens, a minister in the sanctuary, and in the true tabernacle, which the Lord pitched, not man (Heb. 8:1-2; see also 9:23-24).

The Tribulation martyrs likewise may look forward to a heavenly tabernacle.

> For this reason, they are before the throne of God; and they serve Him day and night in His temple; and He who sits on the throne will spread His tabernacle over them (Rev. 7:15).

The inhabitants of the earth during the Millennium will take up where Israel left off.

I will make a covenant of peace with them; it will be an everlasting covenant with them. And I will place them and multiply them, and will set My sanctuary in their midst forever. My dwelling place also will be with them; and I will be their God, and they will be My people. And the nations will know that I am the LORD who sanctifies Israel, when My sanctuary is in their midst forever (Ezek. 37:26-28).

Finally, eternity future involves the perfect expression and experience of God fulfilling His forever purpose of ruling over and dwelling among His people.

And I heard a loud voice from the throne, saying, 'Behold, the tabernacle of God is among men, and He will dwell among them, and they shall be His people, and God himself will be among them' (Rev. 21:3).

Man's Past
As with Adam and Eve in Eden and Israel at the Shekinah's departure, sin disrupts the worship communion between human beings and God. Yet man persistently tries to restore the broken relationship according to his own wisdom. Three forms of bankrupt worship emerge from worship as defined by man.

1. Idolatrous worship involving wrong gods with a wrong heart:

He did away with idolatrous priests whom the kings of Judah had appointed to burn incense in the high places in the cities of Judah and in the surrounding area of Jerusalem, also those who burned incense to Baal, to the sun and to the moon and to the constellations and to all the host of heaven (2 Kings 23:5).

2. Ignorant worship involving wrong gods with a sincere heart:

For while I was passing through and examining the objects of your worship, I also found an altar with this inscription, 'TO AN UNKNOWN GOD.' Therefore what you worship in ignorance, this I proclaim to you (Acts 17:23).

3. Vain worship involving the true God but with a wrong heart attitude:

This people honors Me with their lips, but their heart is far away from Me. But in vain do they worship Me, teaching as doctrines the precepts of men (Matt. 15:8-9).

Satan craves to be worshipped, but should always be denied (Isa. 14:13-14; Matt. 4:8-10). Man inclines to worship angels, but they always reject it (Rev. 19:10; 22:8-9). Humans try to worship other human beings (Acts 10:25; 14:11-15). Paul summarizes the human race's sinful inclination to render worship to someone other than God: 'For they exchanged the truth of God for a lie, and worshipped and served the creature rather than the Creator, who is blessed forever. Amen' (Rom. 1:25).

Only one kind of right worship ever existed—worship in spirit and in truth. 'God is spirit, and those who worship Him must worship in spirit and truth' (John 4:24).

True worship involves the spiritual realm and is always in accord with God's truth concerning both the object and means of worship.

The Bible records many true worship experiences such as:

Abraham and Isaac	Gen. 22:5ff
Eliezer	Gen. 24:26
Israel in Egypt	Ex. 4:31
Joshua	Josh. 5:14-15
Gideon	Judg. 7:15
David	2 Sam. 12:20
Ezra	Neh. 8:6; 9:3
Job	Job 1:20
Wise men	Matt. 2:11
Blind man	John 9:38
Angels	Heb. 1:6

But the most personal and detailed is the experience of Isaiah.

Personal Worship
Prophets normally preach. In one instance, however, Isaiah found himself in the pew, not the pulpit. From his memorable experience, he teaches us about the key elements in the dynamics of true worship.

Whether by personal choice or God's sovereign will, Isaiah found himself gazing on God's uncluttered glory.

In the year of King Uzziah's death, I saw the Lord sitting on a throne, lofty and exalted, with the train of His robe filling the temple. Seraphim stood above Him, each having six wings; with two he covered his face, and with two he covered his feet, and with two he flew. And one called out to another and said, 'Holy, Holy, Holy, is the LORD of hosts, the whole earth is full of His glory.' And the foundations of the thresholds trembled at the voice of him who called out, while the temple was filling with smoke (Isa. 6:1-4).

The significance of this beginning step of worship can be best understood in the historical context of the times.

1. King Uzziah had acted corruptly with regard to temple worship and God had struck him down with leprosy (2 Chron. 26:19-20).
2. Despite this judgment, the people continued to act corruptly (2 Chron. 27:2).

Although Jotham ruled well for sixteen years following his father Uzziah's death, God knew that Israel's prophet needed a fresh glimpse of God's glory and holiness to sustain him in spiritually turbulent times. The same is true for us.

In the midst of God's perfect presence, Isaiah remembered how unholy he was by contrast. He confessed his own sinfulness and Israel's, crying out for God's mercy with a deep sense of need for spiritual cleansing: 'Woe is me, for I am ruined! Because I am a man of unclean lips, and I live among a people of unclean lips; for my eyes have seen the King, the Lord of hosts' (Isa. 6:5).

Isaiah 6:6-7 portrays God's cleansing and forgiveness which the prophet sought. The worship experience—standing in God's presence—brought Isaiah once more to the realization that the Lord reigns supreme in heaven and on earth. Apparently Isaiah had become too bogged down in earthly circumstances (the king's death) and not attentive enough to God's promises and presence. For Isaiah that was sin.

With a freshness of soul and a renewed sense of God's magnificence, Isaiah responded to God's call for service with a new burst of energy.

Then I heard the voice of the Lord saying, 'Whom shall I send, and who will go for us?' Then I said, 'Here am I. Send me!' (Isa. 6:8).

Four elements stand out in Isaiah's worship experience which should be applicable to us on a daily basis.

1. Seeing God's holiness and glory through Scripture
2. Sensing the need to be clean and holy for unhindered fellowship with God
3. Seizing God's promise for forgiveness
4. Serving God with obedience

Corporate Worship

Since eternity will be spent worshipping God, we should be practicing now for the future. What will worship in heaven be like?

Revelation 4-5 paints the most vivid and active picture of heavenly worship in Scripture. What we perceive in heaven should be at the heart of our practice on earth. Six observations prove especially important to shape our worship.

Observation 1—Worship is the exclusive activity. The scenes in both Revelation 4 and 5 conclude with a summary statement about worship:

> The twenty-four elders will fall down before Him who sits on the throne, and will worship Him who lives forever and ever, and will cast their crowns before the throne (4:10).

> And the four living creatures kept saying, 'Amen.' And the elders fell down and worshipped (5:14).

Observation 2—God is the exclusive focus of worship. The Father (4:2, 9-11) and the Son (5:5-6) both feature prominently in the scene. The object and attention of worship is not the congregation, the pastor, the musician, or peripheral features. Worship that is centred anywhere and upon anyone other than God alone is not true worship.

Observation 3—Praise for God laces the worship of heaven. On at least five occasions the participants burst forth with adoration—4:8; 4:9-11; 5:9-10; 5:12; and 5:13.

Observation 4—Truth about God provides the context of worship. Not sermonettes that entertain, not platitudes that produce goosebumps, but reality about God that changes lives marks heavenly worship.

The character of God (4:8), the creation (4:11), God's sovereignty (4:11), salvation (5:9, 12), and the kingdom (5:10) comprise the truth touched upon. This feature expresses itself as preaching in our earthly worship.

Observation 5—All of God's living entourage are united in worship. The four living creatures (4:6-8; 5:8,14), the multitude of angels (5:11), and redeemed humanity represented by the twenty-four elders (4:4; 5:8,14) all joined in corporate worship of God.

Observation 6—The essence of heavenly worship provides the model for earthly worship.

Your kingdom come, Your will be done, on earth as it is in heaven (Matt. 6:10).

Corporate worship will flesh out differently in separate congregations and on different occasions. But these six elements should always be the framework of true corporate worship.

One final thought. No greater experience of worship comes than at times of baptism, which celebrates new life and salvation (Matt. 28:19) and the reproduction of the Upper Room experience, which celebrates Christ's death and its results (John 13:17). These always prove to be blessed times of family worship in the local church.

Contemporary Practice

Personal worship is always appropriate; but what about corporate worship? When should the church gather?

The early church placed special prominence upon the first day of the week for worship (Acts 20:7; 1 Cor. 16:2; Rev. 1:10) because that was the day of Christ's resurrection. Here are some additional reasons for Sunday to be a day of corporate worship. In our culture:

1. It provides the only opportunity during the week for the entire flock to hear the heart, mind, and voice of the Senior Shepherd.
2. It's the only opportunity during the week for God's flock to join their hearts together in unified worship.
3. It's the only time during the week that the flock can blend their voices in one praise together to God.
4. It's the only time during the week to join hands in giving sacrificially to the Lord.
5. It's the only opportunity during the week in which the congregation (both young and old) can have a common shared experience.
6. It's the only time during the week in which the large body can be in a position to encourage and stimulate one another to love and good deeds in accord with Hebrews 10:24-25.

As believers come together to worship, two factors intersect: first, the dynamics of the individual person who prepares and anticipates worship; second, the joining together of like-minded worshippers. Let's focus for a moment on preparation and anticipation.

Externals alone have very little to do with true worship. Only a heart and mind totally devoted to Almighty God can go beyond the 'letter of worship' and fully enter into the authentic 'spirit of worship' that God's holiness demands.

A renewed sense of worship begins each Lord's Day as believers gather to celebrate the greatness of God and the wonderful hope of eternal life in Jesus Christ. This time should set a true worshipper's focus on the glory of God and help to maintain this heavenly perspective throughout the week.

In order to most highly honor God and to prepare yourself for exalting worship, carefully consider the following questions. Every time you prepare to worship, work through them to make sure that you are fully ready to commune with our great God. You might want to tuck these thoughts away in the front of your Bible for easy reference.

1. Am I coming before God to worship Him with a sincere heart? (Heb. 10:22)
2. Am I focusing my full attention on the Lord alone? (Ex. 20:4-6)
3. Am I coming to worship as a true child of the Heavenly Father, knowing that my sins are cleansed through personal faith in the Lord Jesus Christ? (Rom. 10:9-13)
4. Am I coming with a firm grip on the confession of our hope in Jesus Christ? (Heb. 4:14-16)
5. Am I fixing my sight on the Lord of glory in His Word so that my hungering desire is to draw near to Him? (Heb. 7:25; James 4:8)
6. Am I coming with the full assurance that faith provides a sufficient entrance into God's presence—before His throne of grace? (Heb. 11:6)
7. Am I coming to God with the knowledge that the only reason which allows for the privilege of worship is what Christ did for me at Calvary? (Matt. 27:51; 1 Tim. 2:5)
8. Am I coming in purity—cleansed from the daily sin in my life? (1 John 1:9)
9. Am I coming to render honour, glory, praise, and thanksgiving to God rather than to receive anything for myself? (1 Cor. 10:31)
10. Am I praying that, having entered into the presence of God through worship, He will break me, mould me, and make me a pure vessel, useful for the Master's service? (2 Tim. 2:21)

A Testimony

Worship involves the highest privilege and the most exalted of experiences. It is at the apex of Christian living. Worship fuels intimacy with God and heightens our commitment to God's kingdom purpose.

Worship wears appropriately well in all seasons of life—whether one experiences catastrophe like Job (Job 1:13-22) or celebration like Hezekiah (2 Chron. 29:1-30). Clearly, the supreme duty of the creature for time and eternity is to worship the Creator.[2]

One of the psalmists leaves us this legacy expressing his sublime delight over the prospect of worship.

> How lovely are Your dwelling places, O LORD of hosts!
> My soul longed and even yearned for the courts of the LORD;
> my heart and my flesh sing for joy to the living God.
> The bird also has found a house, and the swallow a nest
> for herself, where she may lay her young, even Your altars,
> O LORD of hosts, my King and my God.
> How blessed are those who dwell in Your house!
> They are ever praising You.
>
> Psalm 84:1-4

I will bless the LORD at all times;
His praise shall continually be in my mouth.
Psalm 34:1

13

PRAISING GOD

I vividly remember the dramatic impact this letter had on me when I first read it. My praise life has never been the same.

I spent one and a half years on a kidney machine before getting a transplant. At first I did a lot of complaining, like everyone else. Then one day I stopped all the complaining when I read the account of the Crucifixion.

In the kidney center they helped me get out of my coat; with Jesus they stripped off His robe. When entering the kidney center, the nurses would always speak a kind word to me. But Jesus heard, 'Crucify Him.'

Sometimes on the machine I would develop a headache. They would give me something for it and bring me an ice pack for comfort. Jesus got a crown of thorns. Sometimes I would get thirsty and they would bring me juice and ice water. But Jesus got vinegar and gall. I laid on a comfortable bed for four or five hours, but Jesus hung on a cross.

I hardly felt the needle they put in my arm, but He had nails painfully driven through His hands and feet. My blood was cleansed and recirculated, but His ran out on the ground.

Jesus had turned my days of complaining into days of praising. A careful look into the events that took place that day on Calvary should stop all our complaining. If only we would look in that direction.[1]

He Alone is Worthy

The 70s and 80s brought a revolution in worship music. Choruses popped up everywhere, abounding with Scripture and focusing on God. Praise music arrived with the simplicity of an 'Alleluia' and the grandeur of 'My Tribute' or 'Majesty'. Both the music and the lyrics seemed to catapult Christians closer to God's presence.

Every major change finds its critics and praise music proved no exception. Much criticism came unwarranted, but some was deserved and profitable, in hopes that the spiritual blessings which praise music restored to the Christian community would not be spoiled by its excesses.

Often the 'spiritual high' received from the music overshadowed its purpose. People at times praised 'praise' rather than God. The phrase 'Praise the Lord' grew so common that it became an unthinking response rather than true worship. God must remain the purpose and object of all our praise or it will possess no spiritual value.

But praise music did not originate with our generation. Let's turn to Scripture's praise music. It's mainly found in the Psalms. Recently, with the marvel of computers, I looked at over 260 Scripture references to praise at one sitting. One of my overwhelming impressions from that study was that God is *the* object of praise. Almost always praise divided itself among the name of God, the Word of God, the character of God, and the works of God. This then should be our praise pattern—always God-focused.

God's Name. Here's just a sample: 'Let them praise Your great and awesome name; holy is He' (Ps. 99:3); 'Let them praise the name of the LORD, for His name alone is exalted' (148:13, see also 7:17; 9:2; 69:30; 145:2).

We can praise Him as Elohim, the sovereignly supreme God, or with the name Jehovah (LORD); the eternal God. We can praise His power and strength by calling Him El-Shaddai or God Almighty (Gen. 17:1-2). One of the more popular praise songs has been 'He Is Lord' or Adonai, which exalts God as Master over all.

In the Old Testament, the name Jehovah has several variations, all of which prove praiseworthy.[2]

- *Jehovah-jireh: provider (Gen. 22:14)*
- *Jehovah-rophe: healer (Ex. 15:26)*
- *Jehovah-nissi: banner (Ex. 17:15)*
- *Jehovah-shalom: peace (Judg. 6:24)*
- *Jehovah-tsidkenu: righteousness (Jer. 23:6)*
- *Jehovah-rohi: shepherd (Ps. 23:1)*
- *Jehovah-shammah: presence (Ezek. 48:35)*
- *Jehovah-m'kaddesh: sanctifier (Lev. 20:8)*

God's Word. The Lord's 'love letter' to His people is something that should always elicit our praise. The psalmist certainly thought so.

> In God, whose word I praise, in God I have put my trust; I shall not be afraid (Ps. 56:4).

> Then they believed His words; they sang His praise (Ps. 106:12).

God's character. Since most of these examples represent praise from the Psalms, this list is not exhaustive. Obviously, every characteristic of God deserves praise.

- *Righteousness (Ps. 7:17)*
- *Everlasting lovingkindness (Ezra 3:11; 2 Chron. 5:13; 20:21; Pss. 63:3; 117:2)*
- *Power (Ps. 21:13)*
- *Goodness (Ezra 3:11; Ps. 135:3)*
- *Excellent greatness (Pss. 48:1; 66:3-4; 96:4; 145:3)*
- *Glory (Eph. 1:6, 12, 14)*

The list could be largely expanded to include such qualities as His mercy, grace, patience, holiness, and many others.

God's conduct. Praise proves appropriate for all that God does. Several areas that Scripture particularly focuses on include:

- *Help/deliverance (Ps. 144:2; Jer. 20:13)*
- *Works (Pss. 145:4; 150:2; Isa. 12:5)*
- *Healing (Luke 18:43)*
- *Eternal dominion (Dan. 4:34)*

Praise Instruments
Music seems to be the major way to praise God, particularly when His people have gathered for corporate worship. A survey of the Old Testament points out that praise came from a wide assortment of sources—from a 4,000-piece praise orchestra (1 Chron. 23:5) to a 10-string harp (Ps. 33:2). Specific instruments included:

- *Cymbals (Ezra 3:10; Ps. 150:5)*
- *Lyre (Pss. 43:4; 71:22; 98:5; 147:7; 149:3; 150:3)*
- *Harp (Ps. 71:22; 150:3)*
- *Timbrel (Ps. 149:3; 150:4)*
- *Trumpet (Ezra 3:10; Ps. 150:3)*
- *Pipe (Ps. 150:4)*
- *Stringed instruments (Ps. 150:4)*

It's safe to say that any instrument capable of playing music may be used to praise God and draw attention to Him.

Of course, singing is always in. The first recorded praise song came from Moses (Ex. 15:1-18), who wrote to celebrate God's victory over Pharaoh and Israel's liberation from the Egyptians. 'The Lord is my strength and song, and He has become my salvation; this is my

God, and I will praise Him, my father's God, and I will extol Him' (v. 2).

Deborah and Barak co-wrote a hymn of celebration to give God all the glory for their victory over the Canaanites (Judg. 5:2-31). The psalmist commended song as a means of praise when he wrote, 'I will praise the name of God with song, and magnify Him with thanksgiving' (Ps. 69:30; see also 2 Sam. 22:50; 1 Chron. 16:9; Ps. 9:11).

Famous Praise Gatherings

Leah and Jacob praised God for the birth of Judah, whose name in Hebrew signifies 'praise' (Gen. 29:35). The nation Israel gave a praise offering to God as a part of tabernacle worship (Lev. 19:24). Moses told the Israelites, '[God] is your praise' (Deut. 10:21). The Levites and priests praised God daily for seven days during the Feast of Unleavened Bread (2 Chron. 30:21).

Solomon praised God for His everlasting lovingkindness during the dedication of the temple (2 Chron. 5:13). Four centuries later, Ezra praised the Lord for the rebuilt temple (Ezra 3:10-11). Nehemiah (Neh. 12:46) and Daniel (Dan. 2:23) both praised God for what He had done on their behalf.

The birth of Jesus prompted tremendous praise, first from the angels (Luke 2:13) and then from the shepherds (v. 20).

Perhaps the most unusual praise time, but also the most appropriate, occurred in a prison experience.

> The crowd rose up together against them [Paul and Silas], and the chief magistrates tore their robes off them, and proceeded to order them to be beaten with rods. And . . . they threw them into prison, commanding the jailer to guard them securely; and he, having received such a command, threw them into the inner prison, and fastened their feet in the stocks. But about midnight Paul and Silas were praying and singing hymns of praise to God, and the prisoners were listening to them (Acts 16:22-25).

In times of need or plenty, when life is on the mountaintop or in the dark valley, by yourself or with God's people, with or without music, praise can appropriately be given to God. Even if it comes out as simple as 'Praise the Lord' (Pss. 104:35; 106:1).

A New Song

One of the great scriptural themes focuses on the new song sung by those who have put their faith in God for eternal life. That song comes from God (Ps. 40:3), is encouraged by the psalmists (33:3; 96:1; 149:1), and becomes the righteous response of the redeemed (144:9-10).

It's a song that can only be sung by new creations in Christ (2 Cor. 5:17) who now sing in a new way. It's new in that the song was not sung by us before salvation; thus it is new in time and content.

The new song demonstrates and certifies a new relationship with God. It's a fresh song that proves uncommon to mankind in general.

The Christmas carol 'Joy to the World' came from the pen of Isaac Watts who was touched by the words of Psalm 98. Look there with me a moment as I point out the features of this prototype praise song.

1. It's to be sung to the Lord (v. 1)
2. It's sung about His great deeds (vv. 1-3)
3. It's rendered for the purpose of praise (v. 4)
4. It focuses on the saviourship of God (vv. 2-3)
5. It focuses on the kingship of God (vv. 4-6)
6. It focuses on the judgeship of God (vv. 7-9)

The magnum opus, however, will be sung by the combined voice of heaven's inhabitants.

When He had taken the book, the four living creatures and the twenty-four elders fell down before the Lamb, each one holding a harp, and golden bowls full of incense, which are the prayers of the saints. And they sang a new song, saying 'Worthy are You to take the book, and to break its seals; for You were slain, and purchased for God with Your blood men from every tribe and tongue and people and nation. And You have made them to be a kingdom and priests to our God; and they will reign upon the earth.'

I looked, and I heard the voice of many angels around the throne and the living creatures and the elders; and the number of them was myriads of myriads, and thousands of thousands saying with a loud voice, 'Worthy is the Lamb that was slain to receive power and riches and wisdom and might and honor and glory and blessing.'

And every created thing which is in heaven and on the earth and under the earth and on the sea, and all things in them, I heard saying, 'To

Him who sits on the throne, and to the Lamb, be blessing and honor and glory and dominion forever and ever.'

And the four living creatures kept saying 'Amen.' And the elders fell down and worshipped (Rev. 5:8-14).

Scripture also teaches that God's Spirit orchestrates praise.

And do not get drunk with wine, for that is dissipation, but be filled with the Spirit, speaking to one another in psalms and hymns and spiritual songs, singing and making melody with your heart to the Lord; always giving thanks for all things in the name of our Lord Jesus Christ to God, even the Father (Eph. 5:18-20).

Praise then marks the person who yields to God's Spirit. What could be more appropriate in a spiritual sense than God's Spirit living in God's people directing praise to God the Father and God the Son in heaven?

No wonder 'The Doxology' has long been enthusiastically sung by God's people. If you are as overwhelmed by this theme as I am, you might want to sing now, just as I did when I penned this chapter:

Praise God, from whom all blessings flow;
Praise Him all creatures here below;
Praise Him above, ye heavenly hosts
Praise Father, Son, and Holy Ghost.

Praise Practitioners

It's amazing to read what the Bible says about praise. To sum it up, all things are to the praise of God. The creatures on earth praise Him (Pss. 69:34; 89:5; 148:1) as do the heavens (148:3). Both angels (Job 38:7, KJV; Ps. 148:2) and humans praise God. In case anyone feels left out, the Psalms end with this invitation: 'Let everything that has breath praise the Lord. Praise the Lord!' (Ps. 150:6).

Praise marked Israel's worship in the nation's godly times, for we read: 'And Hezekiah appointed the divisions of the priests and the Levites by their divisions, each according to his service, both the priests and the Levites, for burnt offerings and for peace offerings, to minister and to give thanks and to praise in the gates of the camp of the Lord' (2 Chron. 31:2).

Praise likewise highlighted the early church's experience: 'And all those who believed were together . . . praising God, and having favor with all people. And the Lord was adding to their number day by day those who were being saved' (Acts 2:44, 47).

Praise knew nothing about the separation of church and state. From the lips of Babylon's King Nebuchadnezzar (Dan. 4:34) and from the mouth of the priest Zacharias (Luke 1:64) flowed praise.

Praise equally graced the lips of Christ who was sinless (Matt. 11:25) and Achan who would shortly die for his transgression (Josh. 7:19-20).

Praise is for everyone and everything. 'For it is written: "As I live, says the Lord, every knee shall bow to Me, and every tongue shall give praise to God" ' (Rom. 14:11; see also Isa. 45:23).

Praise Companions
Blessing God and thanking God often accompany praise in Scripture. Indeed, these three form an inseparable trio (see also Pss. 34:1 66:8; 68:26; 115:18).

> Enter His gates with thanksgiving, and His courts with praise. Give thanks to Him; bless His name (Ps. 100:4).

Everyone knows David's famous self-invitation to praise. It makes a great praise chorus.

> Bless the LORD, O my soul; and all that is within me, bless His holy name (Ps. 103:1).

Praise and thanksgiving frequently appear in tandem (see also Pss. 18:49; 30:4; 35:18; 69:30).

> It is good to give thanks to the LORD, and to sing praises to Your name, O Most High (Ps. 92:1).

> Sing to the LORD with thanksgiving; sing praises to our God on the lyre (Ps. 147:7).

The New Testament features thanksgiving just as prominently as the Old.

> In everything give thanks; for this is God's will for you in Christ Jesus (1 Thess. 5:18).

Through Him then, let us continually offer up a sacrifice of praise to God, that is, the fruit of lips that give thanks to His name (Heb. 13:15).

Praise Tips

1. Obey the strong, scriptural call to praise God.

Sing praises to God, sing praises; sing praises to our King, sing praises. For God is the King of all the earth; sing praises with a skillful psalm (Ps. 47:6-7).

Shout joyfully to God, all the earth; sing the glory of His name; make His praise glorious. Say to God, 'How awesome are Your works! Because of the greatness of Your power Your enemies will give feigned obedience to You; all the earth will worship You, and will sing praises to You; they will sing praises to Your name' (Ps. 66:1-4).

2. Look at Psalms 145-150 for worshipful patterns of praise.
3. Praise God every day (Ps. 145:2).
4. Praise God many times daily (Ps. 119:164).
5. Praise God from sunup to sundown (Ps. 71:8).

Praise the LORD! Praise, O servants of the LORD. Praise the name of the LORD. Blessed be the name of the LORD from this time forth and forever. From the rising of the sun to its setting the name of the LORD is to be praised (Ps. 113:1-3).

6. Praise God until death and then forever.

I will sing to the LORD as long as I live; I will sing praise to my God while I have my being (Ps. 104:33).

I will extol You, my God, O King; and I will bless Your name forever and ever (Ps. 145:1).

7. Conduct yourself with praise, for such behavior is becoming to a righteous person at all times.

Sing for joy in the LORD, O you righteous ones, praise is becoming to the upright (Ps. 33:1).

Praise the LORD! For it is good to sing praises to our God; for it is pleasant and praise is becoming (Ps. 147:1).

8. Make praise a continual habit of your life.

I will bless the LORD at all times; His praise shall continually be in my mouth (Ps. 34:1).

9. Think on things that are worthy of praise.

Finally, brethren, whatever is true, whatever is honorable, whatever is right, whatever is pure, whatever is lovely, whatever is of good repute, if there is any excellence and if anything worthy of praise, dwell on these things (Phil. 4:8).

10. Join the throngs in heaven and on earth who find great joy in praising God. Pray that God will fill you with praise.

O Lord, open my lips, that my mouth may declare Your praise (Ps. 51:15).

A Final Note
Augustine wrote that a Christian should be 'an Alleluia' from head to foot. A master of music illustrates this point.

Joseph Haydn was present at the Vienna Music Hall where his oratorio The Creation was being performed. Weakened by age, the great composer was confined to a wheelchair. As the majestic work moved along, the audience was caught up with tremendous emotion. When the passage, 'And there was light!' was reached, the chorus and orchestra burst forth in such power that the crowd could no longer restrain its enthusiasm. The grandeur of the music and the presence of the composer himself brought the vast assembly to its feet in spontaneous applause. Haydn struggled to get out of his wheelchair. Finally up, he motioned for silence. The enraptured crowd heard him call out with what strength he could muster, hand pointed to heaven, 'No, no, not from me, but from thence comes all!' Having given the glory and praise to the Creator, he fell back into his chair exhausted.

Amen!

I will sacrifice a freewill offering to you;
I will praise Your name, O LORD, for it is good.
Psalm 54:6 (NIV)

14

GIVING TO GOD

A young man came out of the Ozark Mountains in his early manhood with the firm purpose of making a fortune. Gold became his god, and putting it first, he won it. He came to be worth millions. Then the crash came, and he was reduced to utter poverty. His reason tottered and fell along with his fortune.

A mere beggar, he took to the road where one day a policeman found him on Eads Bridge gazing down into the waters of the Mississippi and ordered him to move on. 'Let me alone,' the despondent man answered. 'I am trying to think. There is something that is better than gold, but I have forgotten what it is.' They placed him in an institution for the insane. They knew that a man who could forget *that* was not himself.[1]

As the twenty-first century begins, it seems that we have revisited the days when people worship at the shrine of materialism. Our society trusts money to do for them what God has promised to do, in spite of the little motto printed on American coins and bills, 'In God We Trust.'

I recently read that the average giving among Christians in America is only 2.5 percent of their adjusted gross income.[2] That's a far cry from the 23 1/3 percent the Old Testament required (Lev. 27:30; Deut. 12:10-11; 14:28). While I do not believe the New Testament teaches tithing as a legal obligation, the current trend falls enormously below even 10 percent. Therefore, we need to be reminded of what God's Word teaches, and then reorient our budgets to reflect a true worship of God, not of materialism.

Spiritual intimacy demands that we revive our giving to God and reduce our search for the 'good life.' Can you imagine what would happen if every Christian gave just 9 percent as a 'firstfruits' offering? (Prov. 3:9) It would be like the days of Moses (Ex. 36:1-7) and David (1 Chron. 29:1-20). People brought so much back then that they had an over-abundance.

In order to stimulate us all to the appropriate level of blessing (Acts 20:35), our discussion first centres on the greatest message ever written on giving. Then we'll instill some biblical principles on which godly giving can be based. The ABCs of 'grace giving' will top off our thoughts on giving as a means of drawing closer to God.

Paul on Giving

Hard times had struck the church in Jerusalem. It became fitting for the church elsewhere to take up a collection for these distressed brethren in the faith. While on his third missionary journey (Acts 18:23-21:16), Paul carried Jerusalem's cause to the church in Macedonia and Achaia (modern Greece) with the intention of taking their offering to Jerusalem himself (Rom. 15:25-26). In preparation for his up-coming visit, Paul included a major exhortation on giving to the church in Corinth.

He had written briefly about giving once before (1 Cor. 16:1-4); now he writes in earnest. The first major thought focuses on the northern churches in Macedonia—Thessalonica and Philippi (2 Cor. 8:1-5). He commends them as an example of 'grace giving' because, although they possessed little, they gave much. Three major ideas stand out:

1. Even though they were poor, they gave above and beyond the call of duty (vv. 2-3).
2. They did not give because they felt pressured, but because they wanted to (v. 3).
3. They gave according to God's will, not their own (v. 5).

Paul then turns his attention to the Corinthians themselves who had pledged much but given little (vv. 6-15). Central to this exhortation, Paul focuses on the Lord Jesus Christ—how He gave at Calvary—as a model for the Corinthians:

> For you know the grace of our Lord Jesus Christ, that though He was rich, yet for your sake He became poor, so that you through His poverty might become rich (2 Cor. 8:9).

It seems as though the Corinthians wished to wait longer because the time was not right; prosperous times hadn't arrived. So, Paul urges them to give now out of their current riches (8:10-12); and he appeals to the truth that God gives us an abundance as a means to help those who do not have enough, even for the basics (vv. 13-15).

Paul also admonishes them to fulfill their promise to God. He assures them that responsible leaders will render accountable stewardship to the funds collected (vv. 16-24). Even more, their giving 'example' should be bountiful and not minimized by a spirit of covetousness (9:1-5).

Paul closes with instructions on 'grace giving' (9:6-15). He gives the Corinthian Christians four basics:
1. What you plant will determine what you harvest (v. 6).
2. God desires giving with a selfless attitude (v. 7).
3. God will provide the financial seed, if it is to be sown in the cause of righteousness (vv. 8-11).
4. Right giving leads to right worship of God (vv. 12-15).

And my God will supply all your needs according to His riches in glory in Christ Jesus (Phil. 4:19).

Principles for Giving
Someone has noted, 'God is not poor; neither are Christians broke.' Yet at times it seems that way when we look at the finances of many local churches. Why? I believe it results from a combination of factors.

First, many pastors do not teach and practise 'grace giving' in their churches. Consequently, Christians do not know about and cannot give according to grace. Third, Christians who *do* know scriptural standards for giving ignore them, choosing instead to indulge themselves rather than to sacrificially invest in the eternal matters of God's kingdom.

Following are the most basic principles presented in Scripture designed to govern the giving patterns of every Christian:

Recognize that all we have is a gift from God (Ex. 19:5; Ps. 50:10-12; 1 Tim. 6:7). From a communistic viewpoint, the state owns it all. In capitalism, the individual possesses all; but with Christianity, everything belongs to God because He created it (John 1:3).

Job exemplifies the principle, not so much in the good times, but rather at their loss.

And he said, 'Naked I came from my mother's womb, and naked I shall return there. The LORD gave and the LORD has taken away. Blessed be the name of the LORD' (Job 1:21).

Giving should be planned and regular as a part of your personal worship (1 Cor. 16:2). Three elements stand out. First, giving should be done with planned regularity—here Paul teaches to do it weekly on the Lord's Day. Next it is to be personal— 'each one of you.' There are to be no exemptions. Third, give at whatever level God has given to you during that period. So the only possible reason for not giving is that you received nothing. Even then, a person could normally reach back to times when he or she received an over abundance.

Give freely through a 'purposed heart' (2 Cor. 8:3; 9:7). Three types of giving have been identified over the years: the 'flint' giver who must be hammered; the 'sponge' giver who must be squeezed; and the 'honeycomb' giver who overflows. What kind are you?

Jesus first articulated this principle to the disciples as they were about to go out in ministry. 'Freely you received, freely give' (Matt. 10:8). The point is this—grace received is to be grace given.

Giving involves a commitment to the Lord and trust in godly leaders (2 Cor. 8:5). The Macedonians gave first to the Lord by way of a commitment and then executed the plan by actually entrusting the money to Paul and other spiritual leaders. They did this in the same way that the church of Jerusalem laid their gifts at the feet of the apostles (Acts 4:35).

Look at it this way. All of your assets belong to God, who by His will desires you to give for the establishment and extension of His church worldwide. Not only do your resources belong to God, but they are to be received and expended by godly leaders, not you. So it becomes critical that you first find godly leaders who are committed to God's will and then give in abundance.

Giving is not optional (2 Cor. 8:12). Many people believe that they can give non-monetary gifts in lieu of money, or that they can wait until their personal plans are fulfilled and then give abundantly. God soundly rebukes this sort of thinking in Haggai 1:5-11. The Jews worked hard but accumulated little, because building their own homes had higher priority than investing in God's kingdom.

Paul's point is unmistakable—give out of what you have. Don't postpone your giving; for to do so is to tell God that He is less than first in your life.

'Liberality' best describes New Testament giving (1 Cor. 16:2; 2 Cor. 8:2-3; 9:11-13). In your giving, does God get the first and the best or the last and the least? How you give reflects accurately what you think of God and the apple of His eye—the church. The percentage given by each believer will be different with the freedom of grace, but the level should always be sacrificial. Giving should be done with David's heart: 'I will not offer burnt offerings to the Lord my God which cost me nothing' (2 Sam. 24:24; 1 Chron. 21:24).

Giving will be reviewed at the Judgment Seat of Christ (2 Cor. 5:10). Present needs should drive our giving, but so should our future appointment to stand before Christ. Salvation doesn't enter into the issue here, but rewards and loss in eternity, based on how we conducted our Christian life on earth, does (see 1 Cor. 3:15).

Whether God's Spirit has enabled you with the special gift of giving (Rom. 12:8) or you give as a part of your regular Christian duty, there will be a day of accountability.

Giving will bring great blessing to the giver (Acts 20:35). Not only did Jesus and Paul preach this wonderful truth, but the Philippian church experienced the blessing. After receiving a generous gift, Paul writes to remind them that a part of his joy results from the blessing they received in giving. 'Not that I seek the gift itself, but I seek for the profit which increases to your account' (Phil. 4:17).

In some senses, giving becomes the means to gigantic spiritual blessing. God is pleased or blessed with sacrifice (Heb. 13:16). The giver is blessed and the work of God is blessed in that it is enjoying advances continually.

Practice of Giving

So far we've looked at the most influential scriptural text on giving (2 Cor. 8-9) and surveyed the basics of giving. Now, let's turn all of this knowledge into a practical plan that will allow you to be a doer of the Word, not a mere hearer (James 1:22).

First, acknowledge that God really does own all of your assets by taking an inventory of them. Then prayerfully thank Him for loaning them to you.

Think about how you handle other people's property when it is in your possession—with care and a plan to return it in as good or better condition than received. This attitude should also prevail toward God.

A missionary in India once visited a Hindu temple which had been elaborately adorned with precious metals. He asked a nearby worshipper, 'How much did you pay for this?' 'Money?' was the reply. 'We never count the cost when it is for our gods.' And how much more for us who have been redeemed by Christ and worship the true God.

Second, personally accept your spiritual responsibility as a steward of God's possessions. The Jews in Malachi's day failed to take this truth seriously and received biting indictments from God. They had given God second best (Mal. 1:7-9). Even worse, they had robbed God by spending on themselves rather than giving as God instructed (3:8-10).

You might want to ask these questions about both your giving and personal spending:

1. Will this build Christ's church?
2. Will this advance God's kingdom?
3. Will this make an eternal impact?
4. Will this please and glorify God?
5. Will this be in God's will?

Third, pray for God's wisdom and grace in your disbursement of His riches. 'But if any of you lacks wisdom, let him ask of God, who gives to all men generously and without reproach, and it will be given to him' (James 1:5).

When we first became Christians, my wife 'B' and I asked this question; 'Do we give from the gross or the net?' Put another way: 'Do we give before or after taxes?' Wisdom directed that we give to God as He gave to us.

What does this mean practically? Initially, it meant spending according to a plan that put God first. As we reduced our expenditures, that allowed us the freedom to make our first disbursement the money we gave to God.

Then we decided to base our giving on what God gave us before such expenditures as taxes or Social Security. We also decided that what we gave on the Lord's Day didn't need to be our maximum but our minimum. That's been our habit for thirty years now and I joyfully commend it to you.

Fourth, evaluate your giving to the Lord and ask yourself if God would classify your giving as gracious, generous, and/or liberal. The real issue in deciding this is not how much you give, but rather, how much you have left after giving.

Let me illustrate with a day in Jesus' ministry:

And He looked up and saw the rich putting their gifts into the treasury. And He saw a poor widow putting in two small copper coins. And He said, 'Truly I say to you, this poor widow put in more than all of them; for they all out of their surplus put into the offering; but she out of her poverty put in all she had to live on' (Luke 21:1-4).

Look again at Christ's comment on her giving, 'Truly I say to you, this poor widow put in more than all of them.' What did He mean? Four lessons rivet themselves to our souls if we're serious about giving:

1. It was not her social prominence that drew Christ's pleasure—for she was a widow.
2. Her wealth didn't please Him—for she was poor.
3. The amount of her contribution didn't solicit Christ's comments—for the two mites constituted far less than one day's wage.
4. Christ *did* find pleasure in what she had left over after she gave and in what she did without to give—for she put in all that she had to live on.

It could be that God wants you to be like R.G. LeTourneau who practised 'reverse tithing.' He gave 90 percent and kept the other 10.

Fifth, give bountifully to your local church first before you give elsewhere. Both the Bible and logic demand that our primary giving goes to the place where we're fed, loved, cared for, accountable, and where we have spiritual family plus personal involvement. 'And let the one who is taught the Word share all good things with him who teaches' (Gal. 6:6).

Sixth, ask God to make 'grace giving' a joyous, spiritual habit in your life. Then apply the truths, the principles, and the practices we have just discussed.

Sacrificial Giving

After I had preached a message on giving, my secretary asked, 'What is sacrificial giving and how do you know if you're giving at that level?' While I wasn't then and still am not sure of a scientifically precise answer, I am convinced that it involves attitude and action rather than an absolute amount. So my response to Kim sounded something like, 'Sacrificial giving is postponing or foregoing an earthly pleasure to provide for the kingdom's advancement.' If the attitude and actions are right, then the amount will surely please God.

John Wanamaker, a wealthy nineteenth-century Philadelphia merchant, once made a trip to China to determine how well the money he had given to missions was being used. He came upon an old man plowing with a crude apparatus drawn by an ox and a young man. Asking for an explanation, Wanamaker was told that this chapel needed a spire to be visible for miles around. The church members prayed, but the money given was still not enough. Then a son said to his father, 'Let us sell one of the oxen and I will take the yoke of the ox we sell.'

Wanamaker then prayed, 'Lord, let me be hitched to a plow, so that I may know the joy of sacrificial giving.'

O God, You are my God;
I shall seek You earnestly;
my soul thirsts for You, my flesh
yearns for You, in a dry and weary land
where there is no water.
Psalm 63:1

15

EMBRACING GOD

After I preached one Sunday with some strong warnings about psychology, a young 'psych' major at a local university asked for an appointment to discuss my views. His question focused on the biblical basis for my comments.

I had not intended to dismiss the discipline as utterly worthless or leave the impression that anyone who studied psychology had compromised his faith. However, he did catch my less-than-enthusiastic support for the discipline of psychology in general and more pointedly, for its growing emphasis in Christian circles to the point of relegating God's Word to a secondary role.

Later, over breakfast, I explained to him that psychology as a modern discipline rested on godless assumptions and had been promoted mainly by intellectuals who deny God.[1] Thus, they spawned an approach to life that is man-centered, not God-centered. That clearly contradicts the major emphasis of Scripture. My point simply stated is this: Theology might lead to some valid 'psychological' conclusions but psychology will never lead a person to God.

Scripture mandates that godliness become the Christian's quest. In other words, life must be God-centered. 'Therefore you are to be perfect, as your Heavenly Father is perfect' (Matt. 5:48).

Both Paul (1 Tim. 4:7; 6:6) and Peter (2 Peter 1:3, 6) commend godliness as the believer's worthiest aim. As physical children become 'chips of the old block,' so spiritual children should seek to perfect in themselves the image in whose likeness they were created. Christianity demands this; psychology as a modern discipline doesn't even encourage it.

Seeking God

Both theology and psychology explore the inner man. They look beyond the physical. But Paul distinguishes between the temporal and the eternal, while psychology does not.

> Therefore we do not lose heart, but though our outer man is decaying, yet our inner man is being renewed day by day (2 Cor. 4:16).

Then the apostle indicates that through prayer and the power of God's Spirit, our 'inner man' can be strengthened. That's the unique Christian approach to life on this side of heaven.

That He would grant you, according to the riches of His glory, to be strengthened with power through His Spirit in the inner man (Eph. 3:16).

We popularly refer to this truth through the vivid pen of Isaiah:

He gives strength to the weary, and to him who lacks might He increases power. Though youths grow weary and tired, and vigorous young men stumble badly, yet those who wait for the LORD will gain new strength; they will mount up with wings like eagles, they will run and not get tired, they will walk and not become weary (Isa. 40:29-31).

Thus as Christians, Scripture exhorts us to be:
1. Conformed to the image of Christ (Rom. 8:29; Col. 3:10)
2. Transformed into God's glory (2 Cor. 3:18)
3. Imitators of God (1 Cor. 4:16-17; 11:1; Eph. 5:1)
4. Christ-like because we are Christians (Acts 11:26; 1 Peter 4:16)
5. Holy Spirit-like (Rom. 8:6-9;1 Cor. 2:14-15; Gal. 5:22-23)
6. God-like or godly (2 Tim. 3:12; Titus 2:12)

To do this we must seek God as a first priority, not man nor the things of this earth. Moses preached this (Deut. 12:5), as did David (1 Chron. 16:10-11; 22:19). The most memorable exhortation came from Jesus: 'But seek first His kingdom and His righteousness; and all these things will be added to you' (Matt. 6:33).

God makes some tremendous promises to those who seek Him. He gives:

1. Protection	Ps. 9:10
2. Provision	Ps. 34:10
3. Blessing	Ps. 119:2
4. Goodness	Lam. 3:25
5. Reward	Heb. 11:6

How does this all work out in life? A literary snapshot in the life of Justin Martyr (A.D. 100-165) illustrates the ultimate and intimate Christian seeker.

Around 165, Justin and six other Christians were arrested for their faith and brought to trial before Rusticus, the Roman prefect.

Rusticus asked him, 'Are you a Christian?'

'Yes,' Justin answered, 'I am.'

'Then, let's come to the matter at hand,' Rusticus said. 'Sacrifice to the gods.'

'No one who is rightly minded turns from true belief to false.'

'If you do not obey,' the prefect said, 'you'll be punished without mercy.'

'If we are punished for the sake of our Lord Jesus Christ,' Justin said, 'we hope to be saved, for this shall be our salvation and confidence before the terrible Judgment Seat of our Saviour and Lord who shall judge the world.'

The other believers agreed: 'Do what you will,' they said. 'We are Christians, and we do not sacrifice to idols.'

Immediately the sentence fell. All seven were taken from the court and beheaded.[2]

Following Christ

Those who seek will also follow. Jesus came to seek and save those who needed eternal life (Luke 19:10). When He found them, He beckoned them to 'Follow Me!'

On at least eight distinct occasions Jesus issued forth His famous call (see also John 12:26).

1. Andrew and Simon Peter	Matt. 4:18-19
2. John and James	Matt. 4:20-21
3. Unidentified disciples	Matt. 8:22
4. Matthew	Matt. 9:9
5. The Twelve	Matt. 16:24
6. Rich young ruler	Matt. 19:21
7. Philip	John 1:43
8. Simon Peter	John 21:19, 22

The sheep of Christ's flock characteristically follow the Shepherd. 'My sheep hear My voice, and I know them, and they follow Me' (John 10:27).

This simple command reached new levels of impact for me as I read a letter from a man serving time in a federal penitentiary on drugs charges. This former business man gloriously received Christ as his 'Lord and Saviour' in prison.

While reading my book *Unmasking Satan*, he came to a chapter that applied to his married life and wrote to me with a very important question. Its essence was, 'How do I follow Jesus in this situation?'

> *What does a husband and the Bible say to a wife who is committed to waiting? Has my incarceration or rather should my incarceration relieve her of her marital responsibility? In other words, should she suffer while I'm locked up? . . . What does an incarcerated man say to his wife about loneliness, sex, companionship, and temptation? Are our wives commanded by the Bible to hold on and wait for their husbands? Or out of love and concern for our wives should we divorce them and tell them to find another man for companionship?*

This man fervently desired to follow Christ. Both he and his wife just wanted to know what Jesus said so that they could obey. In case you're wondering how I responded, it went something like this— 'Stay married, stay pure, and seek God for the patience and strength to do the humanly impossible.'

Imitating the Holy Spirit

I found it interesting to discover in Scripture that when God commanded us to embrace a certain quality, at times He said 'Be like Me!' We are to be pure, like God (1 John 3:3). Our love should be like God's love (Eph. 5:2;1 John 4:7-17). Since God is holy, we are to be holy also (Lev. 19:2; 1 Peter 1:14-16).

The ultimate test of a vegetable garden or orchard is the produce or fruit which it bears. Likewise, Christian growth is not measured by our size or by how long we have been growing but rather by the quality of fruit manifest in our lives.

God gave us His Spirit as the proper spiritual model so that the fruit harvested in our lives would mark us out as genuine. The degree of Spirit-like fruit growing on the limbs of our lives unmistakably gauges just how intimate we are with God.

Galatians 5:22-23 pictures the Spirit-produced fruit that evidences a truly healthy Christian:

> But the fruit of the Spirit is love, joy, peace, patience, kindness, goodness, faithfulness, gentleness, self-control; against such things there is no law.

Have someone you trust and respect climb through your life and see what kind of fruit they can discover. Will it match up with Holy Spirit-produced fruit like this?

1. *Love.* A sacrificial commitment to the welfare of another person regardless of that person's response or what he or she might give to me in return.
2. *Joy.* A deep, abiding inner thankfulness to God for His goodness that is not interrupted when less desirable life circumstances intrude.
3. *Peace.* Heartfelt tranquility and trust during the storms of life that are anchored in the overwhelming consciousness that I am in the hand of God.
4. *Patience.* A quality of self-restraint which does not hastily retaliate in the face of provoking situations.
5. *Kindness.* A sensitive awareness and willingness to seek out ways in which to serve others.
6. *Goodness.* An unswerving capacity to deal with people rightly in the best interest of God even when correction is required.
7. *Faithfulness.* An inner unyieldingness that results in remaining true to my spiritual convictions and commitments.
8. *Gentleness.* Controlled strength that is dispensed from a humble heart.
9. *Self-control.* An inward, personal mastery that submits my desires to the greater cause of God's will.

We can imitate God's Holy Spirit with His help and power.

Learning from the Master
The sense of 'disciples' and 'discipleship' dominates the pages of the Gospels and Acts, with over 250 mentions. The words refer to a learner/mentor relationship. To become a Christian is to become a learner who sits at the feet of a newfound master—Jesus Christ. 'Take My yoke upon you and learn from Me' has become one of the most memorable of Christ's invitations to eternal life (Matt. 11:29).

In the Book of Acts, where Luke focuses on believers and their activities, every time the concept appears (30 times), with one exception, it refers to a Christian. There is no distinction between being a believer now and a disciple later. The whole church is referred to as disciples (Acts 6:2, 7; 15:10; 18:23). Acts 26:28 compared with

Acts 11:26 equates being a Christian with being a disciple (see also 9:26; 20:30).

One becomes a disciple by responding to God's gospel of grace (14:21; 18:27). There are no instances of a 'non-disciple' believer. One writer summarizes his conclusions about the learner/master relationship with Jesus in an unforgettable way.

The disciple of Jesus is not the deluxe or heavy-duty model of the Christian—specially padded, textured, streamlined and empowered for the fast lane on the straight and narrow way. He stands on the pages of the New Testament as the first level of basic transportation in the kingdom of God.[3]

I recently read a story that riveted itself to my mind. As you read it, remember that Communism bears no eternal value, while Christianity remains humanity's only forever hope.

In the late 1940s Whittaker Chambers was called to witness before a New York Grand Jury against Alger Hiss, one of our high government officials. Chambers, a one-time Communist, accused Hiss of trying to transmit confidential government documents to the Soviet Union through him. When asked what it means to be a Communist by one of the jurors, Chambers struggled to provide a clear answer. Finally he told them that when he was a Communist, he had three heroes.

His first hero was a Pole, a political prisoner in Warsaw. While there, he insisted on cleaning the latrines of the other prisoners because he felt that the most devoted member of any community should take upon himself the lowliest tasks as an example to those who were less devoted. 'That,' said Chambers, 'is one thing it means to be a Communist.'

His second hero was a German Jew who was captured and court-martialed during a revolution in Bavaria. When told that he was now under the sentence of death he replied, 'We Communists are always under the sentence of death.' 'That,' said Chambers, 'is another thing it means to be a Communist.'

His third hero was a Russian exiled to a Siberian prison camp where political prisoners were flogged. He sought some means of protesting that inhumane persecution. Finally in desperation he drenched himself in kerosene, set himself on fire, and burned himself

to death as a protest against what he considered a great indignity.
'That,' repeated Chambers, 'is also what it means to be a
Communist.'[4]

Embracing God is not learning about a system like Communism,
but rather learning from a person—Christ. As we learn, we will
become like Him (Luke 6:40).

Running the Race

The summer of 1984 proved unique to the city of Los Angeles, for
its proud citizens played host to the Olympic games. As part of the
pins and paraphernalia, I heard about an Olympic banner which read,
'Citius, Altius, Fortius.' It's the Latin motto for the Olympics which
means 'swifter, higher, stronger.'

Paul had the similar Isthmian games of ancient Greece in mind
when he wrote:

> Do you not know that those who run in a race all run, but only one
> receives the prize? Run in such a way that you may win. Everyone who
> competes in the games exercises self-control in all things. They then do
> it to receive a perishable wreath, but we an imperishable. Therefore I
> run in such a way, as not without aim; I box in such a way as not beating
> the air; but I discipline my body and make it my slave, so that, after I
> have preached to others, I myself will not be disqualified (1 Cor. 9:24-27;
> see also Phil. 3:12-14).

The place for the race was called the stadium because its course
was a stadium, or 600 Greek feet, in length. The goal rested at the opposite
end from the starting point. There stood the judge with the prize in his
hand. In Paul's day, the crown was made of wilted celery stalks.[5]

For the apostle, his heavenly crown of righteousness (2 Tim. 4:8),
of unfading glory (1 Peter 5:4), of eternal life (James 1:12; Rev.
2:10), and with imperishable quality (1 Cor. 9:25), made the effort
of running the Christian life worth it all. He pressed with all of his
might toward the goal of heaven and glory for the prize of eternal
life. No wonder he could proclaim victory from the Mamertine Prison
in Rome even with the sentence of death imminent. 'I have kept the
faith' (2 Tim. 4:7).

As Paul pressed, so are we to press. We are to pursue with every
ounce of energy these Christian qualities:

1. Hospitality   Rom. 12:13
2. Godliness   1 Tim. 6:11
3. Goodness   1 Thess. 5:15
4. Peace   Rom. 14:19; 2 Tim. 2:22; Heb. 12:14;
                    1 Peter 3:11
5. Love   1 Cor. 14:1; 1Tim.6:11; 2 Tim. 2:22
6. Righteousness   1 Tim. 6:11; 2 Tim. 2:22
7. Faith   1 Tim. 6:11; 2 Tim. 2:22
8. Perseverance   1 Tim. 6:11
9. Gentleness   1 Tim. 6:11

The writer of Hebrews gives us one final tip on our running style. It will equip us for a swifter, higher, and stronger race.

> Therefore, since we have so great a cloud of witnesses surrounding us, let us also lay aside every encumbrance, and the sin which is so easily entangles us, and let us run with endurance the race that is set before us, fixing our eyes on Jesus, the author and perfecter of faith, who for the joy set before Him endured the cross, despising the shame, and has sat down at the right hand of the throne of God (Heb. 12:1-2).

Battling the Enemy

Embracing God also involves traveling through enemy territory, including skirmishes with Satan and his army of hell. The Christian dare not be without his armor.

> Therefore, take up the full armor of God, so that you may be able to resist in the evil day, and having done everything, to stand firm. Stand firm therefore, having girded your loins with truth, and having put on the breastplate of righteousness, and having shod your feet with the preparation of the Gospel of peace; in addition to all, taking up the shield of faith with which you will be able to extinquish all the flaming arrows of the evil one. And take the helmet of salvation, and the sword of the Spirit, which is the word of God (Eph. 6:13-17).

Having been a Naval officer for over five years, including one year of 'shore duty' in Vietnam, I retain a rather vivid image of battlefield reality. However, it reached a new level recently when I invited veteran Christian and Missionary Alliance missionary Herb Clingen into my classroom to share his life and ministry with the moldable young men at The Master's Seminary.

Herb recounted the days that he and his family had been incarcerated by the Japanese in the Philippines during World War II. After treatment became more brutal and just when they and hundreds of others were about to be executed, American army troops pulled off a daring rescue. All of the missionaries were liberated.

Over forty years had passed since that February 24, 1945 release. In 1989, Herb and his wife Ruth met for the first time with the officer who engineered their rescue decades earlier. Herb was able to share that just as this officer had liberated them from the Japanese, they wanted in turn to introduce him to their Liberator from sin and death— Jesus Christ.

The Christian life is a battle, but in the end Jesus wins!

> But in all these things we overwhelmingly conquer through Him who loved us (Rom. 8:37).

> But thanks be to God, who gives us the victory through our Lord Jesus Christ (1 Cor. 15:57).

Travelling Light

We live for a time as aliens in enemy territory (1 Peter 1:1; 2:11). Our spiritual citizenship is in heaven (Phil. 3:20). When final liberation comes in the ultimate sense, we can take nothing with us (Job 1:21; 1 Tim. 6:7). The only investment that lasts will be treasure stored up in heaven (Matt. 6:19-20). Our earthly roots need to be shallow and our anchor in this life should not be set too strongly.

In the ancient near east many of the inhabitants were sojourners or nomads. You can still see bedouins in the Middle East today, constantly moving, without a piece of property to call their own.

That too is our spiritual heritage for a time. Like Abraham (Heb. 11:8-10), David (Ps. 39:12-13), and even Jesus (Heb. 13:12-14), we must not become attached to this world because it will pass away. Our destiny is not here but in heaven.

Our family just received this letter from a fellow spiritual alien. Her experience speaks volumes about our sojourn behind enemy lines.

> *I lost my nursing license in 1988, had it suspended actually. I had cared for a multimillionaire bisexual, influential in the federal government, who developed AIDS. The summer of '87 was a long*

4-month period and he was anxious to 'talk about God.' At the end, he thought he was dying and asked to see a pastor. I gave him my brother David's phone number and at his request, David came for 2½ hours.

The 'lover' was furious and an ethical misconduct and breech of confidentiality complaint was lodged against me. It was taken to the Provincial Nursing Association who took me to a 6-day trial. They could find nothing wrong, except for this and decreed that my license be suspended until I had basic 'refresher' training and submitted an essay stating why my Christian values and moral ethics clouded my nursing judgment when caring for an AIDS patient. Of course that is out of the question. I cannot deny the Lord that bought me, and so after thousands of dollars for legal fees, my earning capacity sank to $8,000 a year working part-time in a local department store selling carpets and lamps.

God never wastes our time or our tears. He could have changed the ruling but chose not to do so. Both patient and 'lover' are now dead, but both knew the Way and the patient spent precious time with David who testified at the trial. When asked what he had discussed with the patient, he said that, 'He asked of me the same questions that Nicodemus asked of the Lord that night. I explained that we are born into a family the first time by water, so the second time we are born into a family by the Spirit of God.' The whole courtroom listened to him simply explain God's plan of salvation; and I am proud to have been there and lose my license for Jesus' sake.[6]

Looking Up

Jim Irwin, *Apollo 15* astronaut, came to a confirming and deepening faith in Christ because of his experience in space. Since those days, he has been used of God to take the Gospel around the world.

It's no wonder that he adopted the following poem as the symbol of his ministry. John Gillespie Magee, Jr., a British aviator who lost his life fighting in World War II, penned 'High Flight.' For Jim Irwin, for me, and for all who would embrace God, John Magee says it all, spiritually speaking.

Oh, I have slipped the surly bonds of earth
    And danced the skies on laughter-silvered wings;
Sunward I've climbed, and joined the tumbling mirth
    Of sun-split clouds—and done a hundred things
You have not dreamed of—wheeled and soared and swung
    High in the sunlit silence. Hov'ring there,
I've chased the shouting wind along, and flung
    My eager craft through footless halls of air.
Up, up the long, delirious, burning blue
    I've topped the windswept heights with easy grace
Where never lark, or even eagle flew.
    And, while with silent, lifting mind I've trod
The high untrespassed sanctity of space,
    Put out my hand and touched the face of God.[7]

Part Four

SPIRITUAL PASSIONS

Not that I have already obtained it, or have already become perfect,
but I press on so that I may lay hold of that for which also I was
laid hold of by Christ Jesus. Brethren, I do not regard myself as
having laid hold of it yet; but one thing I do: forgetting what lies
behind and reaching forward to what lies ahead, I press on toward
the goal for the prize of the upward call of God in Christ Jesus.
Philippians 3:12-14

C.T.'s life stands as some rugged Gibraltar – a sign to all
succeeding generations that it is worthwhile to lose all this
world can offer and stake everything on the world to come.
His life will be an eternal rebuke to easy-going Christianity.
He has demonstrated what it means to follow Christ without
counting the cost and without looking back.[1]
Alfred Buxton
C.T. Studd's co-pioneer in Africa

*Great is the L*ORD*, and highly to be praised;*
and His greatness is unsearchable.
One generation shall praise Your works to another,
and shall declare Your mighty acts.
Psalm 145:3-4

16

GRASPING GOD'S GREATNESS

Former heavyweight boxing champion Muhammad Ali claimed, 'I'm the greatest!' Sports fans continually chant, 'We're number one!' But regardless of what other people think or say, God alone is great.

This hypothetical scene set by Dr. S.M. Lockridge vividly portrays God's greatness:

Where did God come from? He came from nowhere! The reason God came from nowhere is that there was nowhere for Him to come from. Coming from nowhere, He stood on nothing. The reason He had to stand on nothing is there was nowhere for Him to stand. And standing on nothing, He reached out where there was nowhere to reach and caught something where there was nothing to catch and hung something on nothing and He told it to stay there. Now standing on nothing, He took the hammer of His own will; He struck the anvil of His omnipotence and sparks flew. He caught them on the tips of His fingers, flung them out into space and bedecked the heaven with stars, but no one said a word. The reason no one said anything is that there was nobody there to say anything. So God Himself said, 'That is very good.'[1]

The Majesty of God's Greatness

With God, there are no boundaries to His presence, no limits to His knowledge, and no governor on His power. The person of God defines 'greatness.'

We're reminded four times in Scripture of our response to God's greatness. 'Great is the Lord and greatly to be praised' (1 Chron. 16:25; Pss. 48:1; 96:4; 145:3). Nehemiah described God's greatness with terms like *awesome* and *mighty* (Neh. 9:32), as did Daniel (Dan. 9:4) and Jeremiah (Jer. 32:18).

David's prayers habitually acknowledged God's greatness:

For this reason You art great, O Lord GOD; for there is none like You, and there is no God besides You, according to all that we have heard with our ears (2 Sam. 7:22).

Yours, O LORD, is the greatness and the power and the glory and the victory and the majesty, indeed everything that is in the heavens and the earth; Yours is the dominion, O LORD, and You exalt Yourself as head over all (1 Chron. 29:11).

Other Scriptures describe: (1) God's great power (Eph. 1:19); (2) God's great promises (2 Peter 1:4); (3) God's great kingdom (Dan. 7:27); and (4) God's great faithfulness (Lam. 3:23).

'Majesty' also links synonymously with 'greatness,' as the following passages demonstrate:

> The LORD reigns, He is clothed with majesty; the LORD has clothed and girded Himself with strength; indeed, the world is firmly established, it will not be moved (Ps. 93:1).

> For we did not follow cleverly devised tales when we made known to you the power and coming of our Lord Jesus Christ, but we were eyewitnesses of His majesty. For when He received honor and glory from God the Father, such an utterance as this was made to Him by the Majestic Glory, 'This is My beloved Son with whom I am well pleased' (2 Peter 1:16-17).

> And He is the radiance of His glory and the exact representation of His nature, and upholds all things by the word of His power. When He had made purification of sins, He sat down at the right hand of the Majesty on high (Heb. 1:3).

We'll better understand the dimensions of God's greatness by examining the macro-world of space and the micro-world of the human body. Psalm 8:1-4 points to the heavens and Psalm 139:13-16 speaks of our being fearfully and wonderfully made in the womb. These illustrations will help us to grasp, but never completely comprehend, the fullness of our great God.

To grasp the scene, imagine a perfectly smooth glass pavement on which the finest speck can be seen. Then shrink our sun from 865,000 miles in diameter to only two feet . . . and place the ball on the pavement to represent the sun. Step off 82 paces (about two feet per pace), and to represent proportionately the first planet, Mercury, put down a tiny mustard seed.

Take 60 steps more, and for Venus put an ordinary BB.

Mark 78 more steps . . . put down a green pea representing Earth.

Step off 108 paces from there, and for Mars put down a pinhead.

Sprinkle around some fine dust for the asteroids, then take 788 steps more. For Jupiter, place an orange on the glass at that spot.

After 934 more steps, put down a golf ball for Saturn.

Now it gets really involved. Mark 2,086 steps more, and for Uranus . . . a marble.

Another 2,322 steps from there you arrive at Neptune. Let a cherry represent Neptune.

This will take two and a half miles, and we haven't even discussed Pluto! If we swing completely around, we have a smooth glass surface five miles in diameter, yet just a tiny fraction of the heavens—excluding Pluto. On this surface, five miles across, we have only a seed, BB, pea, pinhead, some dust, an orange, golf ball, a marble, and a cherry. Guess how far we'd have to go on the same scale before we could put down another two-foot ball to represent the nearest star. Come on, guess. Seven hundred paces? Two thousand steps more? Four thousand four hundred feet? No, you're way off.

We'd have to go 6.720 miles before we could arrive at that star. Miles, not feet. And that's just the first star among millions. In one galaxy among perhaps thousands, maybe billions. And all of it in perpetual motion . . . the most accurate timepiece known to man.²

Consider your body which proves microscopic compared to our solar system but no less intricate in detail. God made you with over 200 bones plus more than 630 muscles. Your body contains over 30 trillion cells, 16 billion nerve endings, and 4 million pain sensors. Our lungs contain 750 million air sacs and take about 24,000 breaths every 24 hours. Blood flows 168 million miles daily in our bodies, pumped by our heart which beats over 100,000 times a day.³

No wonder the heavens and the human body point unmistakably to God's creative power and greatness.

So great is God's greatness that He will not tolerate anyone who tries to elbow into His exclusive domain. The Philistines tried and painfully backed away (1 Sam. 5:1-12). Nebuchadnezzar, the seventh-century B.C. Babylonian king who ruled the world, tried but retreated in embarrassment (Dan. 4:1-37). Herod Agrippa II tried also and God took his life with worms (Acts 12:21-23).

Job lived to be called 'the greatest of all the men of the east' (Job 1:3). But one day tragedy struck and robbed him of his perceived greatness. He lost his children, servants, possessions, dignity, health, and prominence among men. God then gave Job a lesson on 'greatness.' We would do well to learn from Job's experience, so that we do not have to personally repeat it. He quickly learned that God, not man, serves as the measure of greatness.

There were two sessions—the first in Job 38:1-40:5 and the last in 40:6-42:6. They follow this pattern:

God's challenge	38:3 and 40:6-7
God's test	38:4-40:2 and 40:8-41:34
Job's conclusion	40:3-5 and 42:1-6

Take time to read the scenes as if you were Job being questioned by God. See if you don't begin to both understand and experience something of the One who is uniquely and majestically great.

The Marks of Human Greatness

Man's definition of greatness involves largeness in size or number, remarkableness in magnitude or effect, and superiority in character or quality. It's often measured by appearance, dollars, power, ability, genealogy, position, accomplishment, or possessions. The terms Who's Who, All-American, World Champion, Olympian, World-Class, All-Pro, or Guinness record-holder might apply.

The human race makes a 'great' mistake to think this way. Jesus' disciples proved no exception. They frequently focused on who among themselves was greatest (Matt. 18:1; 20:20-28; Mark 9:33-34; 10:37; Luke 9:46; 22:24; John 13:16). So did the Corinthians in reference to Paul, Apollos, and Cephas (1 Cor. 1:10-17). Both Jesus and Paul put the discussion in perspective.

> He said to them, 'My cup you shall drink; but to sit on My right and on My left, this is not Mine to give, but it is for those for whom it has been prepared by My Father' (Matt. 20:23).

> But we have this treasure in earthen vessels, so that the surpassing greatness of the power will be of God and not from ourselves (2 Cor. 4:7).

While there will never be an earthly counterpart to the eternal greatness of God, the Bible does speak about four marks of kingdom greatness that bear 'great' similarity to God's character. These then are the marks of human greatness as defined by God who alone is great.

Mark #1—Scripturalness. 'Whoever then annuls one of the least of these commandments, and teaches others to do the same, shall be called least in the kingdom of heaven; but whoever keeps and teaches them, he shall be called great in the kingdom of heaven' (Matt. 5:19).

God's Word cannot be broken (John 10:35) because it is a total package. To disallow, annul, or disobey one part is to be guilty of all (Jas. 2:10).

The Jews used to pride themselves in keeping the Law down to the smallest detail. Some rabbis believed the Deuteronomy 22:6-7 statute concerning a mother bird and her chick was the least in importance. Jesus commented on the Pharisees' habit of even tithing mint, dill, and cumin (Lev. 27:30; Matt. 23:23).

What might seem commendable at first, Jesus condemned. Why? Because while fulfilling the minutia of the Law, they neglected the more important matters. They did not keep the whole counsel of God (Matt. 28:20; Acts 20:27). Those who teach and live this way are least in God's kingdom.

The greatest, however, shall first keep or obey and then teach others all of the commandments. The priority of living and *then* communicating is reinforced elsewhere in Scripture (Ezra 7:10; 1 Tim. 4:16). That's why James warns: 'Let not many of you become teachers, my brethren, knowing that as such we will incur a stricter judgment' (Jas. 3:1).

God's view of you is directly proportional to your view of Him. It's evidenced by our commitment to live out and teach others His Word. To be great is to intellectually and obediently embrace all of Scripture.

Mark #2—Submissiveness. 'At that time the disciples came to Jesus and said, "Who then is greatest in the kingdom of heaven?" And He called a child to Himself and set him before them, and said, "Truly I say to you, unless you are converted and become like children, you will not enter the kingdom of heaven. Whoever then humbles himself as this child, he is the greatest in the kingdom of heaven" ' (Matt. 18:1-4).

Humility, or the absence of pride, marks a 'great' convert to God's kingdom.

> But He gives a greater grace. Therefore it says, 'God is opposed to the proud, but gives grace to the humble' (James 4:6).

He has told you, O man, what is good; and what does the LORD require of you but to do justice, to love kindness, and to walk humbly with your God? (Micah 6:8).

Everyone who is proud in heart is an abomination to the LORD; assuredly, he will not be unpunished (Prov. 16:5).

Submission to God's Word and the imitation of Christ's incarnate, humble character identifies 'great' kingdom citizens (Phil. 2:5-8).

Mark #3—Service. 'But the greatest among you shall be your servant' (Matt. 23:11).

This is just the opposite of the way we think—authority not responsibility, strength not weakness, and power not character.

Jesus is the model Teacher/Servant (Matt. 20:28). He came to give, not get; to pay, not receive. We should follow Him. Greatness is not being carried off the field of victory by a cheering throng. Rather, the victor carries off those who would otherwise have lost had he not served them.

Mark #4—Sacrifice. 'But now faith, hope, love, abide these three; but the greatest of these is love' (1 Cor. 13:13).

Faith and hope are unseen—love deals with the visible. Faith looks back to the past, hope to the future, but love is now. The love of which Paul writes is love rendered without being prompted and love that expects nothing in return. That is kingdom greatness. It involves the fifteen action qualities mentioned in 1 Corinthians 13:4-7. Living these out as a pattern of life makes a Christian great. On the other hand, their absence makes one nothing (13:1-3).

Let me share with you a touching eulogy delivered at a service over which I presided on a windy, fall day in the San Fernando Valley. It was delivered by the older brother of a blind, mentally impaired young man who died of cancer. Here's the essence of human greatness as measured by God:

What can be said of the life of Ronald Castersen? Well, it all depends on the way you look at it. From one point of view, he had no great abilities or contributions to society. He was not a well known person, and for sure will never be found in any history books.

But history books are not the only books being written. God is also keeping a book. And who has He chosen to be logged into this book? First Corinthians 1:27-29 says, 'But God has chosen the foolish things of the world to shame the wise, and God has chosen the weak things of this world to shame the things which are strong, and the base things of the world and the despised, God has chosen the things that are not, that He might nullify the things that are, that no man should boast before God.' Ronald's life was very valuable to God, indeed He even sent His own Son to die for him.

Ronald enjoyed the simple things of life. He always loved children, in fact I can remember him sitting in the front yard with his box full of candy generously giving it out to the children who came by. He knew that it was better to give than to receive, and this unselfish attitude was always a strong characteristic of his life.

He wasn't one to complain either. Legally blind from the age of 12, I never can remember him saying, 'I wish I wasn't blind.' In fact he was always one that would encourage others that were in a difficult situation that God was enough for whatever their need might be.

He loved also to work. His condition didn't allow him to do things that were very strenuous, but he was always up early to go to the workshop where he kept busy with various odd jobs. He loved to do small tasks around the house as much as he was capable of.

The greatest attribute that Ronald had in his life was his simple love and reverence for God. He came to know the Lord Jesus as his Saviour as a young boy and loved to tell others about Him also. That is what makes this a joyful time. True, it is a time of sorrow because we miss him, but a great joy because he has graduated from this life and has entered into the joy of the Lord. He has regained his sight. Someday his body will be resurrected from the dead, and we know we will see him again.

I know Ron was a real example to me. Also I thank God for the privilege of knowing him for 26 years. Before I was a Christian he wouldn't give me theological explanations, he would just tell me, 'That's sin,' when he knew something was sin. He knew his God and I'm sure his example was very instrumental in my having gotten saved, for which I thank God.

On Sunday mornings he was always up before me,
enthusiastically waking me up, 'Come on, Steve, let's go worship
the Lord.'

Yes, in ways he was poor in this world, but thank God he had
'treasure in heaven, where moth and rust cannot corrupt, and
thieves do not break in and steal.'[4]

The Mandates of Kingdom Greatness

I once saw this sign in a 'left-handed' shop in Southern California.
'Everyone is born right-handed, only the great overcome it!'
According to the entrepreneur who originated that bit of creative
advertisement, only those who live 'the southpaw way' are great.

God's perspective points in a different direction. Those with 'great'
character and conduct will focus on God's 'great' cause. According
to Jesus this can be summarized in two 'great' activities.

1. *The Great Commandments.* 'One of the scribes came and heard
them arguing and ... asked Him, "What commandment is the foremost
of all?" Jesus answered, "The foremost is, 'Hear, O Israel; the Lord
our God is one Lord; and you shall love the Lord your God with all
your heart, and with all your soul, and with all your mind, and with
all your strength.' The second is this, 'You shall love your neighbor
as yourself.' There is no other commandment greater than these" '
(Mark 12:28-31).

The 613 individual commandments of the Mosaic Law reduce to
two—love God, love man (Lev. 19:18; Deut. 6:5). If we love God,
we'll love to obey and teach all of His will contained in His Word. If
we love men, we'll demonstrate our love for God to them by
submission, service, and sacrifice.

Two young brothers once discussed their life goals. One wanted
to be rich and famous while the other simply desired to obey Christ
fully. Both reached their goal. But in the end, the first was remembered
only by the second's achievements. The epitaph on the rich brother's
tombstone read, 'Here lies the brother of David Livingstone.'

'Great' people manifest God's great love in their lives both for
God and for other human beings.

2. *The Great Commission.* The term *great commission* is never used
in Scripture. However, it is a fitting title to describe Christ's final

instructions to the disciples and in turn to all Christians until Jesus returns. Note the apostles' various renderings of this divine mandate:

> But the eleven disciples proceeded to Galilee, to the mountain which Jesus had designated. When they saw Him, they worshipped Him; but some were doubtful. And Jesus came up and spoke to them, saying, 'All authority has been given to Me in heaven and on earth. Go therefore and make disciples of all the nations, baptizing them in the name of the Father and the Son and the Holy Spirit, teaching them to observe all that I commanded you; and lo, I am with you always, even to the end of the age' (Matt. 28:16-20).

> And He said to them, 'Go into all the world and preach the gospel to all creation' (Mark 16:15)

> And He said to them, 'Thus it is written, that the Christ would suffer and rise again from the dead the third day; and that repentance for forgiveness of sins would be proclaimed in His name to all the nations, beginning from Jerusalem. You are witnesses of these things' (Luke 24:46-48).

> So Jesus said to them again, 'Peace be with you; as the Father has sent Me, I also send you.' And when He had said this, he breathed on them, and said to them, 'Receive the Holy Spirit. If you forgive the sins of any, their sins have been forgiven them; if you retain the sins of any, they have been retained' (John 20:21-23).

> But you will receive power when the Holy Spirit has come upon you; and you shall be My witnesses both in Jerusalem, and in all Judea and Samaria, and even to the remotest part of the earth (Acts 1:8).

The Lord Jesus Christ calls Christians to the greatest of causes—the kingdom of God. The priority activities are:

- *Going*
- *Making disciples*
- *Baptizing*
- *Teaching complete obedience*

Sometimes we take this call to be optional, or to be discussed but never embraced. Not so! The Great Commission must be understood in a military sense. Christ's orders do *not* form the basis for dialogue but rather obedience.

Listen to the testimony of John Wesley who took Christ's words as his personal obligation:

I look upon all the world as my parish; thus far I mean, that in whatever part of it I am I judge it meet, right, and my bounden duty to declare, unto all that are willing to hear, the glad tidings of salvation.[5]

Paul prayed for the Philippians:

And this I pray, that your love may abound still more and more in real knowledge and all discernment, so that you may approve the things that are excellent, in order to be sincere and blameless until the day of Christ (Phil. 1:9-10).

Discerning Christians will always choose the excellence of the Great Commandments and the Great Commission when God's will prevails in their lives.

Models of Godly Greatness
Interestingly, God does not look for great people to manifest His greatness. Neither Israel (Deut. 7:6-8) nor the church (1 Cor. 1:26-31) were chosen because of existing greatness, but rather just the opposite—because of 'great' need.

Some of God's great saints have been well known; others lived in obscurity. Paul saw himself as the greatest of sinners and the least of saints (1 Tim. 1:15; Eph. 3:8). Job (Job 1:1, 3), Ruth (Ruth 3:11), Apollos (Acts 18:27-28), and Daniel (Dan. 10:11, 19) are each called 'great' in Scripture.

Two other names stand out among the many. First is David, a young shepherd boy who was nothing but to whom God promised 'a great name, like the name of the great men who are on the earth' (2 Sam. 7:9). Second is John the Baptist of whom Jesus said, 'Among those born of women there has not arisen anyone greater than John' (Matt. 11:11).

My favourite Bible 'great' is Igdaliah. Chances are that you've never heard a message preached on him; maybe you've never heard of him at all! He represents the majority of committed Christians who live in relative obscurity by comparison to the famous few. Such was the case of Igdaliah whom God refers to in Jeremiah 35:4 as 'the man of God.' Appropriately, *Igdaliah* in Hebrew means 'God is great.' He bore the name that marked his life.

A Parting Word

I once read a sign that said, 'If Moses had a committee, the Jews would still be in Egypt!' God doesn't use great committees but He does enlist great commitment.

Someone asked Francis of Assisi why he accomplished so much. He replied, 'The Lord looked down from heaven upon the earth and said, 'Where can I find the weakest, the littlest, the meanest man on the face of the earth?' Then He saw me and said, 'Now I've found him, and I will work through him. He won't be proud of it. He'll see that I'm only using him because of his littleness and insignificance.''

I'm not Assisi or David or John the Baptist. Maybe you aren't either. But we can pray to be Igdaliahs—weak vessels that contain the greatness of God.

I delight to do Your will, O my God;
Your Law is within my heart.
Psalm 40:8

17

OBEYING GOD'S WILL

Someone recently gifted me with a little porcelain message square. It reads, 'Those who walk with God always reach their destination!' I've often thought since then that it could also be written, 'Those who walk with God always reach *His* destination!' Isn't that the central truth of Jesus' invitation?

> Come to Me, all who are weary and heavy-laden, and I will give you rest. Take My yoke upon you, and learn from Me, for I am gentle and humble in heart; and you will find rest for your souls. For My yoke is easy, and My burden is light (Matt.11:28-30).

Our bottom line in life ought to match God's bottom line. That's the way Jesus, the Son, lived in relationship to God, the Father. He told the disciples, 'My food is to do the will of Him who sent Me, and to accomplish His work' (John 4:34). To the Jews, Jesus answered, 'I do not seek My own will but the will of Him who sent Me' (5:30). The crowds in Galilee heard Him say, 'For I have come down from heaven, not to do My own will, but the will of Him who sent Me' (6:38).

So, if we follow our Lord's example, God's will should frame and drive the priorities of our lives. If we obey His exhortation to join Him in His yoke, then we will walk in God's will. When we walk alongside the One who is consumed with doing the Heavenly Father's will, then His destination will be our destination.

Paul's passion for God's will moved him to pray that the believers in Colossae would be filled with the knowledge of His will in all spiritual wisdom and understanding (Col. 1:9). His prayer encompassed two elements of God's will: (1) that which is known by and is true of every Christian because Scripture reveals it and (2) God's personal will for us as individual Christians which will be discerned, understood, and affirmed through the process of life and passage of time.

Let's begin with the more obvious—God's will revealed in Scripture. Realize that while all of Scripture explains God's will, significant portions stand out because they explicitly state God's will. We want to examine ten such elements of God's will as basic training in godliness.

Salvation

All but four of the Bible's 1,189 chapters (Gen. 1-2 and Rev. 21-22) speak of God's salvation extended to all who would believe in Him through the Lord Jesus Christ. Only in Eden and eternity did or will the human race fully share in God's character of holiness without sin. So it is not surprising to read that it is God's desire or will for people to be saved from their sins (1 Tim. 2:4; 2 Peter 3:9).

Not only is it God's wish, but only by His will can people be saved (Gal. 1:3-5). He predestined us to salvation according to the kind intention of His will (Eph. 1:5) and then worked all things after the counsel of His will (Eph. 1:11). James 1:18 says it best:

> In the exercise of His will He brought us forth by the word of truth, so that we would be a kind of first fruits among His creatures.

One of the chief characteristics identifying one who truly knows God and is part of His eternal family is a compulsion to know and do God's will. It highlights the salvation transaction. Jesus said, 'For whoever does the will of God, he is My brother and sister and mother' (Mark 3:35). A spiritually inherited trait of one who has been born again into God's spiritual family is the lifestyle of doing God's will. So, the one who does God's will abides forever (Matt. 7:21; 1 John 2:17).

May I ask a personal question at this point? Have you ever admitted your spiritual bankruptcy, turned from your self- and sin-centered life, and asked God to forgive you through the Lord Jesus Christ, who died for your sins, rose from the grave on the third day, and extends the free gift of eternal life to all who would believe in Him? If you have, then proceed to the next step. If not, pause and prayerfully do so because you will be unable to take the next steps without having taken that first step out of Satan's dark domain into God's kingdom of light (Acts 26:18; Col. 1:13).

Sacrifice

Sociologist Bronislaw Malinowski notes, 'Magic is when we manipulate the deities so that they perform our wishes; religion is when we subject ourselves to the will of the deities.'[1] In a Christian context, the deceived address God as Lord but then pursue their own will, seemingly at God's expense. But not so the genuine Christian.

Therefore I urge you, brethren, by the mercies of God, to present your bodies a living and holy sacrifice, acceptable to God, which is your spiritual service of worship. And do not be conformed to this world, but be transformed by the renewing of your mind, so that you may prove what the will of God is, that which is good and acceptable and perfect (Rom. 12:1-2).

We have been saved by God's will to do God's will. In some senses we are the human answer to Christ's prayer, 'Your will be done, on earth as it is in heaven' (Matt. 6:10).

So it is reasonable then that we should present ourselves as a 'living sacrifice,' since death has already taken place on the cross when Christ died on our behalf (2 Cor. 5:15). Likewise, we should present ourselves as a 'holy sacrifice' because Christ bore our sins in His body that we might live a holy life (1 Cor. 15:3; 2 Cor. 6:14-7:1; Gal. 1:4; 1 Peter 2:24).

We mustn't jump off the altar, for only there can we experience and demonstrate that the will of God is good and acceptable and perfect. God will change us from the inside out (transform us) rather than the world shaping us from without (conform us).

Spirit Control

Read Paul's words, written to the Christians at Ephesus, very carefully:

So then do not be foolish, but understand what the will of the Lord is. And do not get drunk with wine, for that is dissipation, but be filled with the Spirit, speaking to one another in psalms and hymns and spiritual songs, singing and making melody with your heart to the Lord; always giving thanks for all things in the name of our Lord Jesus Christ to God, even the Father; and be subject to one another in the fear of Christ (Eph. 5:17-21).

God's will involves God's Spirit literally controlling our lives and giving us spiritual direction. How does He do this and how can we cooperate in this spiritual venture? Look at Colossians 3:16-17, and you'll discover that letting the Word of God dwell in you richly produces the same spiritual qualities as letting God's Spirit control you. The simple but profound conclusion is that God's Word energizes man's mind to obey God's Spirit.

If we do this, what will it produce? *First*, godly conversation (Eph. 5:19). We will communicate heavenward with songs of praise to

God and horizontally to each other with words of spiritual joy. *Second*, a thankful reaction to all of life (5:20). *Third*, a submitted relationship to one another in the fellowship of Christ that will extend from our marriage and family life (5:22-6:4) into the work world (6:5-9) and beyond (6:10-20).

This answers the 'how' and 'what' raised by Peter's exhortation 'to live the rest of the time in the flesh no longer for the lusts of men, but for the will of God' (1 Peter 4:2). We fuel the process by taking megadoses of God's Word. We check our progress by looking at three areas of life: (1) our rhetoric, (2) our reactions, and (3) our relationships. If you need a mentor in these areas, let Barnabas be your model (Acts 11:22-24).

Sanctification

Years ago my wife discipled a girl who attended a Christian college. Tragically, this young woman became pregnant outside of marriage and sought my counsel. I told her the first step to recovery involved confessing her immorality as sin against God (Gen. 39:9; Ps. 51:4).

Her response startled me. She blurted out that nowhere in Scripture did God expressly forbid intimate relationships between two people who were in love and intended to marry. I took her to a passage she apparently had overlooked or forgotten.

> For this is the will of God, your sanctification; that is, that you abstain from sexual immorality; that each one of you know how to possess his own vessel in sanctification and honor (1 Thess. 4:3-4).

Nothing violates the holy character of God any more than impure conduct in the physical realm of life. It's true God created us sexual creatures (Gen. 1:27-28). He also gave us explicit directions in its exercise (Ex. 20:14, 17; Lev. 18; Matt. 5:27-28; 1 Cor. 7:1-5; Heb. 13:4). Any attitude or activity outside of these boundaries violates God's will. Sexual purity proves to be a basic measure of spiritual intimacy.

Submission

Apart from rebellion against God, the next two objects of disobedience tend to be governments and employers. Humanity chafes at their kind of authority. For Christians, God wills a different kind of response.

Submit yourselves for the Lord's sake to every human institution, whether to a king as the one in authority, or to governors as sent by him for the punishment of evildoers and the praise of those who do right. For such is the will of God that by doing right you may silence the ignorance of foolish men (1 Peter 2:13-15).

Slaves, be obedient to those who are your masters according to the flesh, with fear and trembling, in the sincerity of your heart, as to Christ; not by way of eyeservice, as men-pleasers, but as slaves of Christ, doing the will of God from the heart (Eph. 6:5-6).

Whether we live in a somewhat free society like America or under a totalitarian system that characterized the Roman world of first-century Christianity, God wills obedience, with the obvious exception of obedience to man that is disobedience to God (Acts 5:27-29).

What can obedience to authority accomplish? It silences the ignorance of foolish men who otherwise would rail against God (1 Peter 2:15). It demonstrates the inner reality of your Christianity in an unmistakable way (Eph. 6:5-6). It provides eternal reward for what you have done (6:7-8).

A citizen's/employee's code of conduct should read:

> GOD'S WILL
> Nothing more,
> Nothing less,
> Nothing else.

Satisfaction

John Newton, former slave trader turned pastor, who wrote the beloved hymn 'Amazing Grace,' proclaimed as he died, 'I am satisfied with the Lord's will.'[2] In so saying, he not only issued a commentary on the Christian life but walked in God's will, even in his last moments on earth. As Paul writes, 'In everything give thanks; for this is God's will for you in Christ Jesus' (1 Thess. 5:18).

Thanksgiving should surround a Christian walking in God's will. It should be:

1. In word   Eph. 5:4; Col. 3:17
2. In deed   Col. 3:17
3. In attitude   Col. 3:15
4. In prayer   Phil. 4:6; Col. 4:2
5. In all things   Eph. 5:20; 1 Thess. 5:18
6. At all times   Eph. 5:20

A spirit of thanksgiving is not limited to America's annual November holiday called Thanksgiving. It's a 365-day-a-year experience. The great saints of old modelled a spirit of thanksgiving in some difficult circumstances.

Job blessed God's name even though he had just suffered the violent death of his children and servants plus the loss of his possessions (Job 1:21). After receiving an unjust but certain judgment of death, Daniel continued in his lifelong habit of thanking God three times daily (Dan. 6:10). Jesus knew His hour of crucifixion had come, but He took time with the disciples to give thanks to God (Matt. 26:27).

The apostles rejoiced that they had been considered worthy to suffer shame for Christ's name (Acts 5:41). Paul and Silas had been unjustly and illegally arrested and then incarcerated at Philippi, but they sang hymns of praise to celebrate (16:25).

What did all these people in diverse situations have in common? I believe they possessed an overwhelming sense of God's sovereign control of life and His goodness. No matter what happened, they could be genuinely thankful, satisfied that God's will was best.

Seeking

Our prayer life should be shaped by God's will. If the Spirit intercepts our prayers to edit them in conformity to God's will, then how much more should we labour to pray in God's will (Rom. 8:27). Our confidence in prayer can be measured by the certainty of praying in God's will.

> This is the confidence which we have before Him, that, if we ask anything according to His will, He hears us. And if we know that He hears us in whatever we ask, we know that we have the requests which we have asked from Him (1 John 5:14-15).

Paul prayed for the Colossians to know God's will (Col. 1:9). Epaphras prayed that they might stand perfect and fully assured in all the will of God (4:12).

Undoubtedly, the most notable prayer with an emphasis on God's will came from the lips of God in human flesh. Jesus prayed in Gethsemane, 'Father, if You are willing, remove this cup from Me; yet not My will, but Yours be done' (Luke 22:42). He prayed this model prayer asking that His will always be conformed to that of the Heavenly Father.

Where should you begin? Let me suggest that you start with the ten elements of God's will noted in this chapter. Pray that God's obvious will outlined in Scripture would characterize your life in Christ.

Serving

Tucked away in the Psalms is an instructive portion of Scripture: 'Bless the Lord, all you His hosts, you who serve Him, doing His will' (Ps. 103:21).

The hosts of God, the ministering band of heavenly angels, serve according to the will of God.

So it was with Paul. In the introductions of five of his letters, he describes himself as 'Paul, an apostle of Jesus Christ by the will of God' (1 Cor. 1:1; 2 Cor. 1:1; Eph. 1:1; Col. 1:1; 2 Tim. 1:1). In writing to the Romans, he noted on several occasions that he deeply desired to come and minister to them, but the will of God would ultimately determine his itinerary (Rom. 1:10; 15:32).

Our service should always be as an ambassador of Christ's bidding, to do His will on His behalf. That can cause frustration at times, particularly when we would like to be in a different location, at another time, in an alternative way than currently prescribed by God. That is a little like Mark Twain's commentary on God's Word and will. 'It is not the parts of the Bible I don't understand that bother me, it's the parts I do understand.' This old adage says it all, 'Serve well where God plants you and let Him be concerned with your next transplant.'

Suffering

Surprised? Let me relieve you by commenting that this is not for every Christian, but we should *all* be prepared. Peter, the apostle of suffering, teaches the truth he lived out.

> For it is better, if God should will it so, that you suffer for doing what is right rather than for doing what is wrong (1 Peter 3:17).

> Therefore, those also who suffer according to the will of God shall entrust their souls to a faithful Creator in doing what is right (1 Peter 4:19).

There is no virtue in suffering for suffering's sake or for unrighteous behaviour. But the highest commendation comes to one who suffers for Christ's cause. Jesus said, 'Blessed are those who have been persecuted for the sake of righteousness' (Matt. 5:10).

Antipas, a saint at Pergamum killed for Christ's sake, was addressed by Jesus as, 'My witness, My faithful one' (Rev. 2:13).

It's a great honour to die serving one's country; patriotism of the highest order costs—even one's life. Our citizenship is in heaven and to die is gain (Phil. 1:21). How much more then should we be willing to suffer like our Saviour and enter more quickly into His heavenly glory (Heb. 10:32-39).

Shepherding

I am personally reminded again that the church is not mine but Christ's, and so is the ministry. Therefore, the church must adhere to His will, not mine. Peter wrote, 'Shepherd the flock of God among you, exercising oversight not under compulsion, but voluntarily, according to the will of God' (1 Peter 5:2).

Kim Yardum Knight, my faithful secretary for over nine years (1980-1989), paused during a busy ministry day and asked me, 'How would you define success?' After reflecting a moment and seeking God's wisdom, I replied, 'Knowing God's will and walking in it.'

That's the *sine qua non* of spiritual fruitfulness. Whether it be in the Christian life or in 'full-time' ministry, we serve according to God's good will and for His pleasure (Phil. 2:12-13).

An Afterthought

These last few pages have really put us on notice. No longer can ignorance be our excuse for walking outside of God's will. We must submit our will to God's. Now, if you feel impatient to get on with 'Seeking God's Will,' pause here a moment more.

Think about several implications of our study:

1. If one or more of these ten explicit statements of God's will is not your pattern of life, then you are out of God's will and God requires change.

2. Certainly we need to be more concerned with what we know than that which we seek to know. While God's personal will unfolds daily, concern yourself primarily with obeying what you know and letting the rest flow out of your maturing obedience.

3. Don't repeat the failure of Israel's disobedience to God's stated will. Count the cost!

Thus says the Lord, your Redeemer, the Holy One of Israel; 'I am the Lord your God, who teaches you to profit, who leads you in the way you should go. If only you had paid attention to My commandments! Then your well-being would have been like a river, and your righteousness like the waves of the sea' (Isa. 48:17-18).

This prayer fittingly caps off our discussion of knowing God's will:

Now the God of peace, who brought up from the dead the great Shepherd of the sheep through the blood of the eternal covenant, even Jesus our Lord, equip you in every good thing to do His will, working in us that which is pleasing in His sight, through Jesus Christ, to whom be the glory forever and ever. Amen (Heb. 13:20-21).

Teach me to do Your will, for You are my God;
let Your good Spirit lead me on level ground.
Psalm 143:10

18

SEEKING GOD'S WILL

For many, finding God's personal will at times seems like searching for something that is capriciously hidden, rarely knowable, or hopelessly lost. But not so for martyred missionary Jim Elliot. Read carefully this 1950 diary entry that expressed his sentiments toward determining God's specific will:

> *Impressed with Ephesians 5, 'understanding what the will of the Lord is,' and Romans 12, 'proving what is the will of God.' Every moment I may be conscious and rejoice in the knowledge of God's will. Obedience to every command puts me on the track and keeps me there. Decisions of course must be made, but as in railroad, so in life—a block signal, a crisis, is lighted only where there is special need. I may not always be in sight of a 'go' light, but sticking to the tracks will take me where the next one is. Understanding the will of the Lord is believing Him, that He will— in all situations where I have obeyed—make that way His own way, effectual for eternity.[1]*

Problem

It's almost comical to hear the bizarre techniques to which Christians often resort to 'squeeze' God's will out of Him. Perhaps the most frequent is the fleece method of Gideon (Judg. 6:36-40). Most do not realize that the fleece represented Gideon's lack of faith and insecurity, not to mention that God never commends 'a fleece' to determine His will. Carefully consider this humble confession:

> *When we were teaching in Winnipeg, the Lord made it very clear that He wanted us to leave teaching to be involved in a local church ministry. At the same time, He made it abundantly clear that we were meant to come to Bethany Chapel in Calgary. It was undeniable guidance both for us and for the elders of the assembly in Calgary. Humanly speaking, the call was unexpected, but it came from God. But we had a house to sell in Winnipeg; so we put out a fleece. It was February, and we began to pray, 'Lord, if You want us to go to Calgary, sell our house by April at such and such price.' You know what? He did not! But we felt sure about His guidance, so we changed the fleece. 'By June, Lord.' Well, to make the story short, the house did not sell. In fact, it did not sell until the very Sunday in August when I first preached in Bethany*

Chapel, and at a price which meant we lost the equity we had in the house. What happened? Wasn't it God's will for us to come to Calgary? Yes, it was. We have never had clearer guidance in our lives about anything, and over and over God has confirmed that to us.

How did we know it was His will? After all, the fleece did not work. I believe God was teaching us not to trust in fleeces. But we knew His will, and that knowledge came by applying some basic principles.[2]

By trusting in the promises of God and applying some basic biblical principles, you too can confidently seek God's guidance. Whether it be in regard to your education, a job, whom you are to marry, where to live, or a myriad of other important life decisions, you can rest in the truth that God's will is always better than your own.

Promises

God is more concerned that we walk in His will than even we are. His Word contains numerous notes of encouragement to reassure us when we travel through life in heavy fog rather than on a clear, sunny day with perfect visibility.

Take courage with these six promises:

1. *Instruction:* I will instruct you and teach you in the way which you should go; I will counsel you with My eye upon you (Ps. 32:**8**).
2. *Counsel:* With Your counsel You will guide me, and afterward receive me to glory (Ps. 73:24).
3. *Guidance* For You are my rock and my fortress; for Your name's sake You will lead me and guide me (Ps. 31:3).
4. *Direction:* Trust in the LORD with all your heart, and lean not on your own understanding; in all your ways acknowledge Him, and He shall direct your paths (Prov. 3:5-6, NKJV).
5. *Establishment:* Commit your works to the LORD, and your plans will be established (Prov. 16:3).
6. *Execution:* Commit your way to the LORD, trust also in Him, and He will do it (Ps. 37:5).

With God's precious and magnificent promises as our foundation, let's move on to what I have kiddingly called over the years 'my 10

Ps in a pod' for affirming God's will. I have personally used them with great profit, particularly in determining God's ministry will in my life. No one principle alone gives clear direction, but the combined sense of direction usually proves unmistakable.

Principles

1. *Presentation.* 'Present your bodies a living and holy sacrifice . . . that you may prove what the will of God is, that which is good and acceptable and perfect' (Rom. 12:1-2).

Realizing that in Christ you are not your own—for you have been bought with a price (1 Cor. 6:19-20)—embrace the 'anywhere, anytime, anything, at any cost' mindset. Be like Samuel (1 Sam. 3:10), Isaiah (Isa. 6:8), and Paul (Acts 22:10) who all were available to carry out God's will.

Unfortunately, some believe that presentation is like buying merchandise on approval. If I like it, I keep it; if not, I'll send it back. The Jews diligently sought God's will through Jeremiah (Jer. 42:2-3). But when Jeremiah revealed that God's will was not what the people had in mind, they called the prophet a liar and went their own way (43:1-4).

Don't be like Jonah, the wrong-way prophet, who headed in the opposite direction of God's will (Jonah 1:1-3). Rather, be like David, a man after God's own heart, who willed to do all of God's will (Acts 13:22).

2. *Prayer.* 'This is the confidence which we have before Him, that, if we ask anything according to His will, He hears us' (1 John 5:14).

Prayer should not be the last court of appeal but rather the first. As a child would seek parental guidance, so we should seek direction from our Heavenly Father.

Jesus expands on this wonderful truth in Luke 11:11-13:

> Now suppose one of you fathers is asked by his son for a fish; he will not give him a snake instead of a fish, will he? Or if he is asked for an egg, he will not give him a scorpion, will he? If you then, being evil, know how to give good gifts to your children, how much more will your Heavenly Father give the Holy Spirit to those who ask Him?

We need not be shy, fearful, or insecure in praying. Rather we can be confident, even bold, to approach God and express our desire to know and walk in His will for our lives.

The late Paul Little recounted this incident from his life:

At the Urbana Convention in 1948, Dr. Norton Sterrett asked, 'How many of you who are concerned about the will of God spend five minutes a day asking Him to show you His will?' It was as if somebody had grabbed me by the throat. At that time I was an undergraduate, concerned about what I should do when I graduated from the university. I was running around campus— going to this meeting, reading that book, trying to find somebody's little formula—1, 2, 3, 4 and a bell rings—and I was frustrated out of my mind trying to figure out the will of God. I was doing everything but getting into the presence of God and asking Him to show me.[3]

What about you?

3. *Priorities.* 'Your word is a lamp to my feet, and a light to my path' (Ps.119:105).

Martin Luther once noted that his conscience was tied to the Word of God. So should ours be. Scripture contains the basics of God's will for us all. It contains the Beatitude attitudes (Matt. 5), the fruit of the Spirit (Gal. 5), the demonstration of love (1 Cor. 13), and the ultimate marks of spiritual maturity (1 Tim. 3). As we focus on making these character qualities the core of our lives, the rest will come in the right way and at the proper time.

We encounter trouble when we disregard the basics in pursuit of the more advanced. Achan (Josh. 7:1-26), Ananias and Sapphira (Acts 5:1-11), and David (Ps. 32) could all tell about their brutal, short-circuiting experiences with God's revealed will. They now know that God's personal will does not bypass or nullify God's revealed will in Scripture.

President Hibben of Princeton once invited Buchman of the Oxford Movement to dinner.

Buchman, an eccentric believer in divine guidance, arrived late and unexpectedly brought three other men with him who had not been invited. When he shook hands with Mrs. Hibben, Buchman said, 'The Lord told me to bring these three other men to dinner, too.'

Mrs. Hibben, who had not expected the three added guests,

replied, 'Oh, I don't think the Lord had anything to do with it.'
    'Why not?' retorted Buchman.
    'Because,' Mrs. Hibben replied, 'God is a gentleman.'[4]

Make sure that what you claim to be God's will is in fact His will, not yours. The principles of Scripture can always test your claim.

4. *People.* 'Without consultation, plans are frustrated, but with many counselors they succeed' (Prov. 15:22; see also 11:14; 20:18; 24:6).

Proverbs continually repeats the basic theme that input from other people to our lives proves invaluable. So does the 'body' principle of the New Testament. 'For the body is not one member, but many' (1 Cor. 12:14).

Paul needed Barnabas (Acts 9:26-27; 11:25), Peter needed Paul (Gal. 2:11-14), and the Israelite kings of the Old Testament needed their prophets and counselors. Unfortunately Rehoboam rejected the counsel of his court and split the kingdom (1 Kings 12:1-15).

Who are your counselors? Your pastor, perhaps, or elders in your church? Your spouse, a close Christian friend, or even your parents? A teacher, a Christian neighbor, or believer at work? Whomever they are, make sure they participate in your process of affirming God's will.

5. *Providence.* 'And we know that God causes all things to work together for good to those who love God, to those who are called according to His purpose' (Rom. 8:28).

There's no better illustration of this than Paul's second missionary journey. He first thought his travelling partner would be Barnabas (who accompanied Paul on the first trip), but it turned out to be Silas and Timothy (Acts 15:39-16:3). Next, they wanted to continue west to Asia but the Holy Spirit forbade it (16:6). So they turned north to Bithynia but the Holy Spirit again rerouted them (16:7). Finally God called them to Macedonia (16:9-10).

That event in Paul's life should encourage us to know that, even for the great apostle, God's will had to be discerned by a process. Paul had two factors in his favour. One, he was available; two, he was in motion and thus easy to redirect.

Can you remember why Paul ministered on the island of Malta? Read about it in Acts 27:1-28:10. Paul never planned to be there but God providentially, through a great storm, directed his path there.

You need to let God's Spirit, in harmony with unchangeable and unavoidable life experiences, be a major director in your odyssey called 'following God's will.'

Here's a last word. Don't be dismayed if it makes more sense looking back than ahead. A Puritan pastor once observed, 'The providence of God is like Hebrew words—it can be read only backwards.'[5]

6. *Patience*. 'But do not let this one fact escape your notice, beloved, that with the Lord one day is like a thousand years, and a thousand years like one day' (2 Peter 3:8; see also Ps. 90:4).

God's concept of time differs from our human perception. He created the world in six days and the world has ever since insisted it took millions if not billions of years. On the other hand, He has been lovingly patient with the human race in allowing for thousands of years of history to believe in Him when He could have brought swift judgment much earlier.

Typically, God's time frame moves slower than ours. On more than one occasion the psalmist cried out, 'How long, O Lord?' (Ps. 13:1-2; see also Pss. 6:3; 35:17; 62:3; 79:5; 80:4; 82:2; 89:46; 90:13; 94:3). If Moses had waited (Acts 7:24-25), or Saul (1 Sam. 13:8-14), or Israel (Num. 21:4-6), biblical history would have been written differently.

Jesus certainly was patient with God's clock. He knew when His time had not yet come (John 7:6) and did not act prematurely. On the other hand, when the hour arrived, He moved (Matt. 26:18). He always had a keen sense of the difference between the immediate and ultimate will of God.

If God is not moving fast enough for you, then slow down and don't run ahead. Allow God's Spirit to manifest His fruit of patience in your life (Gal. 5:22-23). Then agree with the early church, 'If the Lord wills, we will live and also do this or that' (James 4:15).

7. *Persistence*. 'Now He was telling them a parable to show that at all times they ought to pray and not to lose heart' (Luke 18:1).

This story of the nasty judge and needy widow drives home the point of perseverance, particularly in prayer. Don't quit; keep on seeking God's direction.

Beware that there is a wrong kind of 'pressing on.' Balaam continued to follow the path of disobedience even when God told him to stop (Num. 22:21-35). But if no barriers block the way, then continue your quest. Even if you have a false start or two, you can be ultimately rewarded like John Mark (compare Acts 13:13 and 15:37-38 with 2 Tim. 4:11). Continue until God makes it clear that you are to stop, like Paul who prayed three times for the thorn to be removed before he accepted it as God's will (2 Cor. 12:7-10).

By this time you might be asking, 'How do I draw any conclusions from these principles?' Start looking for common points of agreement or intersection. When they come together and agreement exists among most, then you will begin to see the pattern emerge. If your circumstances are taking a lengthy time, I would recommend you keep a diary so that you can easily remember, review, and reflect on each element and its relationship to the others.

8. *Proceed.* 'He who is holy, who is true, who has the key of David, who opens and no one will shut, and who shuts and no one opens' (Rev. 3:7).

There's a time to slack off and a time to surge ahead. So be discerning. Don't move forward to go through a door which God has closed, because you will never open it. Israel tried and failed miserably (Num. 14:26-45).

On the other hand, the church at Philadelphia had only a little power, but they proceeded through the God-opened door that no one could shut (Rev. 3:8). The Asian and Bithynian doors were closed to Paul (Acts 16:6-7), so he marched through the Macedonian door (16:10ff).

In counseling, I always ask two questions before making any commitments. First, 'Are you seeking God's will?' Second, 'When we find it, will you proceed with it?' Only if both questions receive a strong 'Yes!' will I continue. It becomes extraordinarily frustrating to put the brakes on someone who plunges ahead in wild disregard for God's will; it's equally painful to try and blast someone into motion when the time and direction of God's will are obvious.

9. *Peace.* 'Be anxious for nothing, but in everything by prayer and supplication with thanksgiving let your requests be made known to God. And the peace of God which surpasses all comprehension, will guard your hearts and your minds in Christ Jesus' (Phil. 4:6-7).

Paul and Silas, while in the Philippian jail, experienced that peace

(Acts 16:25). So did Peter in the Jerusalem prison (12:6). But it's not always as we might imagine it as if Hollywood filmed the situation.

I received this note of encouragement from the president of a major, conservative seminary in America. It really strikes the balance and rings with reality:

> *I am confident that your decision to remain at Grace Community Church was prayerfully made, and that you are sensitive to the Lord's leading in your life. Knowing the will of God is not as easy to understand as some of the 'manuals' would have us believe, is it? My own experience has been that the clear-cut, 'open and shut' cases are few and far between. It is far more difficult to choose between several opportunities, each of which has great potential. Sometimes all we can do after prayer and reflection is choose one and then see if God gives us reassuring peace. I have also found that 'peace' doesn't always come at once. In fact, my study of Bible personalities indicates that even those who apparently were in the center of God's will did not experience uninterrupted joy and peace in their circumstances. I guess it all boils down to the fact that in this world we are in a battle, and battles are not noted for being easy.[6]*

10. *Praise.* 'In everything give thanks; for this is God's will for you in Christ Jesus' (1 Thess. 5:18).

Regardless of how hopeless the task seems, how foggy the circumstances become, or how long it takes, continue to thank God for who He is and what He is doing in your life. Then live one day at a time fully trusting God with your future.

Postscript

Never forget that God's will is good and acceptable and perfect. If the situation looks bleak, the problem rests with us, not God. We must walk by faith and not always by sight (2 Cor. 5:7).

R.C. Chapman offers this overarching principle:

> *The rule that governs my life is this: Anything that dims my vision of Christ, or takes away my taste for Bible study, or cramps my prayer life, or makes Christian work difficult is wrong for me, and I must as a Christian turn away from it.[7]*

So, by unreserved presentation coupled with uncompromising obedience and unconditional trust, pursue God's will with a holy passion.

In doing so, remember:

God's will will never take you where God's grace cannot keep you.

You will make known to me the path of life;
in Your presence is fullness of joy;
in Your right hand there are pleasures forever.
Psalm 16:11

19

PLEASING GOD

Having just flown home to Los Angeles from Pittsburgh, I rushed to make a seminary graduation speaking engagement. My opening remarks focused on an unusual event from the just completed flight.

Our 737 lost power to an engine and the plane dipped in the direction of difficulty. During the ensuing confusion, I heard the man next to me pray, 'Lord, if You get me back alive, I will give You half of all I own.' The pilot, in the meantime, quickly corrected the problem and we continued toward our destination without further incident. But I couldn't get the man's promise out of my mind.

In the terminal after landing, I came alongside him and joked, 'Sir, I am a representative of God and I'm here to collect your promise to Him.' Without missing a beat he replied, 'Oh, I've made a new vow. I told God that if I'm foolish enough to fly again, I will give Him *all* that I own.' So much for that opportunity!

Now tell me—who was this man trying to please? Himself or God? Admittedly, the story in fact is fiction but oh-so-true in spirit. It typifies the heart of self-centered, self-pleasing mankind whose driving bent focuses inward for self, not upward toward God. It's the spirit of our age; and it's out of sync with the Spirit of God. 'Thou art worthy, O Lord, to receive glory and honor and power: for Thou hast created all things, and for Thy pleasure they are and were created' (Rev. 4:11, KJV).

The Apostle Paul warns that this problem will intensify as time progresses, for in the last days people will be lovers of pleasure rather than lovers of God (2 Tim. 3:1-4). James condemns self-pleasure as counterproductive to our prayer lives: 'You ask and do not receive, because you ask with wrong motives, so that you may spend it on your pleasures' (James 4:3).

God finds no pleasure in mere religious ritual (Ps. 40:6; Heb. 10:6, 8). Nor is He pleased with those who insist on walking by sight rather than according to faith (Heb. 10:38). The degree of spiritual intimacy that we share with God depends uniquely on whom we make our object of pleasure.

God's Pleasure

'I feel sorry for you, Dick. You will not be able to please everyone.' During the first week of a new ministry I heard those words from a well-meaning and perceptive member of the flock. My reply went something like this, 'That may be true, but I only want to please

God.' I would rather know God's pleasure at the expense of man's satisfaction than the reverse.

Why? For two reasons. First, I do not want to compete with God for He will do (in spite of me or you) what He pleases. I desire to move with Him, not against Him.

> But our God is in the heavens; He does whatever He pleases (Ps. 115:3).

> My purpose will be established, and I will accomplish all My good pleasure (Isa. 46:10).

Second, I want to cooperate with God who, in Christ, gave me eternal life. Pleasing Him is an important part of my new faith relationship with God.

> For it is God who is at work in you, both to will and to work for His good pleasure (Phil. 2:13).

> Now the God of peace, who brought up from the dead the great Shepherd of the sheep through the blood of the eternal covenant, even Jesus our Lord, equip you in every good thing to do His will, working in us that which is pleasing in His sight, through Jesus Christ, to whom be the glory forever and ever. Amen (Heb. 13:20-21).

Too many Christians are like the elderly man who was travelling with a boy and a donkey. As they walked through a village, the man was leading the donkey and the boy was walking behind. The townspeople said the old man was a fool for not riding, so to please them he climbed up on the animal's back. When they came to the next village, the people said the old man was cruel to let the child walk while he enjoyed the ride. So, to please them, he got off and set the boy on the animal's back and continued on his way. In the third village, people accused the child of being lazy for making the old man walk, and the suggestion was made that they both ride. So the man climbed on and they set off again. In the fourth village, the townspeople were indignant at the cruelty to the donkey because he was made to carry two people. The frustrated man was last seen carrying the donkey down the road. You cannot please everybody all the time.

Unless our concentrated focus is first upon pleasing God, we too will become spiritually frustrated. Pleasing others or pleasing self falls incredibly short of the spiritual epitome to please God and, in that desire, to also find our own chief source of pleasure. If we seek God and that which His hand provides, we will experience the blessed pleasures of our Lord (Ps. 16:11).

Our Passion

General Omar Bradley in a 1948 Armistice Day address noted, 'We have too many men of science, too few men of God. We have grasped the mystery of the atom and rejected the Sermon on the Mount.' Over five decades have passed and we still face the same spiritual vacuum—too many people pleasing themselves and too few people pleasing God.

It's similar to the time of Malachi. That Old Testament prophet wrote:

A son honors *his* father, and a servant his master. Then if I am a father, where is My honor? And if I am a master, where is My respect?' says the LORD of hosts to you, O priests who despise My name. But you say, 'How have we despised Your name?'

"*You* are presenting defiled food upon My altar. But you say, 'How have we defiled You?' In that you say, 'The table of the LORD is to be despised.'

"But when you present the blind for sacrifice, is it not evil? And when you present the lame and sick, is it not evil? Why not offer it to your governor? Would he be pleased with you? Or would he receive you kindly?" says the LORD of hosts.

The unmistakable symptom of the spiritually anaemic or dead community is desiring more honour for humanity than for God (note the church at Sardis, Rev. 3:1-3).

The exhortation of Scripture gives us a totally different perspective. 'For you were formerly darkness, but now you are light in the Lord; walk as children of light . . . trying to learn what is pleasing to the Lord' (Eph. 5:8, 10). The *King James Version* translates the Greek word for *pleasing* as *acceptable*. Don't miss the point—that which is acceptable to God is also pleasing. There is no middle ground, for if it is unacceptable, it is also displeasing. Only obedience to the truth of God is acceptable, and this alone pleases, delights, and brings joy.

When I served in Vietnam as the pilot of an air cushion vehicle and later as an operational briefer for Vice Admiral Elmo Zumwalt, I had one passion—to please my commanding officer. Daily I experienced an internal ignition that produced external energy which focused on doing those acceptable things that brought pleasure to my leader. By the way, when the Master is pleased, your own life will also become more pleasurable.

Paul writes with a military environment in mind. 'No soldier in active service entangles himself in the affairs of everyday life, so that he may please the one who enlisted him as a soldier' (2 Tim. 2:4).

It's a matter of priorities. You and I must decide who and what is most important—God and His kingdom or me and my world. There are no alternatives for Christians. Since God enlisted us into His 'kingdom corps,' we are soldiers of the Lord and must focus on pleasing Him. Like the centurion, we must be under authority (Matt. 8:8-9) because it is impossible to serve both God and mammon (Matt. 6:24-34). We must choose today whom we will serve (Josh. 24:15).

That's why Paul writes with transparent honesty about the aim of his life. 'Therefore we also have as our ambition, whether at home or absent, to be pleasing to Him' (2 Cor. 5:9). Bury forever the lie that Christians can't be ambitious. The issue is not ambition, rather the object and purpose of our ambition.

The Greek word for *ambition*, translated *labour* in the *King James Version* and *goal* in the *New International Version*, carries the literal idea of seeking that which is honourable with an attitude of love. Seeking the priorities of God ranks as the highest and most honourable of ambitions. Thus, we can anticipate a time of reward at the Judgment Seat of Christ (2 Cor. 5:10). Check out your passion level. Maybe it needs to be stoked up a couple of notches.

If you want to know what it will sound like when applied to life, listen to one of the deputy fire chiefs in Los Angeles who wrote me these unforgettable lines: 'Being a fireman is sufficient to fill the limit of my ambitions in life and to make me serve the general purpose of human society—BUT!! only to the degree that I can sense the Lord's presence, guidance, and approval of that ambition.'[1]

The Biblical Pattern

How can we who have little bring pleasure to God who has everything? Answer: As an obedient child brings pleasure to a parent. No matter how inadequate or insufficient, God takes great pleasure in our obedience and growth.

It all begins with faith—the overarching principle in pleasing God. 'And without faith it is impossible to please Him, for he who comes to God must believe that He is, and that He is a rewarder of those who seek Him' (Heb. 11:6). Faith is indispensable both to salvation and to spiritual intimacy (Col. 2:6).

Here are some childlike steps of faith you can take which will please God because they evidence spiritual health:

1. *Spiritual commitment.* After spending eleven chapters developing doctrinal truths about salvation, Paul exhorts the Romans to decisive action: 'Therefore I urge you, brethren, by the mercies of God, to present your bodies a living and holy sacrifice, acceptable to God, which is your spiritual service of worship' (Rom. 12:1).

The first act is sacrifice—not dead but living. It will be acceptable and pleasing to God. By sacrifice, Paul means yielding all you are and all you have to God in order to become like Christ and fulfill God's kingdom plan for your life. In doing so, you will be in sync with God's will for you.

2. *Submission.* God finds pleasure in the submission of children to parents (Col. 3:20) and in the obedience of servants to their masters (Titus 2:9). As it is in the earthly economy, so it will be in the kingdom domain.

Your submission will not be in vain or without spiritual value. Look at this wonderful promise: 'And whatever we ask we receive from Him, because we keep His commandments and do the things that are pleasing in His sight' (1 John 3:22).

3. *Walking in God's will.* Paul interceded for the Colossians with this wonderful prayer:

> For this reason also, since the day we heard of it, we have not ceased to pray for you and to ask that you may be filled with the knowledge of His will in all spiritual wisdom and understanding, so that you will walk in a manner worthy of the Lord, to please Him in all respects, bearing fruit in every good work and increasing in the knowledge of God (Col. 1:9-10).

Transformation is central to Christianity—being transformed into the likeness of Christ from the inside out, like the caterpillar which becomes a lovely butterfly. 'And do not be conformed to this world, but be transformed by the renewing of your mind, so that you may prove what the will of God is, that which is good and acceptable and perfect' (Rom. 12:2).

4. *Spiritual focus.* The superlative spiritual aspect of being single

lies in the opportunity to concentrate on the Lord without distractions from a spouse, children, and all the accompanying responsibilities of family life. 'But I want you to be free from concern. One who is unmarried is concerned about the things of the Lord, how he may please the Lord' (1 Cor. 7:32).

This does not mean marriage is bad. Just the contrary, since the Bible says, 'It is not good that the man should be alone' (Gen. 2:18, KJV). However, if you are single, God will use it for spiritual good, not social ill, because you have a kingdom advantage over your married counterpart. By application, even for us married folks, a spiritually focused life pleases God.

5. *Purity*. God wants us to become like Him. Because He is holy, He desires that we be holy too (1 Peter 1:16).

> Brethren, we request and exhort you in the Lord Jesus that, as you received from us instruction as to how you ought to walk and please God (just as you actually do walk), that you may excel still more. For you know what commandments we gave you by the authority of the Lord Jesus. For this is the will of God, your sanctification; that is, that you abstain from sexual immorality (1 Thess. 4:1-3).

Immorality abounds among Christians. It displeases our Heavenly Father to know we live lives that contain more darkness than light. To please God, we must flee immorality—like Joseph (Gen. 39:12; see also 1 Cor. 6:18).

A friend penned these significant words. I think of them often as a reminder that God wants me to reflect His purity.

> *My life is all Yours to shape as You will.*
> *I'll be the glove for Your hand to fill.*
> *I want to be pleasing to You. May it be,*
> *that You might be glorified somehow in me.* [2]

6. *Doing good.* It's so uncomplicated. 'And do not neglect doing good and sharing; for with such sacrifices God is pleased' (Heb. 13:16).

The Philippians sent a gift to Paul by the hand of Epaphroditus. The apostle reports it pleased God (Phil. 4:18).

7. *Worship*. Praise, deeds of righteousness, and worship bring immense pleasure to God. Catch this repetitious idea in the Psalms:

I will praise the name of God with song, and magnify Him with thanksgiving. And it will please the LORD better than an ox or a young bull with horns and hoofs (Ps. 69:30-31).

Let them praise His name with dancing; let them sing praises to Him with timbrel and lyre. For the LORD takes pleasure in His people; He will beautify the afflicted ones with salvation (Ps. 149:3-4).

8. *Living in God's Spirit.* 'Those who are in the flesh cannot please God' (Rom. 8:8; see also Gal. 5:16-17). It demands that we forsake our rights for the rights of God.

Therefore do not let what is for you a good thing be spoken of as evil; for the kingdom of God is not eating and drinking, but righteousness and peace and joy in the Holy Spirit. For he who in this way serves Christ is acceptable to God and approved by men (Rom. 14:16-18).

It means we act like Christ. 'For even Christ did not please Himself; but as it is written, 'The reproaches of those who reproached You fell upon Me'' (Rom. 15:3).

9. *Preaching the truth.* When Paul preached, he did so to please God, not necessarily his audience (Gal. 1:10). Elsewhere he writes, 'But just as we have been approved by God to be entrusted with the gospel, so we speak, not as pleasing men but God, who examines our hearts' (1 Thess. 2:4).

All three persons of the Godhead are associated with truth—Father (John 3:33), Son (14:6), and Holy Spirit (16:13). To abandon truth is to abandon God. To compromise God's Word is to compromise God. With neither is God pleased (1 Cor. 1:20-21).

Fruitful Practitioners

With the many activities required and with this high level of spiritual demand, you might be asking, 'Has anyone ever brought pleasure to God?' Let me answer in the affirmative and give you some examples.

Enoch proved to be a man of faith, and he pleased God.

By faith Enoch was taken up so that he would not see death; and he was not found because God took him up; for he obtained the witness that before his being taken up he was pleasing God. And without faith it is impossible to please Him, for he who comes to God must believe that He is, and that He is a rewarder of those who seek Him (Heb. 11:5-6).

As a young man, Solomon desired wisdom and truth more than riches. This pleased God. 'It was pleasing in the sight of the Lord that Solomon had asked this thing' (1 Kings 3:10).

Paul energetically reached out to please God. 'Therefore we also have as our ambition, whether at home or absent, to be pleasing to Him' (2 Cor. 5:9).

Jesus testified to a lifestyle designed to please God. 'And He who sent Me is with Me; He has not left Me alone, for I always do the things that are pleasing to Him' (John 8:29).

All of these men depended on God's Word for life direction and God's Spirit for a life dynamic. We have the same resources and the same opportunity for spiritually pleasing God.

Spiritual Payoffs

Making your priority in life to please God is not without its rewards. If you invest in God's pleasure, you will reap these divine dividends:

Peace	'Glory to God in the highest, and on earth peace among men with whom He is pleased' (Luke 2:14).
Prayer Answered	'And whatever we ask we receive from Him, because we keep His commandments and do the things that are pleasing in His sight' (1 John 3:22).
Personal Relationships	'When a man's ways are pleasing to the Lord, He makes even his enemies to be at peace with him' (Prov. 16:7).

In the Academy Award-winning film *Chariots of Fire,* Eric Liddell, famed Olympian and missionary to China, conversed with his sister Jenny on a Scottish moor about the timing of his return to missionary work. His response remains etched in my memory. 'I believe that God made me for a purpose—for China—but He also made me fast. And when I run I feel His pleasure.'

What did God make you for? Do you sense His pleasure? Do you have God's pleasure as your highest ambition? Are you willing to put God's pleasure first?

Aim your life at the bull's eye of God's pleasure and you will never miss the spiritual mark. You'll not be disappointed, and neither will God. Your heart will be filled with this great sense of commitment.

I rise up to worship, I stand to acclaim
The King of all ages, Christ Jesus His name.
I ask you, King Jesus, fulfill this desire,
Ignite me and make me, aflame and afire.
Come rule all my life,
Lord Jesus Christ, be Master and King.
Come rule all my life,
Lord Jesus Christ, be my everything. [3]

*I will give thanks to You, O Lord my God, with all my heart,
and will glorify Your name forever.*
Psalm 86:12

20

GLORIFYING GOD

It's fitting that I pen this during the Christmas season. The lyrics from so many carols speak of God's glory and fill our hearts with praise.

'Glory to God, all glory in the highest' comes from 'O Come, All Ye Faithful' as does the line, 'O Jesus, to Thee be all glory given.' In 'Hark the Herald Angels Sing,' the angels shout out, 'Glory to the newborn King.' My favourite, however, remains the refrain from 'Angels We Have Heard on High'—'Gloria in excelsis Deo.' Glory to God in the highest!

After I preached one Sunday night, a young man inquired, 'Since God's glory is complete, how can we possibly add anything to it? Why does Scripture command us to give Him glory?' We opened our Bibles to 2 Corinthians 3:18:

> But we all, with unveiled face beholding as in a mirror the glory of the Lord, are being transformed into the same image from glory to glory, just as from the Lord, the Spirit.

I explained to him that by analogy God is to us as the sun is to the moon. As the sun is the exclusive source of light, so God is the sole source of glory; as the moon reflects light, so we reflect God's glory.

But because God's image in us was fractured by the Fall, sinful mankind refracts God's glory more than they perfectly reflect it back to Him. However, once we are transformed into the same image at the moment of salvation, we reflect more than we refract. Thus, God's glory is more and more returned to Him just as He transmitted it to us. That's how we can give to God something that He alone possesses and shares with no one (Isa. 42:8; 48:11).

God's glory dominates Scripture. Some have suggested 'glory' as the Bible's unifying theme. Over 400 appearances of the word in Scripture support this thesis.

After studying every passage, it seems to me that from the perspective of, 'What can I do to glorify God?' three distinct realms need to be identified and discussed. So I have listed the glorifying activities of a believer under these categories: (1) God directed, (2) Christian directed, and (3) unbeliever directed.

Upward Direction

Being God by definition includes being glorious. Many titles reflect God's glory:

- *The Lord of Glory (1 Cor. 2:8)*
- *The Majestic Glory (2 Peter 1:17)*
- *The King of Glory (Ps. 24:7-10)*
- *The Spirit of Glory (1 Peter 4:14)*
- *The Word of Glory (John 1:14)*

Most of God's glory reflected back to Him by us comes through acts of personal devotion and adoration that are God directed. Please note the activities of personal worship that glorify God.

1. *Living with purpose.* 'Whether, then, you eat or drink or whatever you do, do all to the glory of God' (1 Cor. 10:31).

The famous eighteenth-century American preacher Jonathan Edwards applied this to his life by resolving, 'That I will do whatsoever I think to be most to the glory of God.' His respects and yours frame the picture of life that is lived in all respects for God's glory. In so doing we will be an answer to Paul's prayer for the Philippians (1:9-11; see in contrast Dan. 5:23).

2. *Confessing sins.* 'Then Joshua said to Achan, 'My son, I implore you, give glory to the LORD, the God of Israel, and give praise to Him; and tell me now what you have done. Do not hide it from me'' (Josh. 7:19).

To continue in sin shames God (Rev. 16:9). But to confess our sins acknowledges His holiness and brings Him glory.

3. *Praying expectantly.* 'Whatever you ask in My name, that will I do, so that the Father may be glorified in the Son' (John 14:13).

Your prayers in Christ's name bring the Father glory. Let's begin our prayers with Moses' petition, 'I pray You, show me Your glory' (Ex. 33:18).

4. *Living purely.* 'Flee immorality. Every other sin that a man commits is outside the body but the immoral man sins against his own body. Or do you not know that your body is a temple of the Holy Spirit who is in you, whom you have from God, and that you are not your own? For you have been bought with a price: therefore glorify God in your body' (1 Cor. 6:18-20).

It glorifies God to live in the light of His holy character.

5. *Submitting to Christ.* 'For this reason also God highly exalted Him, and bestowed on Him the name which is above every name, so that at the name of Jesus every knee will bow, of those who are in heaven, and on earth, and under the earth, and that every tongue will

confess that Jesus Christ is Lord, to the glory of God the Father' (Phil. 2:9-11).

6. *Praising God.* 'For all things are for your sakes, so that the grace which is spreading to more and more people may cause the giving of thanks to abound to the glory of God' (2 Cor. 4:15).

The Samaritan healed of leprosy glorified God with praise as did the angels at Christ's birth (Luke 17:18, 2:14). Let your mouth be filled with the Lord's praise and glory all day long (Ps. 71:8).

7. *Obeying God.* 'Because of the proof given by this ministry they will glorify God for your obedience to your confession of the gospel of Christ, and for the liberality of your contribution to them and to all' (2 Cor. 9:13).

8. *Growing in faith.* 'Yet, with respect to the promise of God, he [Abraham] did not waver in unbelief, but grew strong in faith, giving glory to God, and being fully assured that what God had promised, He was able also to perform' (Rom. 4:20-21).

9. *Suffering for Christ's sake.* 'Make sure that none of you suffers as a murderer, or thief, or evildoer, or a troublesome meddler; but if anyone suffers as a Christian, he is not to be ashamed, but is to glorify God in this name' (1 Peter 4:15-16).

Peter knew of what he wrote, for years earlier Christ had told him by what kind of death he would glorify God (John 21:19).

10. *Rejoicing in God.* 'Glory in His holy name; let the heart of those who seek the LORD be glad' (1 Chron. 16:10).

11. *Worshipping God.* 'All nations whom You have made shall come and worship You, O Lord; and they shall glorify Your name' (Ps. 86:9).

12. *Bearing spiritual fruit.* 'My Father is glorified by this, that you bear much fruit, and so prove to be My disciples' (John 15:8).

Inward Dimension

The Christian life begins by being right with God, but it does not end there. From the upward direction, we now turn inward to ways that believers can glorify God in the church and among themselves.

The catchy note that follows captures the normal process in the church. However, we know that whatever is accomplished goes to the credit and glory of God, who has everything to do with spiritual victories (Eph. 3:20-21).

There are six stages in all great projects. First there is enthusiasm. Next comes doubt. This is followed by panic. Phase four is the search for the guilty . . . then punishment of the innocent. The final stage? Giving credit to those who didn't have anything to do with it.[1]

13. *Proclaiming God's Word.* 'Finally, brethren, pray for us that the word of the Lord will spread rapidly and be glorified, just as it did also with you' (2 Thess. 3:1).

14. *Serving God's people.* 'As each one has received a special gift, employ it in serving one another, as good stewards of the manifold grace of God. Whoever speaks, is to do so as one who is speaking the utterances of God; whoever serves, is to do so as one who is serving by the strength which God supplies; so that in all things God may be glorified through Jesus Christ, to whom belongs the glory and dominion forever and ever. Amen' (1 Peter 4:10-11).

15. *Purifying Christ's church.* 'That He might present to Himself the church in all her glory, having no spot or wrinkle or any such thing; but that she would be holy and blameless' (Eph. 5:27).

16. *Giving sacrificially.* 'Because of the proof given by this ministry they will glorify God for your obedience to your confession of the gospel of Christ, and for the liberality of your contribution to them and to all' (2 Cor. 9:13).

17. *Unifying believers.* 'And the glory which You have given Me I have given them; that they may be one, just as We are one' (John 17:22).

As Christ accepted us, so we are to accept one another to God's glory (Rom. 15:7).

Outward Dynamic

First up, then in, and now out. That completes the cycle. Someone may ask, 'Which of these three is most important?' Let me respond with a question, 'What leg on a three-legged stool is most important?' All are equally important, but the order in which we glorify God is crucial. We must first be fixed on Him before we can minister to one another. Then, unless we are right in the body of Christ, we can never hope to reach out to the lost with the Gospel of Christ.

18. *Salvation of the lost.* 'His glory is great through Your salvation, splendor and majesty You place upon him' (Ps. 21:5).

'To the praise of His glory' dominates Paul's comments on salvation (Eph. 1:6, 12, 14). It proved that way in the salvation of Paul (Gal. 1:23-24) and Cornelius (Acts 11:18). Since the lost have fallen short of God's glory (Rom. 3:23), then to be saved is to have that glory restored.

19. *Shining Christ's light.* 'Let your light shine before men in such a way that they may see your good works, and glorify your Father who is in heaven' (Matt. 5:16).

20. *Spreading God's Gospel.* 'For all things are for your sakes, so that the grace which is spreading to more and more people may cause the giving of thanks to abound to the glory of God' (2 Cor. 4:15).

This proved to be Paul's experience on his first missionary journey. When the Gentiles heard the gospel, they rejoiced, glorified God, and believed (Acts 13:48).

A converted Hindu addressing a number of his countrymen once said, 'I am by birth of an insignificant and contemptible caste, so low that if a Brahman should chance to touch me he must go and bathe in the Ganges for the purpose of purification; and yet God has been pleased to call me not merely to a knowledge of the gospel, but to the high office of teaching it to others. My friends,' said the converted Hindu, 'do you know the reason of God's comfort? It is this: If God had selected one of you learned Brahmans and made you a preacher, on becoming successful in making converts, bystanders would have said it was an amazing learning of the Brahman and his great weight of character that were the cause; but now, when anyone is convinced by my instrumentality, no one thinks of ascribing any praise to me; and God, as is His due, has all the glory.'[2]

A Concluding Comment

Ichabod, which means 'no glory' in Hebrew, would be the worst thing imaginable for a believer (1 Sam. 4:21). For God's glory to be absent from a believer or the church is unthinkable. The glory of God needs to be our consuming quest.

The initial question is asked in *The Westminster Shorter Catechism*, 'What is the chief end of man?' Answer: 'Man's chief end is to glorify God, and to enjoy Him forever.' The ultimate object of our thoughts and priorities should be the glory of God. Our total being should be absorbed by this thrilling prospect which is the pinnacle experience of spiritual intimacy.

I've often marvelled at a commemorative sign which stands in front of a building complex devoted to ministry. It captures the 'shoe leather' sense of glorifying God. The plaque reads:

ARROWHEAD SPRINGS VILLAGE

DONATED BY FIVE BUSINESSMEN WHO
WANT TO GIVE GOD *ALL* THE GLORY

So, like these men, let the beatitude of the psalmist and the doxology of Paul be yours now and forever more.

Blessed be the LORD God, the God of Israel, who alone works wonders. And blessed be His glorious name forever; and may the whole earth be filled with His glory. Amen, and Amen (Ps. 72:18-19).

Now to our God and Father be the glory forever and ever. Amen (Phil. 4:20).

Part Five

SPIRITUAL PURSUITS

But speaking the truth in love,
we are to grow up in all aspects into Him,
who is the head, even Christ.
Ephesians 4:15

But grow in the grace and knowledge
of our Lord and Savior Jesus Christ.
To Him be the glory, both now
and to the day of eternity. Amen.
2 Peter 3:18

I feel like a man who has no money in his pocket
but is allowed to draw for all he wants upon
one infinitely rich; I am, therefore, at once
both a beggar and a rich man.[1]
John Newton

Then in fellowship sweet
We will sit at His feet,
Or we'll walk by His side in the way;
What He says we will do,
Where He sends we will go -
Never fear, only trust and obey.[1]

John H. Sammis

21

SPIRITUAL CONDITIONING

Ben Johnson and Pete Rose share several similar life experiences. They are well-known, former athletes who disqualified themselves to participate in sports because they broke the rules. Possible spiritual parallels can be drawn to the Christian life, since the New Testament more than once compares the rigours of Christian living to disciplined athletic training and competition.

> Therefore, since we have so great a cloud of witnesses surrounding us, let us also lay aside every encumbrance, and the sin which so easily entangles us, and let us run with endurance the race that is set before us, fixing our eyes on Jesus, the author and perfecter of faith, who for the joy set before Him endured the cross, despising the shame, and has sat down at the right hand of the throne of God (Heb. 12:1-2).

> Do you not know that those who run in a race all run, but only one receives the prize? Run in such a way that you may win. Everyone who competes in the games exercises self-control in all things. They then do it to receive a perishable wreath, but we an imperishable. Therefore I run in such a way, as not without aim; I box in such a way, as not beating the air; but I discipline my body and make it my slave, so that, after I have preached to others, I myself should be disqualified (1 Cor. 9:24-27).

> Not that I have already obtained it, or have already become perfect, but I press on so that I may lay hold of that for which also I was laid hold of by Christ Jesus. Brethren, I do not regard myself as having laid hold of it yet; but one thing I do: forgetting what lies behind and reaching forward to what lies ahead, I press on toward the goal for the prize of the upward call of God in Christ Jesus (Phil. 3:12-14).

> But have nothing to do with worldly fables fit only for old women. On the other hand, discipline yourself for the purpose of godliness; for bodily discipline is only of little profit, but godliness is profitable for all things, since it holds promise for the present life and also for the life to come(1 Tim. 4:7-8).

> Also if anyone competes as an athlete, he does not win the prize unless he competes according to the rules (2 Tim. 2:5).

Consistent spiritual victories, like a string of wins in sports, depend upon several factors. They include being experienced in using these disciplines.

1. The discipline of conditioning—holiness cultivation
2. The discipline of skill—spiritual growth
3. The discipline of obedience—biblical submission
4. The discipline of focus—spiritual priorities

All these features come into play as Paul introduces us to a Christian way of life comprised of ten separate but vitally related elements. In keeping with an athletic motif, the apostle suggests 'a Christian decathlon' of sorts. These ten events comprise the ABCs of Christian conditioning.

> We urge you, brethren, admonish the unruly, encourage the fainthearted, help the weak, be patient with everyone. See that no one repays another with evil for evil, but always seek after that which is good for one another and for all people. Rejoice always; pray without ceasing; in everything give thanks; for this is God's will for you in Christ Jesus. Do not quench the Spirit; do not despise prophetic utterances. But examine everything carefully; hold fast to that which is good; abstain from every form of evil (1 Thess. 5:14-22).

Assist the Spiritually Needy

> We urge you, brethren, admonish the unruly, encourage the fainthearted, help the weak, be patient with everyone (1 Thess. 5:14).

Four kinds of people receive notice for the second time in this letter: *the unruly* (cf. 4:11-12); *the fainthearted* (cf. 4:13-18); *the weak* (cf. 4:1-8); and *all men* (cf. 3:12). These people are undisciplined, fearful, lacking strength, and unsaved.

The obligation to minister to them is a function of the entire body of believers. Every Christian needs to be involved, not just the pastor and other church leaders. Paul's strong urging assumes that 'the brethren' have spiritual resources lacking in these four groups. Christians in the body should be spiritually disciplined, courageous, strong, and true believers. Then they will be in a position to minister to those in need.

The first group involves the unruly or undisciplined, people who are 'out of step' with the marching orders of Scripture. Their lives tend to be anything but quiet, focused, and industrious. These folks do not take 4:11-12 seriously:

> Make it your ambition to lead a quiet life and attend to your own business and work with your hands, just as we commanded you; so that you may behave properly toward outsiders and not be in any need.

Believers are to lovingly confront or admonish these people to change their behaviour. Paul illustrates this when he confronts a certain segment of the Thessalonians about their undisciplined and lazy ways (2 Thess. 3:6-12).

Those with 'a small soul,' the fainthearted or fearful, need encouragement or comfort. Paul demonstrates what he means in 1 Thessalonians 4:13-18 where he writes with truth and comfort concerning the destiny of loved ones who have already died. These words then are to be used in ministering to one another.

Mature believers are to hold onto those who are spiritually weak or lacking strength. They are to be a strength for those who might be morally weak (4:3-8). The best picture of this kind of ministry can be found in Paul's correspondence to the Corinthian church.

Finally, they are to be patient or endure with those who have not yet embraced Christ (all men). Long-suffering decidedly identifies one whom the Spirit controls (Gal. 5:22) and who characteristically loves people (1 Cor. 13:4). Paul prays that the Thessalonians will abound in love for unbelievers (3:12).

Be Concerned for the Good of Others

> See that no one repays another with evil for evil, but always seek after that which is good for one another and for all people (1 Thess. 5:15).

Good, not evil, is to be the goal of our involvement with other people. No one is ever to seek evil as a repayment for evil; everyone is always to seek to do good for believers (one another) and unbelievers (all men; see Gal. 6:10).

Jesus comments on this radical departure from normal human response in His great Sermon on the Mount.

> You have heard that it was said, 'An eye for an eye, and a tooth for a tooth.' But I say to you, do not resist an evil person; but whoever slaps you on your right cheek, turn the other to him also. If anyone wants to sue you, and take your shirt, let him have your coat also. Whoever forces you to go one mile, go with him two. Give to him who asks of you, and

do not turn away from him who wants to borrow from you.

You have heard that it was said, 'You shall love your neighbor, and hate your enemy.' But I say to you, love your enemies, and pray for those who persecute you so that you may be sons of your Father who is in heaven; for He causes His sun to rise on the evil and the good, and sends rain on the righteous and the unrighteous. For if you love those who love you, what reward do you have? Do not even the tax collectors do the same? If you greet only your brothers, what more are you doing than others? Do not even the Gentiles do the same? Therefore you are to be perfect, as your heavenly Father is perfect (Matt. 5:38-48).

Paul, Peter, and John all echo the same idea.

Never pay back evil for evil to anyone. Respect what is right in the sight of all men. If possible, so far as it depends on you, be at peace with all men. Never take your own revenge, beloved, but leave room for the wrath of God, for it is written, 'Vengeance is Mine, I will repay,' says the Lord. 'But if your enemy is hungry, feed him, and if he is thirsty, give him a drink; for in so doing you will heap burning coals upon his head.' Do not be overcome by evil, but overcome evil with good (Rom. 12:17-21).

To sum up, all of you be harmonious, sympathetic, brotherly, kind-hearted, and humble in spirit; not returning evil for evil, or insult for insult, but giving a blessing instead; for you were called for the very purpose that you might inherit a blessing (1 Peter 3:8-9).

Beloved, do not imitate what is evil, but what is good. The one who does good is of God; the one who does evil has not seen God (3 John 11).

By obeying these Scriptures, you will be a consistent doer of good and minimize the times you want to retaliate.

Cultivate a Joyful Heart

Rejoice always (1 Thess. 5:16).

If you are regularly assisting the spiritually needy and consistently concerned for the good of others, you will need to rejoice always in order to maintain your sanity.

Whether you're on top of life or underneath it, joy should be your constant companion (James 1:2-4). Joy in the Lord, even while you suffer, marks spiritual maturity (Pss. 31:7; 35:9; 40:16; 70:4).

> But it is still my consolation, and I rejoice in unsparing pain, that I have not denied the words of the Holy One (Job 6:10).

> Now I rejoice in my sufferings for your sake, and in my flesh I do my share on behalf of His body, which is the church, in filling up what is lacking in Christ's afflictions (Col. 1:24).

> But to the degree that you share the sufferings of Christ, keep on rejoicing, so that also at the revelation of His glory, you may rejoice with exultation (1 Pet. 4:13).

The focus of your joy should be on the Lord and the things of eternity. Here's a sample of biblically recommended objects for joy.

The mighty acts of God	Psalm 66:6
The name(s) of God	Psalm 89:16
The Word of God	Psalm 119:162
The salvation of God	Isaiah 61:10
The Holy Spirit of God	Romans 14:17

Paul put it most directly to the Philippians, 'Rejoice in the Lord always; again, I will say, rejoice!' (4:4).

Joy coloured Paul and Barnabas' jail term in Philippi where they sang hymns of praise to God after they had been beaten and illegally incarcerated (Acts 16:25). For the joy set before Him, Jesus endured the cross (Heb. 12:2).

Depend on Prayer

> Pray without ceasing (1 Thess. 5:17).

People who haven't made prayer a habit in good times won't usually pray in a crisis. The genius of Paul's exhortation lies in prayer's duration — 'without ceasing.' The idea is not that you are praying every single second of every hour, but rather that prayer is a consistent pattern of your life.

No one better exemplifies the consistency and resulting effect of unceasing prayer than Daniel. His professional enemies could find no fault with his life other than that he remained faithful to God

(Dan. 6:4-5). So they persuaded the king to sign into law a mandate that only the king could be worshipped for the next thirty days. A trip to the lions' den would reward those who disobeyed. Look at Daniel's response:

> Now when Daniel knew that the document was signed, he entered his house (now in his roof chamber he had windows open toward Jerusalem); and he continued kneeling on his knees three times a day, praying and giving thanks before his God, as he had been doing previously (Daniel 6:10).

He dared to continue his habit of prayer in the face of a death threat. After an overnight stay with the lions, Daniel lived while his accusers died (6:21-24).

Paul practised what he preached. As you read his letters in the New Testament, you see prayer as a common theme. Paul prayed without ceasing (Rom. 1:9-10; 1 Cor. 1:4-9; 2 Cor. 13:7; Eph. 1:16; Phil. 1:4; Col. 1:3; 1 Thess. 1:2; 2 Thess. 1:3; 2 Tim. 1:3; and Phile. 4).

No one has equalled the regularity of our Lord in prayer. He prayed in public at His baptism (Luke 3:21). Christ habitually prayed in solitude, whether it was in the wilderness or the mountains—at times all night long (Luke 5:16; 6:12; 9:18). He took some of the disciples to pray on the mountain (Luke 9:18-29). Later they asked Him to teach them how to pray (Luke 11:1). He prayed for others (Luke 22:32) and for Himself (Luke 22:41, 44).

Enter God's Gates with Thanksgiving

> In everything give thanks; for this is God's will for you in Christ Jesus (1 Thess. 5:18).

God's will demands that we live in a habitual state of thankfulness. Elsewhere Paul wrote, 'always giving thanks for all things' (Eph. 5:20). The psalmist said,

> Enter His gates with thanksgiving,
> And His courts with praise.
> Give thanks to Him; bless His name.
> For the LORD is good;
> His lovingkindness is everlasting,
> And His faithfulness to all generations (Psalm 100:4-5).

Whether in life or death, thanksgiving remains God's order of the day. When speaking of death, Paul wrote, 'But thanks be to God, who gives us the victory through our Lord Jesus Christ' (1 Cor. 15:57).

As our Lord instituted the bread and cup which would symbolize His soon death for our sins, He gave thanks before partaking of both the bread and the cup (Mark 14:22-23; Luke 22:19-20).

To live maturely in Christ means to live with a 'gratitude attitude.'

Fire Up the Spirit

Do not quench the Spirit (1 Thess. 5:19).

The NIV translates this phrase, 'Do not put out the Spirit's fire.' The focus here is on the Spirit's activity in the life of a true believer. 'Do not quench' appropriately responds to the picture of God's Spirit as fire (Acts 2:3).

How does one quench the Spirit? Very simply—with sin. As water is to fire, so sin is to God's Spirit working in us.

If I quench the Spirit, I will hate; if I walk in the Spirit, I will love. If we look at the fruit of the Spirit in Galatians 5:22-23, we can see the opposite effect of quenching the Spirit.

Fueled by the Spirit	*Quenching the Spirit*
Joy	Gloom
Peace	War
Patience	Anger
Kindness	Meanness
Goodness	Evil
Faithfulness	Selfishness
Gentleness	Malice
Self-control	Out of control

Paul contrasts these ideas in Ephesians 4:30-32 as he commands the Ephesians not to grieve the Holy Spirit. Then he commands them to put away the kinds of attitudes and responses that are grievous to God (4:31). They include:

Bitterness	Clamour
Wrath	Slander
Anger	Malice

These attitudes need to be replaced with Spirit-generated qualities that mark out true spirituality and minimize the deeds of the flesh (4:32). Kindness, tenderheartedness, and forgiveness stand in contrast to meanness, hardheartedness, and vengefulness.

Give Prophetic Truth Honour

> Do not despise prophetic utterances (1 Thess. 5:20).

Here Paul is talking about the authoritative words of God through a prophet. Prophecies can refer to the spoken word (1 Cor. 14:6; 1 Tim. 1:18; 4:14; Rev. 11:6), but more often it refers to the written Word of God.

The prophecy of Isaiah	Matthew 13:14-15
The prophecy of Scripture	2 Peter 1:20-21
Words of the prophecy	Revelation 1:3
Words of the prophecy of this book	Revelation 22:7, 10, 18-19.

In Paul's day there were both. In our day, we have neither kind of prophecy. The fruit of the historic prophetic ministry is what we call Scripture. So we could paraphrase the intent of Paul's words for today as, 'Do not despise Scripture.' The Greek word for 'despise' means 'to look down upon, to deny, to make or to find contemptible.' There are three basic levels of despising God's Word.

Level 1—Despise by not listening, as those with whom God's Spirit did not strive forever; they were judged in the Noahic flood (Gen. 6:3).
Level 2—Despise by listening but not believing, as Judas who betrayed Christ or the followers of Christ who withdrew because of difficult statements (John 6:60, 66).
Level 3—Despise by listening, believing but not obeying, as illustrated by Peter in his three denials (Matt. 26:69-75) or Demas in his desertion of Paul (2 Tim. 4:10).

To avoid any hint of despising Scripture, we need to do three things: listen to understand; believe by faith; and obey to glorify God.

Hold All Things Up to the Light of God's Word

> But examine everything carefully (1 Thess. 5:21a).

This expands on the previous command. It not only includes teaching which can be either true or false, but involves the experiences of life which can be good or evil.

Here, Paul teaches absolutism, not relativism. The standard for testing all things is the Word of God. Everything requires examination or testing.

> All Scripture is inspired by God and profitable for teaching, for reproof, for correction, for training in righteousness; so that the man of God may be adequate, equipped for every good work (2 Tim. 3:16-17).

Scripture continually bids us to test or to discern:

For false gods	Deuteronomy 13:1-5
For false prophets	Deuteronomy 18:20-22
For distorted truth	Isaiah 8:20; Revelation 22:18-19
For false teachers	1 John 4:1-3

Two historical tests of eternal significance come to mind. Eve tested Satan's words, but unfortunately not against God's words. She compared his words to her own thoughts, and finding them in agreement, she rejected God and fell into sin (Gen. 3:1-6). The human race has lived in sin ever since.

Jesus tested Satan's words too, but against the Word of God. In each instance, Satan disagreed with God so Jesus reaffirmed God's Word and utterly rejected Satan (Matt. 4:1-11). Thus Christ remained without sin (2 Cor. 5:21; 1 John 3:5).

Involve Yourself in Good Things

Hold fast to that which is good (1 Thess. 5:21b).

Determine what is good and then grip it firmly—don't let it go. Paul prayed for this for the Philippians.

> And this I pray, that your love may abound still more and more in real knowledge and all discernment, so that you may approve the things that are excellent, in order to be sincere and blameless until the day of Christ (Phil. 1:9-10).

Daniel serves as a life study of one who continually sought the most spiritual excellent way.

> But Daniel made up his mind that he would not defile himself with the king's choice food or with the wine which he drank; so he sought permission from the commander of the officials that he might not defile himself (Daniel 1:8).

They tried to give Daniel a Babylonian education (1:4), name(1:7), and diet (1:8). He went along with the teaching because he could test it with Scripture and reject that which was a lie. A new name did not change the character of Daniel and besides, he could not stop them from calling him whatever name they wanted.

Why then did he reject the food, which at first glance seems to be insignificant? When Daniel tested the food against Scripture, he decided that the Levitical standard declared it unclean (Lev. 11, Deut. 14); also, the food had been offered to idols (Ex. 34:15; Num. 25:1-2; Deut. 32:37-38).

Scripture declared food and drink offered to idols to be evil; therefore, Daniel refused to take hold of that which was not good.

Join Not with Evil

> Abstain from every form of evil (1 Thess. 5:22).

Paul prohibited involvement or perceived interest in anything that did not test out as good by the guidelines in Scripture. Like Daniel, we too should abstain from that which God declares evil.

> If anyone comes to you and does not bring this teaching, do not receive him into your house, and do not give him a greeting; for the one who gives him a greeting participates in his evil deeds (2 John 10-11).

A Final Tip

Your daily life and your church will continuously provide 'the workout facility' for your conditioning routine. Like physical exercise, spiritual exercise gives best results when it is a daily part of your schedule. The challenge is now yours to grow strong in the things of Christ.

Consecrate me now to Thy service, Lord,
By the pow'r of grace divine;
Let my soul look up with a steadfast hope,
And my will be lost in Thine.[1]

Fanny J. Crosby

22

SPIRITUAL SUBMISSION

During the time of the Czars in Russia, one of the Czars walked out of his palace into the garden where he found a sentry walking in front of a plot of weeds. He asked the soldier, 'Why are you here? What are you guarding?'

The sentry said, 'Sir, I do not know. I have been told that this is my post, and I am serving faithfully.'

The Czar thought that was strange, and so he went to the captain of the watch and asked him, 'What are they guarding?' The captain replied, 'Sir, I know not what they are guarding, but we have done it for years.'

That still seemed strange to the Czar, so he asked that the post be investigated. They delved back into history and discovered that 100 years before, Catherine the Great was given a rosebush as a gift. She planted it in that place and asked for a sentry so that the plot would not be overrun by people.

Six months later, the rosebush died, but the post continued on for over 99 years until somebody asked the strategic question: Why? What is the reason for it? For more than 99 years, a weed-infested bed that had no purpose to anyone was guarded by the best of the Russian Army!

I pray, when we stand before God in heaven, that kind of experience will not have been true in our lives. We don't want to have to answer God's question, 'Why did you do this?' with 'Sir, I do not know, but I have done it that way for years and did not think to ask why.' To avoid such a possibility, let's go back to Scripture and rediscover our original marching instructions.

The Principle of Paradox

While most people would question their paradoxical connection, freedom and submission belong together. Think about it! If I submit to the law of gravity, I will be able to live freely; but an attempt to free myself from it could lead to a moment of instant exhilaration and then sudden death.

Scripture abounds with kingdom paradoxes. Let me remind you of a few. 'But many who are first will be last; and the last, first' (Mark 10:31). 'Whoever wishes to become great among you shall be your servant' (Mark 10:43; see also Matt. 23:11). 'Whoever wishes to be first among you shall be slave of all' (Mark 10:44). 'Whoever then humbles himself as this child, he is the greatest in the kingdom of heaven' (Matt. 18:4). 'For the one who is least among all of you, this is the one who is great' (Luke 9:48).

Before we became Christians, we were dead in our sins and trespasses (Eph. 2:1) but after salvation, although now alive with Christ (Eph. 2:5), we are dead to sin (Rom. 6:11).

Somehow it's Christ who lives my Christian life (Gal. 2:20); yet at the same time I too live my Christian life.

The most important of these apparent contradictions, however, is the spiritual paradox between freedom and slavery.

> For when you were slaves of sin, you were free in regard to righteousness ... But now having been freed from sin and enslaved to God, you derive your benefit, resulting in sanctification, and the outcome, eternal life (Rom. 6:20,22).

We have been freed from the bondage of obedience to sin, and concurrently enslaved to God's righteous authority in our lives. This paradox is nowhere more evident than in the New Testament texts which refer to Christians as servants, slaves, or bondservants. True liberation comes from enslavement to God's kingdom. As such, we were freed (saved) to serve the Lord of lords and King of kings.

> For they themselves report about us what kind of a reception we had with you, and how you turned to God from idols to serve a living and true God (1 Thess. 1:9).

The corollary paradox simply put is this, 'We distinguish ourselves as servants by what we are becoming in character, and by constancy of mature, Christian lifestyle, rather than by the deeds we perform.'

This truth found its fullest expression in Paul's instructions to Timothy for the Ephesian church. We'll be looking at a passage which gives qualifications for those seeking a church office but which, in fact, sets the character standard for the paradoxical phenomenon of being a servant and thereby being free to honour Christ in the church.

A Preview
First Timothy 3:8-13 explains God's servantship pattern for the church, but its application really extends to all Christians. This is the pattern of living which God commends to us.

Deacons likewise must be men of dignity, not double-tongued or addicted to much wine or fond of sordid gain, but holding to the mystery of the faith with a clear conscience. These men must also first be tested; then let them serve as deacons if they are beyond reproach. Women must likewise be dignified, not malicious gossips, but temperate, faithful in all things. Deacons must be husbands of only one wife and good managers of their children and their own households. For those who have served well as deacons obtain for themselves a high standing and great confidence in the faith that is in Christ Jesus.

These six verses contain what God intends the church to know about a servant/slave of Jesus Christ. What makes this text so important? Why is this passage so different from any of the other New Testament texts on servanthood?

It is true that the New Testament has much to say about serving. There are four different words for serving—*doulos*, normally translated bondslave; I own nothing and I am owned by someone else (Rom. 6:16); *hupērētes*, an under rower, a third-level galley slave and rower (that's about as low as you can get; Paul calls himself that in 1 Cor. 4:1); *leitourgos*, which has to do with spiritual service to God; it might be used of one who served in a priestly function (Acts 13:2); and *diakonos*, just a simple table waiter, one who does the menial tasks of life (1 Tim. 3:8, 12).

Since these four words are used over 250 times in the New Testament, it is safe to say that servanthood is a major thread in the gospel. Jesus modelled servanthood for all. He said that He did not come to be served, but to serve (Matt. 20:28). He also said, 'The greatest among you shall be your servant' (Matt. 23:11).

All Christians, without exception, are gifted to serve. Peter said, 'As each one has received a special gift, employ it in serving one another' (1 Peter 4:10). Scripture reports that God gave apostles, prophets, evangelists, and pastor-teachers for the equipping of the saints—that is, you and me—for the work of service to the building up of the body of Christ (Eph. 4:11-12).

Scripture commands us all to serve. Paul wrote in Galatians 5:13, 'Through love serve one another.' All those who have been brought into the family of God by His grace are to be servants.

The Prototype

Let's look at the prototype for servantship in Acts 6. Here, the church was in its infant stage. Acts 5:42 reports that while the church was teaching and preaching Jesus as the Christ, and the disciples were increasing in number, even while there was great joy in the church, there was a complaint.

This clamour arose on the part of the Hellenistic Jews against the native Hebrews. Those who were Greek by birth, but Jewish by religious preference, said that their widows were being overlooked in the daily serving of food. It had nothing to do with doctrine per se, but it had everything to do with the essential, albeit mundane, task of who got fed and who got the most.

So the apostles summoned the congregation and said, 'It is not desirable for us to neglect the Word of God in order to serve tables' (6:2). They were setting priorities in the church.

I don't believe for a minute that they would have minded putting their hands in soapy dishwater to clean up the plates, or donning an apron and cooking food and serving it. But they knew that doing so would cause them to neglect the Word of God. If we have to choose between food for the body and food for the soul, food for the soul always comes first.

So they said, 'We have a problem. We have more ministry than we have men, so we have to expand the leadership corps to get the job done.'

They went to the congregation and said, in effect, 'We as apostles delegate to you the responsibility of selecting from among you seven men of good reputation, full of the Spirit and of wisdom, whom we may put in charge of this task' (6:3). They meant, 'We are going to need some more people to come alongside and help us, because it is important that we feed all the widows, and that there be no complaining in the church.'

The apostles concluded, 'We will devote ourselves to prayer and to the ministry of the Word of God' (6:4). The statement found approval with the whole congregation. They knew the apostles and they knew God worked through them, so they chose Stephen, a man full of faith and of the Holy Spirit, along with Philip, Prochorus, Nicanor, Timon, Parmenas, and Nicolas, a proselyte from Antioch.

Then these men came before the apostles, and after praying, the apostles laid their hands on them. I love what it says in verse 7. As people were in tune with the Spirit of God and were committed to the priorities of God, 'the Word of God kept on spreading.' The number of the disciples continued to increase greatly in Jerusalem, and a great many of the priests became obedient to the faith.

Early on, the apostles discovered that they couldn't do it all. So the initial leadership of the church consisted of apostles and those servants called out of the congregation and delegated by the apostles to serve with them. That is the prototype of the pattern the church later developed.

God's Pattern for Men

The model for servanthood in the church starts with a person displaying a habitual lifestyle of Christian maturity. The classic biblical passage that outlines these character qualities is 1 Timothy 3:8-13. This passage talks about those who would serve as deacons and deaconesses in the church, special servants who were recognized because they modelled mature Christianity. These standards then stand as a measure of maturity for all Christians.

Verses 8-9 and 12 contain seven qualities of a servant. Verse 11 gives four qualities which really summarize those previous seven. As you look at the pattern for servanthood, ask yourself, 'How am I doing?'

Servants must be marked by dignity. That doesn't mean that they dress up in a three-piece suit and wear wing-tips all the time. It doesn't mean they sleep in a tie. Dignity has nothing to do with their outward appearance. It has everything to do with how they are dressed on the inside. The *King James Version* calls them 'men who are grave.' That doesn't mean that servants walk around with a big frown on their faces, but that they are people who have respectability and dignity.

I like the *New International Version* translation. It calls them people 'worthy of respect because of who they are.' They are noble. They are honourable. They are responsible. That quality is for all Christians. It is the way mature, older men are to be and the way they are to teach younger men to be, according to Titus 2:2. To sum it up, it is *maturity that commands respect.*

Servants are not to be double-tongued. Literally, they are not to engage in double-talk, but to be consistent in their living.

That is why the *New International Version* translates this simply as 'sincere'. Such people say what they mean and mean what they say. They are not looking out for their own advantage but are asking, 'How can we advance the church?'

Servants are not 'addicted to much wine.' Servants are not only worthy of respect because of their maturity and their consistency, but also because they are being controlled by God's Spirit and not by some outside influence.

In our day and age, there are all sorts of control problems beyond alcohol, such as drugs, for instance. The point is that those who have the serious responsibility to serve need to be in total control of their senses. Their minds need to be clear. They need to be full of energy and totally controlled by God's Spirit. This is why it says in Ephesians 5:18, 'Do not get drunk with wine, for that is dissipation, but be filled with the Spirit'—not distilled spirits but the Divine Spirit.

Servants should not be 'fond of sordid gain.' In twentieth-century lingo, they are not to be money-grabbers, but are to be more interested in the things of God than the things of earth. That is why Jesus said, 'But seek first His kingdom and His righteousness; and all these things will be added to you' (Matt. 6:33).

By the way, this same quality applies for elders or pastors. In Titus 1:11 we read that overseers should not work in the church 'for the sake of sordid gain;' 'greedy for filthy lucre,' says the *King James Version*. Money is never to be the object of ministry. A person with an unhealthy outlook on money will either neglect the ministry or pervert it for money.

Servants are to hold to the mystery of the faith with a clear conscience. What does this mean? Very simply, that they are to have a firm grasp on, and an unfaltering allegiance to, the Word of God. They believe that it came from God through men and was written down accurately in the original autographs, and that all within it is truth to be obeyed.

What did Paul mean by 'the mystery of the faith'? He meant that we would not know the mystery unless God revealed it to us. That which has been revealed by God is to be grasped firmly by those who would serve. They are to be doctrinally sound and not confused. Also, they are to serve with a clear conscience.

They are to believe in their hearts what they have affirmed with their lips; and what they believe, they are to live out in the servantship of the church. There is to be no shallow veneer of outward spirituality without inward scriptural substance.

Later on Paul tells us something of what that mystery of the faith is, for he says 'by common confession, great is the mystery of godliness' (1 Tim. 3:16). This is talking about the incarnation of Christ.

> He who was revealed in the flesh,
> was vindicated in the Spirit,
> seen by angels,
> proclaimed among the nations,
> believed on in the world,
> taken up in glory.

Servants don't let go if things get a little rough. They will hold on even if it causes the loss of their lives. That is what a slave is to be, according to God's standard.

In Acts 6, when they selected those seven men full of wisdom and full of the Spirit of God, do you remember who was first on the list? It was Stephen. It says that Stephen went forth and ministered great signs, wonders, and miracles in the power of God. Later in Acts 7 he preached a fantastic message, so powerful that it convicted the Jews until they took up stones to kill him. He faithfully held to the faith until the end.

Servants are to be the husband of only one wife. It says the same thing in 1 Timothy 3:2 for elders. For all servants, God has the same standard for the home. You are to be a one-woman man. Women, you are to be a one-man woman. You are not to have eyes for anyone else, but are to be wholly devoted to your mate.

The greatest cure for immorality and adultery is, first, to be deeply in love with Jesus Christ; and, second, if you are married, to be deeply growing in love with your wife.

Servants will be good managers of their children and of their own households. They must have a demonstrated ability to be servants/leaders of their families.

Those are the seven qualities given for men: dignified, not double-tongued, not given to much wine, not fond of sordid gain, holding firmly to the mystery of the faith with a clear conscience, having eyes only for his wife, and maintaining a good reputation as a leader in the home.

When God said that servants must qualify in this pattern of life, He was talking about direction, about lifestyle, about consistency in one who would be a servant of Jesus Christ.

God's Pattern for Women

Paul went on to speak about women servants (1 Tim. 3:11). The text says, 'Women must likewise ...' If you have the *King James Version*, it says 'wives.' That is an unfortunate translation, because Paul was not talking about the wives of deacons, but about women qualified to serve in the church.

The little word 'likewise' is referring back to 3:8. Just as deacons are to be qualified, as elders are to be qualified, so are deaconesses. The Greek noun *diakonos* has a masculine gender, but that has nothing to do with the sex of a person. There is no female form of *diakonos*.

There are only four qualities listed in verse 11. But let me suggest that there is not a lesser standard for women than for men. Paul just decided to be a little briefer.

Women must likewise be dignified. He uses the same word that he did in verse 8. Women must also be worthy of respect because of their maturity.

Women are not to be malicious gossips. The Greek noun is *diabolos,* the word translated 'devil' in the New Testament. He says they are not to be devil-like in their conversation—slandering, starting rumours and with their tongues setting fires that righteousness can't put out. So the tongue of a deacon and the tongue of a deaconess are incredibly important.

Women are to be temperate. This word was used for elders in 1 Timothy 3:2, who were also to be temperate or sober, that is, moderate, balanced, and clear-headed; it would encompass all that he has already said about wine, money, and faith in relation to the deacon in vv. 8-9.

Women are to be 'faithful in all things'—faithful with regard to the Word and to their family relationships.

Examine Yourself

How do we recognize a mature servant? What is the ultimate test? Verse 10 says 'These men must also first be tested.' How does one become a deacon or deaconess? There is a twofold process: let them first be tested, and then let them serve.

To grow in the grace and knowledge of the Lord Jesus Christ is the mandate of every Christian. It is important that you cultivate the qualities of Christ in your life. Some of you feel that if you aspire to leadership, it is yours to go for. Others think you can sit back and fold your arms and say, 'Let somebody else do it, I'll be just a second-class citizen in the kingdom of God.'

We recognize in our assemblies those who are maturing to become like Christ. Let them cultivate the qualities of Christ, and then let them submit themselves for testing and affirmation.

It is rather like a take-home exam. There are no trick questions and no surprises. It is obvious what God's standards are, and you can take the test as many times as you want to. Look at what it says: ' These men must also first be tested and then let them serve as deacons if they are beyond reproach.' Paul's point is not perfection, but a consistent, obvious, outward pattern demonstrated over a long enough time. Then people can determine if spiritual maturity is real.

I'm amazed it doesn't talk about giftedness. It doesn't say, 'If you can speak well,' 'If you can teach kids well,' or 'If you can do this or that.' It talks about who you are, about godly character, about being beyond reproach.

This is where churches go astray. Most churches which are committed to the Word of God appoint someone to be a deacon or deaconess and believe that by the appointment he or she will become a servant. God's Word indicates that this is backward. They are first to be tested and only if they pass the test are they to be chosen. Never is the church to choose and then test. It is to test, pass, and choose. If you have been in many churches, you know that once a person gets a deacon or deaconess badge, they don't want to give it back!

Let me tell you what a deacon is in the church of God—just a simple table waiter. Deacons are not the people at the table eating the food and paying for it. They are just the waiters. They constantly go into the kitchen. It's tiring and laborious. There is nothing glorious about it from an earthly perspective. But deacons have a heart to serve God in the midst of God's people; they are godly in their character, and they live out Jesus Christ in their lives.

The Prize
We have seen the prototype, that is, how God began that pattern and worked it out until it became the normal pattern of the church. There is to be testing. And for those who submit themselves and pass the test, there is a real prize.

Maybe some of you are asking, 'Is it worth it? Should I go through all this? I'll make myself too vulnerable if I do that! What if I don't pass?'

There is no shame in not passing. It just means that you need to grow a little more. The only shame is if there is no desire in your heart or mind to grow in Christ. It is not a shame to be an infant, is it? We don't go around saying, 'Look at all those shameful kids in the nursery. They wear diapers and I am in big people's clothes!' There is no shame, as long as I am becoming what God wants me to be.

What is the prize? I love verse 13, for it says that those who have served well, rightly, correctly, acceptably, and commendably unto God as deacons and deaconesses, receive a high standing. I don't think it is talking so much about a high standing in the presence of God as a high standing in the assembly of God's people. We have submitted ourselves to an incredibly rigorous test and having made ourselves vulnerable, we have passed the test.

Jesus said that if you want to be high in the assembly, you go low. If you want to soar, you dive. If you want to be first, be last. If you want to be a lord, be a servant. If you want a high standing in the assembly, don't go up—go down. That is the paradox of submission.

There is a second prize that He gives, that is perhaps even greater. You will obtain a great confidence in the faith that is in Christ Jesus. Nothing is more exhilarating, nothing will better launch you to more growth than to learn that the Bible works, to experience the walk of faith, and to know that the greatest spiritual freedom comes to the most committed servants of Jesus Christ.

Like a mighty army
Moves the Church of God;
Brothers, we are treading
Where the saints have trod.
We are not divided,
All one body we —
One in hope and doctrine,
One in charity.[1]

Sabine Baring-Gould

23

SPIRITUAL SERVICE

Satan loves disturbance and disruption in the church. His strategy of 'divide and conquer' works as well today as it did when he first used it on Eve to separate her from God (Gen. 3:1-7).

On the other hand, biblical history sends signals about false unity which is just as dangerous as division and is to be avoided. Jehoshaphat paid the price of ecumenism with Ahab (2 Chron. 19: 1-2). Christ confronted the ecumenism of the churches in Pergamum (Rev. 2:14-15) and Thyatira (Rev. 2:20-24). Ephesus rejected the Nicolaitans and received the Saviour's 'Well done!' (Rev. 2:6). Jude encouraged Christians to contend earnestly for the faith (Jude 3).

Unity that pleases God and advances His kingdom will not be at the expense of His Word or character. Unity at the expense of God's Word or character is not true or holy. The oneness Jesus prayed for in John 17 will not compromise truth and righteousness.

Paul's charge to oneness (Phil. 2:1-4) did not countermand his high view of and total commitment to Scripture. The clarion call to one Lord, one faith, and one baptism sounded forth from the same apostle who wrote that all Scripture comes from God; it serves therefore as the measure by which true Christians can discern if a beckon to unity is really of God (Eph. 4:5; 2 Tim. 3:16-17).

The ideals of many ecumenists are peace and love. To interpret this approach accurately, believers must view these commendable qualities through the context of truth. True peace cannot be experienced apart from God's truth (Jer. 33:6; Zech. 8:19); neither can true love (Eph. 4:15; 1 John 3:18).

A major mark of spiritual maturity is to promote unity without comprising truth and righteousness or sacrificing relationships. The alert Christian will be watching for potential disruption and be prepared to deal with it biblically.

> Blessed are the peacemakers for they shall be called the sons of God (Matt. 5:9).

The Bible on Unity
The Jews sang Psalms 120-134 when ascending to Jerusalem for worship; one of them focused on unity.

> Behold, how good and how pleasant it is
> For brothers to dwell together in unity!
> It is like the precious oil upon the head,
> Coming down upon the beard,

Even Aaron's beard,
Coming down upon the edge of his robes.
It is like the dew of Hermon,
Coming down upon the mountains of Zion;
For there the LORD commanded the blessing —
life forever (Psalm 133).

To them, unity appeared as pure as the newly anointed priest (Ex. 29:7; Lev. 8:12). The life-giving water flowing off Mt. Hermon to bring precious water to the rest of Israel pictures the positive dynamic of peace among believers. When the Jew read this psalm, he would likely think of Abraham who said to Lot, 'Please let there be no strife between you and me . . . for we are brothers' (Gen. 13:8).

Our Lord Jesus Christ indicated His concern for unity among the disciples. During His last time with them before the cross, He prayed,

I am no longer in the world; and yet they themselves are in the world, and I come to You. Holy Father, keep them in Your name, the name which You have given Me, that they may be one, even as We are (John 17:11).

I do not ask on behalf of these alone, but for those also who believe in Me through their word; that they may all be one; even as You, Father, are in Me, and I in You, that they also may be in Us; so that the world may believe that You sent Me. The glory which You have given Me I have given to them; that they may be one, just as We are one (John 17:20-22).

His prayer focused on the disciples (17:11), but it also extended to all who would believe in the future—including us (17:20). Christ clearly wants believers to be promoting oneness among the family of God.

The answer to Christ's prayer stands out prominently in the Acts narrative about life in the new church at Jerusalem. On at least five occasions, their unity is highlighted.

One mind in prayer	Acts 1:14
One mind in worship	Acts 2:46
One accord in prayer	Acts 4:24
One heart and soul in sharing their possessions	Acts 4:32
One accord in Christ	Acts 5:12

Paul portrayed oneness in the body of Christ beautifully to the Romans:

> Now may the God who gives perseverance and encouragement grant
> you to be of the same mind with one another according to Christ Jesus;
> so that with one accord you may with one voice glorify the God and
> Father of our Lord Jesus Christ (15:5-6).

They were to share the same mind, accord, and voice, and in so doing
glorify God. On the other hand, he would quickly confront potential
or actual division (Rom. 16:17; 1 Cor. 3:3).

Later on, Paul wrote to the Philippians that conduct worthy of the
gospel involved unity of mind and spirit (1:27-30). He added that ultimate
joy could be experienced only by believers who found unity in the same
mind, the same love, the same spirit, and the same purpose (2:1-2).

The Key to Unity
When the King of kings abandoned His heavenly throne, he had to
borrow a place to be born, live in a home not His own, ask for a boat
to preach from, and be buried in a tomb on loan. Though He was
rich, for our sakes He became poor (2 Cor. 8:9). The Apostle Paul
explained such radical behaviour in Philippians 2:5-8:

> Have this attitude in yourselves which was also in Christ Jesus, who,
> although He existed in the form of God, did not regard equality with
> God a thing to be grasped, but emptied Himself, taking the form of a
> bondservant, and being made in the likeness of men. Being found in
> appearance as a man, He humbled Himself by becoming obedient to the
> point of death, even death on a cross.

With unmistakable authority, Paul commanded believers to think
about one another as Christ thought about them. This idea first entered
the discussion in verse 2: 'Make my joy complete by being of the
same mind . . . united in spirit, intent on one purpose.' With humility,
they were each to 'regard one another as more important than himself.'
These thoughts precede his explanation for Christ's departure from
the presence of God. Christ left heaven:

To seek and save the lost	Luke 19:10
To reveal God	John 1:18
To provide eternal life	John 10:10
To experience human life	Hebrews 2:17-18
To destroy the work of Satan	1 John 3:8

In Philippians 2:5ff, Paul added another reason—to model the mind-set that God demands Christians possess and practise.

Attitudes result in actions. Christ's attitude of sacrifice led Him first to make Himself as nothing; then the attitude of submission caused Him to humble Himself on the cross — all of this to voluntarily fulfill the role of a servant. He served God by accomplishing His salvation purposes (Isa. 42:1; 53:11), and He served us by giving Himself as a ransom for many (Matt. 20:28).

The great doctrine known as the 'kenosis' emerges from Paul's literary and theological masterpiece. Christ emptied Himself not of His deity, to be sure, but rather of the independent exercise of His divine attributes. He 'stripped Himself of the insignia of majesty' and then added to Himself both the internal and external reality of humanity. He took 'the form of a bondservant' and was 'made in the likeness of men.' Servant thinking drove Christ to appear in a body as the God-man—one person both fully God and fully human.

Paul later commented on the Incarnation, 'Beyond all question, the mystery of godliness is great' (1 Tim. 3:16, NIV). While all this rich theology and depth of thought eludes our full mental grasp, Paul simply believed that as Christ served so should Christians, for we are to think and then act like Christ (Phil. 2:3-4). D.L. Moody said, 'The measure of a man is not how many servants he has, but how many men he serves.'

The attitude of sacrifice says, 'I am willing, like Christ, to give up my present God-given privileges to follow God's servant-direction for my life.' The attitude of submission says, 'I am willing, like Christ, to obey God's servant-will for my life even when it involves humiliating life circumstances.' This kind of thinking drove Christ to act. Thus He:

1. Sacrificed His royal residency in heaven for the slums of this earth (John 6:51).
2. Sacrificed His intimate fellowship with holy God to talk among sinful people (John 1:1, 14).
3. Sacrificed comforts and pleasures for the pain of an imperfect world (Matt. 27:46).
4. Sacrificed His role as the sovereign of the universe to be a servant of man-kind (Matt. 20:28).
5. Lowered His quality of life from peace to war (Matt. 10:34; 1 John 3:8).

6. Lowered His environment from purity to sin-bearing (1 Peter 2:24).
7. Lowered His lifestyle from riches to poverty (2 Cor. 8:9).
8. Lowered His ministry from independence to dependence (John 5:30; 8:28; 12:49).
9. Lowered His experience from glory and life to shame and death (John 17:5).

Christian thinking should cause us to give, not get—to let go rather than to grasp selfishly. But the giving up is not without immediate blessing, for Jesus said, 'It is more blessed to give than to receive' (Acts 20:35). And don't forget our delayed reward. Concerning Jesus, Paul wrote:

> For this reason also God highly exalted Him, and bestowed on Him the name which is above every name, so that at the name of Jesus every knee will bow, of those who are in heaven, and on earth, and under the earth, and that every tongue will confess that Jesus Christ is Lord, to the glory of God the Father (Phil. 2:9-11).

God honoured Christ's servant role, and attitude of sacrifice and submission, with exaltation. In similar ways, God will exalt the Christian who consistently models Christ's behaviour.

> The greatest among you shall be your servant. Whoever exalts himself shall be humbled; and whoever humbles himself shall be exalted (Matt. 23:11-12).

> Therefore humble yourselves under the mighty hand of God, that He may exalt you at the proper time (1 Peter 5:6).

Our society believes that Christian thinking—servanthood, humility, and submissive obedience—leads to earthly insignificance. But for Jesus and those who follow Him, following the mind of Christ results in eternal impact. So, 'Have this attitude in yourselves which was also in Christ Jesus' (Phil. 2:5). As Christ responded to us, Christians are to act toward one another. But, what does this involve?

Promoting Unity

> For just as we have many members in one body and all the members do not have the same function, so we, who are many, are one body in Christ, and individually members of one another (Rom. 12:4-5).

For the body is not one member, but many (1 Cor. 12:14).

First, the *principle*. None of us can exist fruitfully and peacefully by ourselves. We belong to a spiritual body of many parts which God intended to work together. Just as an athletic team must work in unison, the parts of a jet airplane operate as one, or the voices of a choir blend in harmony, so the members of Christ's body need to each contribute their part and receive the needed contribution of others.

Oftentimes we think of *functional* unity in terms of each person exercising a spiritual gift (1 Cor. 12: 4-11). However, a more foundational unity is called for by the 'body principle.' We can call it *relational* unity. It's built around the myriad of New Testament exhortations regarding 'one another.'

Second, the *practice*. Family behaviour in the body of Christ all starts with 'Love one another.' Our Lord told the disciples:

By this all men will know that you are My disciples, if you have love for one another (John 13:35).

The epistles refer to this overarching principle at least ten times (Rom. 13:8; 1 Thess. 3:12; 4:9; 2 Thess. 1:3; 1 Peter 1:22; 1 John 3:11,23; 4:7, 11; 2 John 5).

From this broad statement, the epistles then move to explain the various features of unity which should be active in the church. They are numerous and in general are self-explanatory. So let me list them for you and ask that you slow down here to look up all the passages.

Be devoted	Romans 12:10
Honour by giving preference	Romans 12:10
Be of the same mind	Romans 12:16; 15:5
Build up	Romans 14:19; 1 Thessalonians 5:11
Be at peace	Romans 14:19
Receive/accept	Romans 15:7
Admonish/comfort	Romans 15:14; 1 Thessalonians 4:18; 5:11
Greet	Romans 16:16; 1 Corinthians 16:20; 2 Corinthians 13:12; 1 Peter 5:14
Care	1 Corinthians 12:25

Serve	Galatians 5:13
Bear burdens	Galatians 6:2
Forbear, be patient	Ephesians 4:2; Colossians 3:13
Be kind	Ephesians 4:32
Submit	Ephesians 5:21
Esteem highly	Philippians 2:3
Forgive	Colossians 3:13
Seek the good	1 Thessalonians 5:15
Stimulate	Hebrews 10:24
Confess sins	James 5:16
Pray for	James 5:16
Be hospitable	1 Peter 4:9
Be humble	1 Peter 5:5
Fellowship in the light	1 John 1:7

While total unity is *doctrinal, functional*, and *relational*, when problems exist, we look first at the relational element.

Preventing Disruption

Not only are we to add positive responses to our lifestyle, but we need to eliminate or avoid other responses which Scripture prohibits. Take a careful look at the 'do not' side of the 'one anothers.'

Owe anything but love	Romans 13:8
Judge	Romans 14:13
Defraud/deprive in marriage	1 Corinthians 7:5
Devour/consume	Galatians 5:15
Provoke/challenge	Galatians 5:26
Envy	Galatians 5:26
Lie	Colossians 3:9
Hate	Titus 3:3
Speak against/complain	James 4:11; 5:9

Whether it be a marriage, a family, or the body of Christ, when these mature behaviour patterns consistently colour life, great harmony and peace will be the experience.

Live in Peace

With the Father called 'the God of peace' (2 Cor. 13:11), the Son entitled 'the Prince of peace' (Isa. 9:6), and the Spirit producing 'the fruit of peace' in believers (Gal. 5:22), it's no wonder then that Paul writes several exhortations to unity.

> If possible, so far as it depends on you, be at peace with all men (Rom. 12:18).

> Live in peace with one another (1 Thess. 5:13b).

When peace like a river attendeth my way,
When sorrows like sea billows roll;
Whatever my lot, Thou has taught me to say,
It is well, it is well with my soul.[1]

Horatio Spafford

24

MEASURING SPIRITUALITY

Some people calculate their godliness by how well they keep a man-made list of do's and don'ts. That is *legalism.* Those at the other end of the scale determine spirituality by how close they can get to the edge and still not seem to be involved in sin. That is *licence.*

Neither way takes God's Word or God's holiness seriously. Both appeal to man's approval or disapproval rather than to God's.

Regardless of what any person thinks, including ourselves, God will one day render His divine judgment about our spirituality. His critique will count for eternity.

> Therefore we also have as our ambition, whether at home or absent, to be pleasing to Him. For we must all appear before the judgment seat of Christ, so that each one may be recompensed for his deeds in the body, according to what he has done, whether good or bad (2 Cor. 5:9-10).

Now God has not left us in the dark as to what evidences true spirituality or what we should strive for in our Christian life. Scripture repeatedly outlines the elements of character and lifestyle that God highly values. Paul's words to the Roman Christians lay a foundation.

> Therefore do not let what is for you a good thing be spoken of as evil; for the kingdom of God is not eating and drinking, but righteousness and peace and joy in the Holy Spirit. For he who in this way serves Christ is acceptable to God and approved by men (Rom. 14:16-18).

This shows that God is not so much interested in the physical side of life as He is in the spiritual side. Other portions of Scripture more explicitly outline God's spiritual goals for us.

The Call to Measure Our Spirituality

Paul had been arrogantly challenged by the Corinthians to check his own life for proof of Christ's reality (2 Cor. 13:2-3). He countered with this rebuke:

> Test yourselves to see if you are in the faith; examine yourselves! Or do you not recognize this about yourselves, that Jesus Christ is in you—unless indeed you fail the test? (2 Cor. 13:5).

That raises the question, 'What should they have examined and looked for?' Maybe they thought back to Micah 6:8.

> He has told you, O man, what is good; And what does the Lord require of you but to do justice, to love kindness, and to walk humbly with your God?

But that's not specific enough. The Apostle John wrote in more detail.

> These things I have written to you who believe in the name of the Son of God, so that you may know that you have eternal life (1 John 5:13).

By what characteristics would his readers know that they possessed eternal life? John listed three broad criteria. The entire book is based on these tests. Here is a brief summary.

1. The Test of Obedience (1:5-2:6; 2:29-3:10): 'By this we know that we have come to know Him, if we keep His commandments' (1 John 2:3).

2. The Test of Love (2:7-11; 3:11-24; 4:7-5:5): 'We know that we have passed out of death into life, because we love the brethren. He who does not love abides in death' (1 John 3:14).

3. The Test of Truth about Jesus Christ (2:18-28; 4:1-6; 5:6-12): 'We are from God; he who knows God listens to us; he who is not from God does not listen to us. By this we know the spirit of truth and the spirit of error' (1 John 4:6).

Standards of Spirituality

While these statements are helpful for most of us, they still do not give enough details. So we ask for more.

I want to introduce the chief passages in Scripture which provide additional details. In some sense, they serve as spiritual dimensions which we need to measure daily. They involve both positive and negative qualities.

1. According to Moses. For most, this would be the first standard. Just remember that since it was first written, the heart or spirit of the fourth commandment, about the Sabbath day, has moved from the seventh day to the first day of the week in celebration of Christ's resurrection (1 Cor. 16:1-2; Col. 2:16; Rev. 1:10).

> Then God spoke all these words, saying, 'I am the LORD your God, who brought you out of the land of Egypt, out of the house of slavery.
> 1. You shall have no other gods before Me.
> 2. You shall not make for yourself an idol, or any likeness of what is in heaven above or on the earth beneath or in the water under the earth. You shall not worship them or serve them . . .

3. You shall not take the name of the LORD your God in vain, for the Lord will not leave him unpunished who takes His name in vain.

4. Remember the Sabbath day, to keep it holy. Six days you shall labor and do all your work, but the seventh day is a Sabbath of the Lord your God . . .

5. Honor your father and your mother, that your days may be prolonged in the land which the Lord your God gives you.

6. You shall not murder.

7. You shall not commit adultery.

8. You shall not steal.

9. You shall not bear false witness against your neighbor.

10. You shall not covet your neighbor's house; you shall not covet your neighbor's wife or his male servant or his female servant or his ox or his donkey or anything that belongs to your neighbor (Ex. 20:1-17).

2. According to Jesus

Blessed are the poor in spirit, for theirs is the kingdom of heaven.

Blessed are those who mourn, for they shall be comforted.

Blessed are the gentle, for they shall inherit the earth.

Blessed are those who hunger and thirst for righteousness, for they shall be satisfied.

Blessed are the merciful, for they shall receive mercy.

Blessed are the pure in heart, for they shall see God.

Blessed are the peacemakers, for they shall be called the sons of God.

Blessed are those who have been persecuted for the sake of righteousness, for theirs is the kingdom of heaven.

Blessed are you when people insult you and persecute you, and falsely say all kinds of evil against you because of Me.

Rejoice and be glad, for your reward in heaven is great; for in the same way they persecuted the prophets who were before you.

Matthew 5:3-12

3. According to Paul

The fruit of the Spirit is love, joy, peace, patience, kindness, goodness, faithfulness, gentleness, self-control; against such things there is no law (Gal. 5:22-23).

Love is patient, love is kind, and is not jealous; love does not brag and is not arrogant, does not act unbecomingly; it does not seek its own, is not provoked, does not take into account a wrong suffered, does not rejoice in unrighteousness, but rejoices with the truth; bears all things, believes all things, hopes all things, endures all things (1 Cor. 13:4-7).

4. According to Peter.

Applying all diligence, in your faith supply moral excellence, and in your moral excellence, knowledge; and in your knowledge, self-control, and in your self-control, perseverance, and in your perseverance, godliness; and in your godliness, brotherly kindness, and in your brotherly kindness, love. For if these qualities are yours and are increasing, they render you neither useless nor unfruitful in the true knowledge of our Lord Jesus Christ (2 Peter 1:5-8).

Remember this! Each writer exhorted the believers to live with greater consistency each day and to make these qualities their pattern of living. The Bible does not teach 'perfectionism' as a goal or hope in this life. Never does Scripture demand or expect a continuous, sinless experience. That's why God has made provision for believers to be cleansed of the immediate filth of sin (James 5:16; 1 John 2:1-2).

What is your response? If you say, 'Forget it! These are irrelevant, plus they are too difficult. No one can do that!' you need to examine yourself, as Paul told the Corinthians. People who want a form of godliness without the Spirit's power to transform their lives have not really embraced Christ (2 Tim. 3:2-5). They are shallow soil or the weed-infested soil, as in Jesus' parable of the four soils (Matt. 13:5-7, 20-22).

You might be saying, 'That's the deep desire of my heart! I know that's right and I want to make godliness a greater part of my life and a more consistent pattern of my Christian walk.' That is the expected response of a true believer and one in whom the Spirit lives and works.

On the other hand, we should be so consumed by what we have just read that not one of us should ask, 'Since I'm doing so well, is there more?' But for the sake of being true to Scripture, let me show you the ultimate. Without this final quality, our quest for godliness would remain incomplete.

The Final Standard — Contentment

Phillip Keller, keenly aware of what true spirituality involves, notes, 'Contentment should be the hallmark of the man or woman who has put his or her affairs in the hands of God.'[2]

Paul outlines four elements which build spiritual contentment in the believer, as a conclusion to his letter to the Philippians. In an era of materialistic selfishness, nothing could be more appropriate for a Christian to understand and implement. It crowns the head of spiritual maturity.

Element One—Confidence in God's Power.

> But I rejoiced in the Lord greatly, that now at last you have revived your concern for me; indeed, you were concerned before, but you lacked opportunity. Not that I speak from want; for I have learned to be content in whatever circumstances I am. I know how to get along with humble means, and I also know how to live in prosperity; in any and every circumstance I have learned the secret of being filled and going hungry, both of having abundance and suffering need. I can do all things through Him who strengthens me (Philip. 4:10-13).

Paul spoke from the crucible of his own life, outlining the basic truths which flow out of a firm belief in God's sovereign and all-powerful control of this world and our lives.

Contentment looks first to God (4:10).
Contentment can be learned (4:11-12).
Contentment does not depend on life circumstances (4:11-12).
Contentment is not based on self-sufficiency (4:13).
Contentment finds its source in Christ's strength (4:13).

Element Two—Confidence in God's Providence

> Nevertheless, you have done well to share with me in my affliction . . . Not that I seek the gift itself, but I seek for the profit which increases to your account. But I have received everything in full, and have an abundance; I am amply supplied, having received from Epaphroditus what you have sent, a fragrant aroma, an acceptable sacrifice, well-pleasing to God (Phil. 4:14-18).

Paul didn't encourage the Philippians to look for the miraculous, such as God's care for the Israelites in the wilderness (Deut. 8:3-4). Rather, he explained how God had provided for him through their gifts.

Element Three—Confidence in God's Promises.

> And my God will supply all your needs according to His riches in glory in Christ Jesus (Phil. 4:19).

This certainly stands as one of the great promises of Scripture. Christians in other times and different places have appreciated and experienced it even more vividly than we do today. Paul encouraged them that God would meet their needs, just as they had met his. It is a companion to other great texts on God's promises such as,

> Blessed be the LORD, who has given rest to His people Israel, according to all that He promised; not one word has failed of all His good promise, which He promised through Moses His servant (1 Kings 8:56).

> For as many as are the promises of God, in Him they are yes; therefore also through Him is our Amen to the glory of God through us (2 Cor. 1:20).

> For by these He has granted to us His precious and magnificent promises, so that by them you may become partakers of the divine nature, having escaped the corruption that is in the world by lust (2 Peter 1:4).

Element Four—Confidence in God's Eternal Purposes.

> Now to our God and Father be the glory forever and ever. Amen (Phil. 4:20).

> So David blessed the Lord in the sight of all the assembly; and David said, 'Blessed are You, O LORD God of Israel our father, forever and ever. Yours, O LORD, is the greatness and the power and the glory and the victory and the majesty, indeed everything that is in the heavens and the earth; Yours is the dominion, O LORD, and You exalt Yourself as head over all. Both riches and honor come from You, and You rule over all, and in Your hand is power and might; and it lies in Your hand to make great, and to strengthen everyone. Now therefore, our God, we thank You, and praise Your glorious name' (1 Chr. 29:10-13).

Contentment then is a satisfied spiritual view of life that yields all personal rights to the higher purposes of God's will and glory. It also has the ultimate confidence in God to sustain and strengthen, regardless of what life brings. It's not a stoic self-suffering, but is a spiritual God-dependency.

Now why is this the final standard? Listen to Paul!

But godliness actually is a means of great gain, when accompanied by contentment. For we have brought nothing into the world, so we cannot take anything out of it either. If we have food and covering, with these we shall be content (1 Tim. 6:6-8).

Unless contentment completes our godliness, then we fall short of the spiritual goal. If we want to be godly, then we must also be confident that He will take care of us. With that comes contentment.

Pressing On

In this chapter I have given you some of the key Scriptures by which we can measure our spirituality as God measures it. No one will ever fully become all that the New Testament exhorts us to be. Yet, we are to continue toward full maturity. Paul puts it all in proper perspective for the Philippians. So, we let him have the last word in our discussion.

Not that I have already obtained it, or have already become perfect, but I press on so that I may lay hold of that for which also I was laid hold of by Christ Jesus. Brethren, I do not regard myself as having laid hold of it yet; but one thing I do: forgetting what lies behind and reaching forward to what lies ahead, I press on toward the goal for the prize of the upward call of God in Christ Jesus. Let us therefore, as many as are perfect, have this attitude; and if in anything you have a different attitude, God will reveal that also to you; however, let us keep living by that same standard to which we have attained (Phil. 3:12-16).

Holy, holy, holy!
Lord God Almighty!
Early in the morning
Our song shall rise to Thee;
Holy, holy, holy!
Merciful and mighty!
God in three Persons,
Blessed Trinity![1]

Reginald Heber

25

PRACTICING SPIRITUALITY

One of our fine students at The Master's Seminary sent me this touching letter.

Dear Dr. Mayhue,

The past six months of my life have been a time of great learning for me. God used many circumstances in my life to show me why I need to depend on Him much more than I do. However, in the midst of the learning, I found myself lacking motivation for the task (preparation in seminary) God has called me to. It seemed as if the harder I tried to 'get back on track,' the worse things became. I would ask myself what happened to the desire I once had; how could I not do my best, when men's lives depend on it?

Over the holidays, I had a chance to reflect on some of these events; and God made clear to me the reason behind the struggles I faced. Simply put, I had misplaced my priorities. By that I mean I had fallen into the tragedy of placing seminary and the ministry before communing with our Divine Father. Yes, I still spent time with God; however, the time was not the consecrated communion I have enjoyed in the past.

What a fool I was to allow such a thing to happen. However, our gracious Father has shown to me the steps I need to take to prevent it from happening again. I believe seminary is helpful; however, nothing can ever better prepare a man for serving the King than consistent and consecrated communion before His throne. Ministry is the reason for our pilgrimage on earth, but ministry placed before our 'First Love' is vain.[2]

He poignantly expressed the regret that the spiritual character being formed *in* him had not manifested itself fully by emerging *out* of him in his spiritual conduct and communion with God. I suspect that most of us have needed to write more than one letter like this in our Christian life.

If he had asked, 'How can I tell when I'm back on track?' I would have directed his thoughts to Psalm 15. We need to look there too.

1   O LORD, who may abide in Your tent?
    Who may dwell on Your holy hill?
2   He who walks with integrity, and works righteousness,
    And speaks truth in his heart.
3   He does not slander with his tongue,

Nor does evil to his neighbor,
Nor takes up a reproach against his friend;

4   In whose eyes a reprobate is despised,
But who honors those who fear the LORD;
He swears to his own hurt and does not change;

5   He does not put out his money at interest,
Nor does he take a bribe against the innocent.
He who does these things will never be shaken.

Psalm 15 does not speak to the fact of salvation but, rather, to the fruit of redemption. It spells out the unchanging desire and standard of God for His redeemed children to be transformed into His never-changing character which is summed up in *holiness*.

When the character of God really begins to shape a person's life, what does it look like? The psalmist lays out three major characteristics to authenticate genuine, growing, godly character and conduct in the life of a true believer.

The Right Concern

O LORD, who may abide in Your tent? Who may dwell on Your holy hill? (Ps. 15:1).

To the psalmist and prophets in the tenth century B.C., these questions would produce immediate thoughts of the tabernacle on Mt. Zion where the Israelites worshipped. The two terms 'tent' and 'holy hill' signified God's presence over the ark of the covenant (Ex. 25:22). Located in the holy of holies, the ark of the covenant was where the Shekinah glory of God dwelt. For every true worshipper of God, this represented the most sacred spot on earth. The psalmist begins with this inquiry, 'Who is qualified to stand in the presence of the Lord?'

The tent of meeting or tabernacle is where God's people met God (Ex. 25). It accompanied the Jews as they wandered in the wilderness and went to battle with them when Joshua captured the Promised Land (Josh. 6:8). Hundreds of years later it found its rightful place in Jerusalem under King David's leadership (2 Sam. 5-6).

God's 'tent' rested on a holy hill where a holy God was to be worshipped by a holy people. This 'hill' finds prominent mention in the Psalms (2:6; 3:4; 24:3; 43:3-4; 74:2; 99:9).

When Moses stood in the presence of God in the wilderness, the Lord told him, 'Remove your sandals from your feet, for the place on which you are standing is holy ground' (Ex. 3:5). When faced with God's holiness, the Prophet Isaiah cried out, 'Woe is me, for I am ruined! Because I am a man of unclean lips, and I live among a people of unclean lips; for my eyes have seen the King, the LORD of hosts' (Isa. 6:5). Both of these men experienced the essence of the question voiced in Psalm 15:1, and they understood God's uncompromising demand for holy behaviour.

> As obedient children, do not be conformed to the former lusts which were yours in your ignorance, but like the Holy One who called you, be holy yourselves also in all your behavior; because it is written, 'You shall be holy, for I am holy' (1 Peter 1:14-16).

This thought of standing or dwelling in the presence of God is one of the great unifying themes of Scripture. This marks the beginning point for the psalmist—seeking God on His terms, not ours. Whatever qualifies a person to abide in God's sacred tabernacle and to dwell on His holy hill must be decided by God, not by us. So the psalmist asks the appropriate question of the right Person when he begins, 'O Lord . . .'

The Right Conduct

Some have asked, 'Does Psalm 15 teach salvation by works?' Let me answer emphatically, 'No!' This psalm beautifully portrays the fruit of sanctification in the life of one who is already saved. It pictures a person who submits to God's instructions on holiness and begins to exhibit the character qualities of God in his own personal right.

There are at least three good reasons to strongly insist that this psalm pictures the life of an authentic believer. First, the Old Testament teaches that salvation is by grace without human works (Joel 2:32; see Rom. 10:13). Second, the New Testament teaches identically the same truth (Eph. 2:8-10; Titus 3:5-7). Third, Psalms 13 and 14 teach salvation by God's doing, not by man's works.

The gracious, overarching answer to the question of Psalm 15:1 is found in the following verse.

> *He who walks with integrity, and works righteousness, and speaks truth in his heart (Ps. 15:2).*

The psalmist pinpoints a person's walk, works, and words as the key elements. They will be seen in the integrity of one's life, the

righteousness of one's labour, and the truthfulness of one's speech.
Psalm 24:4 develops the same theme in different phrasing.

Psalm 15:2	*Psalm 24:4*
walks with integrity	pure heart
works righteousness	clean hands
speaks truth	no falsehood

'How does this flesh out in everyday life?' As if anticipating our question, the psalmist continues and outlines the details in these three arenas of life.

The Interpersonal Arena. *'He does not slander with his tongue.'* (15:3a). Our dealings with people are not to be characterized by slander or backbiting (Gal. 5:15), for a slanderer will not see the salvation of God (Ps. 50:20-23). We should never bless God and turn right round and curse men (James 3:9-10). James states strongly, 'My brethren, these things ought not to be this way.'

The Hebrew word for 'slander' literally means 'to walk about.' We are not to have walking tongues that bear slanderous tales about other people. This instruction is not unique to Psalm 15.

> Let no unwholesome word proceed from your mouth, but only such a word as is good for edification according to the need of the moment, that it will give grace to those who hear (Eph. 4:29).

> If anyone thinks himself to be religious, and yet does not bridle his tongue but deceives his own heart, this man's religion is worthless (Jas. 1:26).

In our conversation, we are to be like the Lord Jesus Christ of whom it is written, 'And all were speaking well of Him, and wondering at the gracious words which were falling from His lips' (Luke 4:22).

'Nor does evil to his neighbor' (15:3b). Unlike what Ahab did to Naboth (1 Kings 21), or David to Uriah (2 Sam. 11), or Haman to Mordecai (Esther 2-7), we are to do good to our neighbour.

But who is our neighbour? Jesus defined neighbour as anyone in the normal sphere of our life who is in need of mercy (Luke 10:25-37). So we are not surprised to read repeatedly in Scripture, 'Love your neighbor as yourself' (Lev. 19:18; Matt. 22:39; Rom. 13:9-10; Gal. 5:14).

The psalmist warns, 'Whoever secretly slanders his neighbor, him will I destroy' (Ps. 101:5). 'Do not devise harm against your neighbor,' warns the writer of Proverbs (3:29). We are to be like Jesus who looked at people with compassion (Matt. 9:36).

'Nor takes up a reproach against his friend' (15:3c). The psalmist has moved from people in general to a neighbour, and now to a close, intimate acquaintance. Proverbs variously describes a 'friend' as one who loves at all times (17:17); who sticks closer than a brother (18:24); and whose wounds are faithfully designed to help, not destroy (27:6). A friend is one who walks into your life when the others walk out.

The Hebrew word for 'reproach' means 'to scorn or treat with contempt.' Rather, we are to treat our friends with respect and a desire to build up, not to tear down. If we are faithful to our friendships, then we will be like our Lord who befriended the sinners and publicans for whose sins He would die (Matt. 11:19), who befriended Peter who denied Him three times (John 21:15-23), and who befriended Thomas even though he doubted (John 20:26-29).

The Spiritual Arena. *'In whose eyes a reprobate is despised'* (15:4a). At first glance this may sound as if it contradicts the love of God and seem overly harsh; yet, Jesus condemned the Pharisees (Matt. 23) and cleansed the temple twice (Matt. 21; John 2). So, there is a right kind of despising.

A 'reprobate' is one who has rejected God and the things of God as utterly worthless. Therefore, we who value God most highly are to reject the reprobate's conclusions about God as worthless and untrue, and the reprobate's lifestyle as destructive and without value. In terms of our behaviour toward them, listen to another Psalm.

> How blessed is the man who does not walk
> in the counsel of the wicked,
> Nor stand in the path of sinners,
> Nor sit in the seat of scoffers!
> But his delight is in the law of the LORD,
> And in His law he meditates day and night.
>
> Psalm 1:1-2

Does this mean we are not to evangelize the wicked? No—quite the opposite! We are to tell them about their sins and our holy Saviour, but we are not to walk in their ungodly footsteps. Jesus best exemplifies this in Mark 2:15-17. After being criticized by the religious establishment for socializing with publicans and sinners, He responded, 'I did not come to call the righteous, but sinners.'

'But who honours those who fear the LORD' (15:4b). We are to love the brethren (Heb. 13:1). Those who fear the Lord share the same concern for standing in the presence of God because they have confessed and repented of their sin, and then have embraced the Lord Jesus Christ in His death, burial, and resurrection. Thus they now walk in His way (Ps. 128:1) and keep His commandments (Ecc. 12:13). Fearing God has become a lifestyle for them (Prov. 23:17; Col. 3:22; 1 Peter 2:17).

We are to treat our brothers and sisters (James 2:15) in the Lord with honour and love (John 1:12; Rom. 8:14, 16). We share the same faith (Rom. 8:15); we are fellow-heirs (Rom. 8:17); we all have one Father (Eph. 4:6); we have all been adopted (Eph. 1:5); we were all unworthy (Rom. 3:23); we were all saved the same way (Eph. 2:8-10); and we all were saved for the same ultimate purpose (1 Cor. 10:31; Eph. 2:10).

Jesus manifested this quality of honouring others. A striking example was when He commended the widow for giving her two mites (Luke 21:1-4). And John reports, 'Jesus knowing that His hour had come . . . having loved His own who were in the world, He loved them to the end' (John 13:1).

The Community Arena. The psalmist has looked at the key lifestyle indicators that evidence an inward quest for holiness. They lie in the realm of interpersonal relationships plus spiritual relationships and, finally, in community relationships.

'He swears to his own hurt, and does not change' (15:4c). Honesty marks the man of holiness who purposes never to be guilty of perjury in the courtroom of God. He knows that the Lord hates a lying tongue (Prov. 6:17). He commits himself to total truth and honesty, even when he will lose or be hurt by it.

Scripture clearly teaches the premium that God places on truth. We need to put deceiving lips away (Prov. 4:24); if we do not, our lies will be punished (Prov. 19:5, 9).

Jesus described Himself as 'the truth' (John 14:6). When the soldiers maliciously approached Him in Gethsemane, he did not hedge, but rather forthrightly acknowledged that He was Jesus of Nazareth (John 18:1-9). When being tried before Pilate and Herod, instead of pleading the Fifth Amendment or using some other legal ploy to avoid the truth, He answered directly, and they crucified Him for it.

The writer of Proverbs gives us a great little prayer which I retreat to often, 'Keep deception and lies far from me' (30:8).

'He does not put out his money at interest' (15:5a). This is not necessarily an anti-banking verse. Jesus affirmed normal business dealings involving interest (Matt. 25:14-30; Luke 7:40-43). However, it is a strong condemnation of charging usurious interest rates that take advantage of the poor.

In ancient times, the rich really did get richer and the poor much poorer. Exorbitant interest rates of 33 percent or even 50 percent were not uncommon. In some cases, double interest was charged whereby people had to pay interest on the original interest. These gouging rates would be charged for the barest necessities of life such as food, clothing, and shelter.

The Old Testament clearly prohibited the practice of charging interest to fellow Jews (Ex. 22:25-27; Lev. 25:35-38; Deut. 23:19-20). The basic meaning of the Hebrew word translated 'at interest' is 'to bite with the intention of hurting.' In effect, the psalmist says, 'Those of you who are rich, because you have more than the basics, do not grow more prosperous by making money at the expense of those who do not even have enough to survive.' Of our Lord it is written:

> For you know the grace of our Lord Jesus Christ, that though He was rich, yet for your sake He became poor, so that you through His poverty might become rich (2 Cor. 8:9).

'He does not take a bribe against the innocent' (15:5b). Men who can be bribed to condemn the innocent are labelled 'worthless' in Scripture (1 Kings 21:10, 13). Those who bribe deserve to be called 'evil' (1 Kings 21:17-26). The ultimate bribe was paid to Judas, the son of perdition, who betrayed the Lord Jesus Christ (Matt. 26:14-16; 27:1-5).

Jesus exemplified this prohibition in His life. Satan attempted to bribe Him with the promise of bypassing the cross and immediately ruling the world, if He would just denounce God the Father and worship Satan (Matt. 4:8-9). With this curt reply, 'Go, Satan!' (4:10), Jesus put Satan on notice that He could not be bought.

The Right Confidence

'He who does these things will never be shaken' (15:5c). No verse in Scripture states more clearly how one can personally be assured of the genuineness of salvation.

One whose salvation is real has every right to be continually confident about an abiding relationship with God and to feel certain that he qualifies to abide in God's tabernacle and stand on the Lord's holy hill (15:1). The psalms elsewhere echo this same blessed truth.

> I have set the LORD continually before me;
> Because He is at my right hand, I will not be shaken (Psalm 16:8).

> For the king trusts in the LORD,
> And through the lovingkindness of the Most High
> he will not be shaken (Psalm 21:7).

> He only is my rock and my salvation,
> My stronghold; I shall not be greatly shaken (Psalm 62:2).

The outward marks of spiritual maturity which validate the inner character of holiness that comes through God's regenerating work in the life of a repentant sinner include:

1. A concern to seek God's holiness.
2. A conduct submitted to God's standards of holiness.
3. A confidence in the assurance of salvation brought about by habitually living out God's holiness.

O hope of every contrite heart,
O joy of all the meek,
To those who fall, how kind Thou art!
How good to those who seek![1]

Bernard of Clairvaux

26

RESTORING SPIRITUALITY

Life boils down to one word—WARFARE. Life consists of a daily struggle to meet deadlines, satisfy people, balance the checkbook, mow the lawn, clean the house, avoid mistakes, fight the freeway, earn passing grades, watch the waistline, or just simply keep our heads above water.

Our most formidable foe, Satan, attacks through constant confrontation with sin. The conflict rages without ceasing. For example, David, the God-anointed king of Israel, fought a battle one day with this arch-enemy and lost. In Psalm 51 we read how he succumbed to the opposition but, nevertheless, won the war. From him we can learn how to overcome sin's damaging blow when it throws an uppercut to the chin of a true believer.

David doesn't stand alone, either. Peter denied Christ three times (Matt. 26:69-75). Moses once failed to treat God in a holy manner (Deut. 32:51). John Mark proved unfaithful in his first major ministry assignment (Acts 13:13; 15:38). The church at Ephesus left its first love (Rev. 2:4). Demas deserted Paul (2 Tim. 4:10). Israel lost favour with God (Rom. 11:11-24). Achan disobeyed (Josh. 7:22-26). Nadab and Abihu profaned the tabernacle service (Lev. 10:1-2). Ananias and Sapphira lied to God (Acts 5:1-11). Uzziah made an unauthorized sacrifice (2 Chron. 26:16-21). Uzzah touched the ark (2 Sam. 6:6-7).

Some died immediately for their transgressions; others lived a while before God's judgment. Still others lived a full life by God's mercy. But none chronicled the details of their sin and God's dealing with them as David did after his transgression with Bathsheba (2 Sam. 11-12). David's diary presents his spiritual spill and subsequent recovery in order to assist others who have gravely sinned but whom God has sovereignly and mercifully let live. Psalm 51 answers the question, 'What if this happens to me?'

David's Situation

David was not a 'one-woman man'; 2 Samuel 3:1-5 names six of his wives. Because Jerusalem lived in peace and the tabernacle resided on God's mountain, David's attentions turned from God's agenda to more women. While his troops were out securing the kingdom, their king stayed at home and attempted to conquer a woman's heart (2 Sam. 11:1-5).

In so doing, he directly violated the last five of the Ten Commandments—four of the five demanding the death penalty (Ex.

20:13-17). David murdered, committed adultery, stole Bathsheba's heart from her husband, gave false witness against Uriah, and coveted his neighbour's wife.

In fact, David also dishonoured his parents, profaned the Sabbath with unholy worship, took God's sacred name in vain, made women his idol, and disobediently viewed them as idolatrous objects of worship. David represents the classic case of breaking the law in one point and thus violating it in all points (James 2:10). No wonder the divine commentary on David's escapade reads, 'But the thing that David had done was evil in the sight of the LORD' (2 Sam. 11:27).

Second Samuel 12:1-23 and Psalm 32 detail David's initial denial and his later confession of sin. He suffered greatly before he admitted his sins to Nathan; and even with this, his life would be plagued to the end by tragedies in his own household, by the enemies of the Lord having occasion to blaspheme God because of his sin, and by the death of Bathsheba's child (12:11-14). But the Lord mercifully took away David's sin and let him live (12:13).

Psalm 51 outlines the steps of spiritual rehabilitation that David took in the midst of an apparently hopeless situation. First he confessed his sin before God—open repentance (51:1-6). Second, David prayed for God's restoration (51:7-12). Finally, the king of Israel recommitted himself and prayed that God would use him as before (51:13-19). If you are now facing similar circumstances, then David's response to God needs to be your course of action.

David's Repentance

David's testimony illustrates eight characteristics that distinguish between true repentance like David's and the selfish regret that Judas displayed (Matt. 27:3). You can measure your own honesty and genuineness by comparing them to David's account (51:1-6).

1. David openly admitted his sin when confronted by a godly man (2 Sam. 12:13). He didn't lie about it, deny it, make excuses, bargain, minimize the sin, deflect the conversation to the sin of others, talk about extenuating circumstances, seek to explain it from his childhood, blame his weaknesses, call sin a sickness, or attempt to justify what he had done. He forthrightly announced, 'I have sinned against the Lord.' He courageously owned up to his transgressions.

2. David's guilt drove him to cry out for God's mercy, grace, and cleansing (Ps. 51:1-2). Nathan stalked David on the outside and guilt

pursued him on the inside—both being God's spiritual agents. The physical and emotional wounds of sin drove David to despair before he asked for God's healing hand (Ps. 32:3-5). He appealed to God's compassionate character (Ex. 34:6), asking God to use a spiritual peroxide and clean out his sinful wound. He could not live with the pain of unresolved sin any longer.

3. David openly acknowledged his unrighteous disposition (Ps. 51:3-5). David affirmed what God knew all along—his sins and transgressions. In a day when the Christian community seems to minimize or explain away sin, a fresh dose of David's honesty is greatly needed (see 1 Kings 8:46; 2 Chron. 6:36; Pss. 130:3-4; 143:2; Rom. 3:23). He did not excuse his behaviour on the grounds of psychological predisposition, childhood traumas, or sexual addiction. Rather, he took personal responsibility for his own sin.

4. David understood that the ultimate issue involved is sin (Ps. 51:4a). There is no sin that is not first against God who is holy (Isa. 6:3). That's why Joseph, when confronted by the sexual lure of Potiphar's wife, cried out, 'How then could I do this great evil and sin against God?' (Gen. 39:9) Until this level of understanding sin can be acknowledged, true repentance has not been genuinely manifested.

5. David submitted to God's standards of moral right and wrong (Ps. 51:4b). 'And done what is evil in Your sight.' David did not judge his actions from the perspective of societal norms, government standards, the legal, educational, or religious communities, the moralists of his day, or even his own values. He allowed God to determine what constituted righteous or unrighteous behaviour (Pss. 19:8; 33:4). God's Word stood as the ultimate authority in David's experience.

6. David willingly accepted whatever punishment God deemed just (Ps. 51:4c). When Nathan told David of the rich man wronging the poor shepherd (2 Sam. 12:1-4), David sentenced the rich man to die; and in that case, it only involved the rich stealing from the poor. When David realized that he was the man, it is no wonder that he cried out with a truly repentant spirit, 'You are justified when You speak, and blameless when You judge.' He had, in fact, broken all Ten Commandments, and anything less than death would be unimaginable and a superlative extension of mercy.

7. David enrolled in the school of truth (Ps. 51:6). I think it is safe to say that if David had been faithful to the classroom of God's Word

all along, he never would have misused his idle time to get involved with Bathsheba (Ps. 119:9-11). He had been absent too long from a daily diet of truth; here he expressed his renewed hunger for truth and wisdom.

8. David publicly shared his brutal battle with sin to warn others who might otherwise walk in the same sinful way (Ps. 32:5). When Jesus warned Peter that Satan would sift him, He concluded, 'When once you have turned again, strengthen your brothers' (Luke 22:32). David demonstrated in his confession a deep desire to direct others away from sin, even at the expense of his own reputation. For thousands of years, David's autobiographical account has been available in Scripture for all to read.

> Search me, O God, and know my heart;
> Try me and know my anxious thoughts;
> And see if there be any hurtful way in me,
> And lead me in the everlasting way (Psalm 139:23-24).

David's Prayer for Restoration
In Revelation 2:4-5, the Lord of the church confronted the Ephesian church over leaving their first love and abandoning their beginning works. He gave them three steps to follow if they wanted to continue enjoying God's blessing:

1. Remember back to your first love and beginning works.
2. Repent of your present sin.
3. Return to your roots of love and good deeds.

The alternative was not pleasant. ' . . . or else I am coming to you, and will remove your lampstand out of its place—unless you repent' (2:5). Jesus could not have been clearer—repent and I will continue in your presence. *Or*, continue to sin and I will remove your ministry.

This pattern for Ephesus repeats the pattern of David established 1,000 years earlier. Because of its timeless nature, the same process is also in place today. David prayed in Psalm 51:7-12 that God would restore to him the blessings (not the reality) of his salvation which were forfeited during his spree of unconfessed sin. It is amazing how much David gave up, in light of how little he had to gain by his sin.

Personal Holiness (Ps. 51:7, 9b-10a). 'Purify me with hyssop, and I shall be clean; wash me, and I shall be whiter than snow . . . and

blot out all my iniquities. Create in me a clean heart, O God . . .'
David came to the right Person—for only God can forgive sin. When
He does, we are made white as snow, even though our sin be like
scarlet (Isa. 1:18). He removes sin as far as the east from the west
(Ps. 103:12). Our forgiven sin is cast into the depth of the sea (Micah
7:19). God casts our sin behind His back where He will never see it
again (Isa. 38:17). David was dirty with sin, and so he asked God to
cleanse him.

Emotional Peace (Ps. 51:8a). 'Make me to hear joy and gladness.'
Both of these internal instruments had been silenced by sin and David
agonizingly desired their return. God graciously responded and David
declared in a burst of testimony and exhortation:

> Be glad in the LORD and rejoice you righteous ones, and shout for joy all
> you who are upright in heart (Psalm 32:11).

Physical Health (Ps. 51:8b). 'Let the bones which You have
broken rejoice.' His physical pain was as intense as if David had
multiple fractures. He described it in Psalm 32:3-4 as his body wasting
away, groaning throughout the day, and losing his energy as with the
intense heat of summer. It seems that David experienced what doctors
call 'emotionally induced illness.' The heaviness of guilt took a major
toll on his physical well-being.

Intimacy with God (Ps. 51:9a). 'Hide Your face from my sins.'
David was ashamed of his sin and did not want God to look on him in
that state. Perhaps David had in mind the words he had written earlier.

> The eyes of the LORD are toward the righteous, and His ears are open to
> their cry. The face of the LORD is against evildoers, to cut off the memory
> of them from the earth (Ps. 34:15-16).

Spiritual Integrity (Ps. 51:10b). 'Renew a steadfast spirit in me.'
In sin, David lost his loyalty, faithfulness, and dependability. What
he once was known for, sin had destroyed. Most of all, David had
violated God's trust. Now with his sin behind both him and God, he
turned again to his Lord to seek provision of what he had lost.

Assurance (Ps. 51:11a). 'Do not cast me away from Your presence.'
David was not pleading for his salvation, but that he might once
again resume his usefulness to the Lord. Paul wrote of such things,
discussing how he had with meticulous discipline conducted his life
according to God's standard lest he be disqualified (1 Cor. 9:24-27).

Spiritual Power (Ps. 51:11b). 'And do not take Your Holy Spirit from me.' David was referring here to the Holy Spirit's presence for empowerment in the kingship. David knew full well what happened to Saul when he sinned—the Spirit departed (1 Sam. 16:14). He knew that God would be equally just to remove the Spirit's power which had been given at his own anointing to the kingship of Israel (see 1 Sam. 16:13).

The Joy of Salvation (Ps. 51:12a). The norm had already been expressed by David (Ps. 13:5-6).

> But I have trusted in Your lovingkindness; my heart shall rejoice in Your salvation. I will sing to the LORD, because He has dealt bountifully with me.

David had forfeited the joy of salvation, and he could not sing of his redemption as he once had.

Sustaining Grace (Ps. 51:12b). David was totally uncertain of his future as he cried out. He had done the only reasonable thing—thrown himself on the mercy of the court (cf. 51:4). Remembering that God withdrew His graces from Saul, David prayed in fear and trust combined.

The radical route of spiritual recovery which David took involved not only total repentance, but also an earnest, prayerful plea for God to bring a revival of what had once been experienced but was now overshadowed by sin.

David's Recommitment

With repentance and revival behind him, the king now recommitted himself to some basics that once characterized his life but had been absent for a season of sin. In the final seven verses of Psalm 51, David focused on the spiritual priorities of personal testimony (v.13); song of salvation (v.14); praises to the Saviour (v.15); true worship (vv.16-17); prayer for Israel (vv.18-19).

There can be no doubt that God sovereignly used David's experience to warn us. The price and pain of sin are too great. For those who miss this divine **CAUTION** and sin, it's God's word of hope. As David found personal restoration in his redemptive relationship with God, so can those who have tragically followed him in sin, if they are willing also to find their way out through repentance.

God's Reaffirmation of David

Did God accept David's repentance as genuine? Did God answer David's revived plea for restoration? Did God respond to David's prayer of recommitment? Listen carefully to God's affirmation, 'I have found David the son of Jesse, a man after my heart, who will do all my will' (Acts 13:22). Since these words were penned a millennium after David's sin, we can assume that God brought recovery to David's life. You can read of these events in David's life in 2 Samuel 12-1 Kings 2.

No sin is so great that God cannot forgive it. But it must be dealt with on God's terms according to God's will. In all cases God's terms begin with true repentance. In David's case, God's will involved restoration.

Were the whole realm of nature mine,
That were a present far too small;
Love so amazing, so divine,
Demands my soul, my life, my all.[1]

Isaac Watts

POSTSCRIPT

No spiritual shepherd worthy of his charge would dare lead the flock without first praying for them. When he prays, he acknowledges Christ as the Chief Shepherd (1 Peter 5:4) and invokes God's strength to accomplish His purposes in the church. Remember, Epaphras prayed that the Colossians would 'stand firm in all the will of God, mature and fully assured' (Col. 4:12, NIV).

I do not want to close without expressing my heart to pray for you. If you're curious to know how I should pray, look at Paul's petitions on behalf of Christians in his day. They are my models.

> I pray that the eyes of your heart may be enlightened, so that you may know what is the hope of His calling, what are the riches of the glory of His inheritance in the saints, and what is the surpassing greatness of His power toward us who believe. These are in accordance with the working of the strength of His might (Eph. 1:18-19).

> For this reason, I bow my knees before the Father . . . so that Christ may dwell in your hearts through faith, and that you, being rooted and grounded in love, may be able to comprehend with all the saints what is the breadth and length and height and depth, and to know the love of Christ which surpasses knowledge, that you may be filled up to all the fullness of God (Eph. 3:14, 17-19).

> And this I pray, that your love may abound still more and more in real knowledge and all discernment, so that you may approve the things that are excellent (Phil. 1:9-10).

> We have not ceased to pray for you ... so that you will walk in a manner worthy of the Lord, to please Him in all respects, bearing fruit in every good work and increasing in the knowledge of God (Col. 1:9-10).

According to the pattern of Paul's prayers, the highest priority in your Christianity will be to cultivate a growing likeness to God in character and conduct by submitting to the transforming power of God's Word and God's Spirit.

As spiritual intimacy and maturity become your experience, these wonderful words will more frequently be on your lips.

I'll love Thee in life,
I will love Thee in death,
And praise Thee as long
As Thou lendest me breath;
And say when the death-dew
Lies cold on my brow;
If ever I loved Thee,
My Jesus, 'tis now.[2]

William R. Featherstone

NOTES

INTRODUCTION
1. Quoted by Albert M. Wells, Jr. in *Inspiring Quotations* (Nashville, TN: Thomas Nelson, 1988) 121.
2. Gordon MacDonald, *Restoring Your Spiritual Passion* (Nashville, TN: Oliver Nelson, 1986) 10-11.

PART ONE – SPIRITUAL PROGRESS
1. Carl F.H. Henry, 'Evangelical Courage in an Age of Darkness,' in *Table Talk*, 14:1 (January, 1990) 11-12.

ONE – KNOWING GOD
1. Gordon Verrell, 'Hershiser Closer to History,' in *Long Beach Press – Telegram* (September 25, 1988) C5.
2. A.W. Tozer, *The Pursuit of God* (Harrisburg, PA: Christian Publications, 1948) 14-15.
3. Philip Yancey, 'Gandhi and Christianity' in *Christianity Today* (April 8, 1983) 16.
4. Max Wertheimer, *How a Rabbi Found Peace* (Lansing, IL: American Messianic Fellowship, n.d.) 2, 3, 7, 11.
5. Myra Brooks Welch, 'The Touch of the Master's Hand' in *The Treasury of Religious Verse* (Westwood, NJ: Fleming H. Revell, 1962) 87-88.
6. John Mohr, 'A Note From the Composer' in *He Holds the Keys* (Chatsworth, CA: The Sparrow Corporation, 1987). International copyright secured. All rights reserved. Used by permission.

TWO – TAKING THE FIRST STEP
1. Charles Wesley, 'And Can It Be?' stanza 1.

THREE – GROWING IN GRACE
1. Charles Wesley, 'Love Divine, All Loves Excelling,' stanza 4.
2. Richard F. Lovelace, 'Evangelical Spirituality: A Church Historian's Perspective' in *Journal of the Evangelical Theological Society*, 31:1 (March, 1988) 33.
3. John Brown, *The First Epistle of Peter*, v. 1 (Edinburgh: The Banner of Truth Trust, rpt., n.d.) 106.

4. John Owen, *The Holy Spirit: His Gift and Power* (Grand Rapids: Kregel, rpt., 1954) 230.

5. Amy Carmichael, *If* (Grand Rapids: Zondervan, rpt., 1980).

FOUR – WHAT IS GOD LIKE?
1. Walter Chalmers Smith, 'Immortal, Invisible,' stanza 1.

FIVE – TO BE LIKE GOD!
1. Ancient Irish hymn of unknown authorship, 'Be Thou My Vision,' stanza 1.

2. Jerry Bridges, *The Practice of Godliness* (Colorado Springs, CO: NavPress, 1983) 69.

PART TWO – SPIRITUAL POWER
1. J.C. Ryle, *Holiness* (Old Tappan, NJ: Fleming H. Revell, rpt., n.d.) vii.

SIX – INVADED BY GOD'S SPIRIT
1. Edwin Hatch, 'Breathe on Me, Breath of God,' stanzas 1 and 2.

2. This chapter does not intend to deal with the issues commonly associated with pentecostal, charismatic, and Third Wave tradition. For a complete biblical treatment of these areas, please consult John MacArthur, Jr., *Charismatic Chaos* (Grand Rapids: Zondervan, 1992) and Richard Mayhue, *The Healing Promise* (Ross-shire, Scotland: Mentor, 1997).

SEVEN – LISTENING TO GOD
1. Larry Crabb, 'Facing the Pain in Relationships,' *Discipleship Journal*, 43 (1988) 16.

2. Published by Fleming H. Revell. Also see the newly published *MacArthur Topical Bible* (Nashville: Word Publishing, 1999).

3. For further instruction on how to use these practical steps for fruitful Bible study, see Richard Mayhue, *How to Interpret the Bible for Yourself* (Ross-shire, Scotland, Christian Focus, 1997).

EIGHT – IMPACTED BY GOD'S WORD
1. John Burton, 'Holy Bible, Book Divine,' stanzas 1 and 2.

2. John F. MacArthur, Jr., *Our Sufficiency in Christ* (Dallas: Word Publishing, 1991) 261.

3. For background on Bible study, see Richard Mayhue, *How to Interpret the Bible for Yourself* (Ross-shire, Scotland, Christian Focus, 1997).

4. John Owen, *Thinking Spiritually* (London: Grace Publication Trust, rpt., 1989) 21-22.

5. For a fuller discussion see Willem A. Van Gemeren, 'Psalms' in *The Expositor's Bible Commentary*, vol. 5 (Grand Rapids: Zondervan, 1991) 737-38.

6. My favorite helps to make this a reality are (1) *The Daily Walk*, published monthly by Walk Thru the Bible Ministries, which can be purchased at your local church bookstore or ordered by writing to *The Daily Walk*, P.O. Box 478, Mt. Morris, IL 61504 and (2) *The One Year Bible* (Wheaton, IL: Tyndale House, 1986).

7. Ruth Harms Calkins, *Lord I Keep Running Back to You* (Wheaton, IL: Tyndale House, 1979) 82-83.

NINE – THINKING LIKE GOD

1. Jim Downing, *Meditation* (Colorado Springs, CO: NavPress, 1976) 7-8.

2. Harry Blamires, *The Christian Mind* (Ann Arbor, MI: Servant Books, 1963) 110-11.

3. Richard Mayhue, *Unmasking Satan* (Wheaton, IL: Victor Books, 1988) 21.

4. Charles Colson, *Against the Night* (Ann Arbor, MI: Servant Publications, 1989) 26-27.

TEN – TRANSFORMED BY GOD'S WISDOM

1. Thomas O. Chisholm, 'O to Be Like Thee!' stanza 1.

2. Henry Beach and Roy McKie, *Sailing: A Sailor's Dictionary* (New York: Workman Publishing, 1981) cover.

PART THREE – SPIRITUAL PRIORITIES

1. William Wilberforce, *Real Christianity* (Portland, OR: Multnomah Press, 1982) 125.

ELEVEN – TALKING TO GOD

1. Ray Stedman, *Jesus Teaches on Prayer* (Waco, TX: Word Books, 1975) 7.

2. A.T. Pierson quoted by John MacArthur, Jr. in *Grace to You* (January, 1983) 1.

TWELVE – WORSHIPPING GOD
1. A.W. Tozer, *Whatever Happened to Worship* (Camp Hill, PA: Christian Publications, 1985) 7.

    2. John MacArthur, Jr., *The Ultimate Priority* (Chicago: Moody Press, 1983) vii.

THIRTEEN – PRAISING GOD
1. *Grace to You* (June/July, 1985) 8.

    2. See Nathan Stone, *Names of God* (Chicago: Moody Press, 1944) for an expanded discussion.

FOURTEEN – GIVING TO GOD
1. Clovis Chappell in *Christian Medical Society Journal*. VII:4 (Fall, 1976) 1.

    2. Ron Blue in *Discipleship Journal* (September/October, 1989) 20.

FIFTEEN – EMBRACING GOD
1. Affirmed by Gary Collins, *The Rebuilding of Psychology* (Wheaton, IL: Tyndale House, 1977) 73-92.

    2. Bruce Shelley, 'Justin: Witness and Martyr' in *Moody Monthly* (June, 1986) 27.

    3. Dallas Willard, 'Discipleship for Super-Christians Only?' in *Christianity Today* (October 10, 1980) 23.

    4. Don Hescott, 'A Lesson on Commitment from a Communist,' in *Masterpiece* (September/October, 1989) 24.

    5. Oscar Broneer, 'The Apostle Paul and the Isthmian Games,' in *The Biblical Archaeologist*. XXV:1 (February, 1962) 17.

    6. Used by permission.

    7. *The Treasury of Religious Verse* (Westwood, NJ: Fleming H. Revell, 1962) 8.

PART FOUR – SPIRITUAL PASSIONS
1. Norman Grubb, *C.T. Studd: Cricketer and Pioneer* (Fort Washington, PA: Christian Literature Crusade, 1982) 3.

SIXTEEN – GRASPING GOD'S GREATNESS
1. Used by permission.

    2. Charles R. Swindoll, *Come Before Winter* (Portland, OR: Multnomah Press, 1985) 294-95.

3. Jerry Bergman, 'The Pinnacle of Divine Creativity,' in *Ministry* (November, 1984) 28-29.

4. Used by permission.

5. Howard A. Snyder, *The Radical Wesley* (Grand Rapids, MI: Zondervan, 1980) 92.

SEVENTEEN – OBEYING GOD'S WILL

1. Quoted by Philip Yancey in *Christianity Today* (September 16, 1983) 27.

2. Quoted in *Famous Last Words,* compiled by Jonathon Green (London: Omnibus Press, 1979) 28.

EIGHTEEN – SEEKING GOD'S WILL

1. Elisabeth Elliot, *Shadow of the Almighty* (Grand Rapids, MI: Zondervan, 1958) 128.

2. Gary Inrig, *Hearts of Iron, Feet of Clay* (Chicago: Moody Press, 1979) 116-17.

3. Paul Little, *Affirming the Will of God* (Downers Grove, IL: InterVarsity, 1971) 17-18.

4. T.S. Rendall, 'The Lord Led Me – But Did He?' in *The Prairie Overcomer* (May, 1982) 201.

5. John Flavel quoted by Sinclair Ferguson in 'The Task of Seeking God's Mysterious Will,' in *Eternity* (May, 1988) 25.

6. Used by permission of Dr. Homer A. Kent, Jr., then President of Grace Theological Seminary.

7. Paul L. Tan, *Encyclopedia of 7,700 Illustrations* (Rockville, MD: Assurance Publishers, 1979) 738.

NINETEEN – PLEASING GOD

1. Used by permission of LAFD Deputy Chief Dave Parsons.

2. Music and lyrics by Don Kistler (Yucaipa, CA: Oak Tree Music, 1979). Used by permission of the composer.

3. Author unknown.

TWENTY – GLORIFYING GOD

1. Unknown author quoted by Charles Swindoll, *Newsbreak* (November 13, 1988) 4.

2. Author unknown.

PART FIVE – SPIRITUAL PURSUITS
1. John Newton, *John Newton* (Chicago: Moody Press, n.d.) 159.

TWENTY-ONE – SPIRITUAL CONDITIONING
1. John H. Sammis, 'Trust and Obey,' stanza 5.

TWENTY-TWO – SPIRITUAL SUBMISSION
1. Fanny J. Crosby, 'I Am Thine, O Lord,' stanza 2.

TWENTY-THREE – SPIRITUAL SERVICE
1. Sabine Baring-Gould, 'Onward, Christian Soldiers,' stanza 3.

TWENTY-FOUR – MEASURING SPIRITUALITY
1.Horatio Spafford, 'It Is Well with My Soul,' stanza 1.
    2. Phillip Keller, *A Shepherd Looks at Psalm 23* (Grand Rapids, MI: Zondervan, 1970) 30.

TWENTY-FIVE – PRACTICING SPIRITUALITY
1. Reginald Heber, 'Holy, Holy, Holy,' stanza 1.
    2. Used by permission.

TWENTY-SIX – RESTORING SPIRITUALITY
1. Bernard of Clairvaux, 'Jesus, the Very Thought of Thee,' stanza 3.

POSTSCRIPT
1. Isaac Watts, 'When I Survey the Wondrous Cross,' stanza 4.
    2. William R. Featherstone, 'My Jesus, I Love Thee,' stanza 3.

SUBJECT INDEX

Scripture Index

FIGHT THE GOOD FIGHT

ISBN 1-85792-470-3

Richard Mayhue examines twelve character examples in the Bible, some who failed, some who recovered after failing, and some who achieved God's goal in their lives.

They failed to win: Solomon: shipwrecked saint; Jonah: wrong-way prophet; Eve: long-shot loser; Saul: 'my way' monarch.

They fell but recovered: Elijah: lone prophet; Samson: wayward warrior; Habakkuk: the 'show me' man; Moses: successful failure.

They fought to victory: Joseph: God's valedictorian; Job: righteous victor; Ruth: God's Cinderella; Daniel: man of high esteem.

Contains a great deal of practical application for Christians of this age and culture. I am confident that parents, pastors, teachers and all Christians will find this book to be a good investment. I heartily recommend it both for your reading enjoyment and for teaching purposes' (Tim LaHaye).

HOW TO INTERPRET THE BIBLE

ISBN 1-85792-254-9

This book discusses the obstacles that keep us from a truly biblical interpretation of Scripture.

'We all need help in approaching the Bible ... this book is not a heavy theological treatise addressed to academics. It is intended for all types of Christian people who are serious about studying the Bible carefully ... I warmly commend it' (Eric Alexander).

WHAT WOULD JESUS SAY ABOUT YOUR CHURCH?

ISBN 1-85792-150-X

Richard Mayhue shows a clear pathway for our churches to follow. It is a pathway with a history of success because it is the one given to the churches in the New Testament. With startling clarity he shows us that there is more than enough guidance for us to turn the world upside down just as the early church did.

It is time for the church to listen directly to her Lord and He has spoken clearly, confrontively and compassionately. My thanks and yours should be to Richard Mayhue for taking us back to hear the audible voice of the Saviour as He pleads with His beloved (John MacArthur).

THE HEALING PROMISE
Is it always God's will to heal?

ISBN 1 85792 302-2

In *The Healing Promise* Richard Mayhue provides straight answers without compromising the Bible or God's miraculous power.

The Healing Promise includes –
A special interview with **Joni Eareckson Tada** where she talks about coping with the attitudes towards healing she encounters every day.

A chapter by **André Kole**, the man behind many of **David Copperfield's** illusions, on techniques used in healing meetings.

A special interview with **John and Patricia MacArthur** about their experiences when Patricia was badly injured in a car accident.

1 and 2 Thessalonians

Triumphs and Trials of a Consecrated Church

ISBN 185792452-5

The Thessalonian epistles give us relevant glimpses of the church's earliest times. When looking at the early church many contemporary questions arise such as –

- How serious was Jesus about the Great Commission?
- What is the TRUE Gospel?
- How do you plant a church?
- Which doctrines should you teach to new believers?
- What is the pastor's role amongst his flock?
- What methods should pastors use to deal with doctrinal error?
- What is prophetic teaching and how important is it?
- How does a believer live a righteously against Satanic assault?

'After meticulously defining the background for the Thessalonian epistles, Richard Mayhue unfolds Paul's pastoral concerns and theological instruction. Verse by verse he expounds the epistles with impeccable precision. Having been thus immersed in these epistles, the reader will be challenged to live out their teachings. That is the ultimate compliment that can be paid to any sermon or commentary' (William D. Barrick, The Master's Seminary, Los Angeles)

'Dr. Mayhue's lucid exposition of the Thessalonian epistles is merely the tip of a very deep iceberg of information. The author transports us to the past (how these epistles fit within the first century world), and propels us into the future (how these epistles equip today's reader). In addition, Mayhue's ability to blend grand themes yields 33 Overviews, which should place this work on the desk of any student of Scripture' (Dr. W. Gary Phillips, Bryan College, Dayton, Tennessee).